Engineering Expansion

AMERICAN GOVERNANCE: POLITICS,
POLICY, AND PUBLIC LAW

Series Editors: Richard Valelly, Pamela Brandwein, Marie Gottschalk,
Christopher Howard

A complete list of books in the series is available from the publisher.

ENGINEERING EXPANSION

The U.S. Army and Economic Development, 1787–1860

William D. Adler

PENN

UNIVERSITY OF PENNSYLVANIA PRESS

PHILADELPHIA

Published by
University of Pennsylvania Press
Philadelphia, Pennsylvania 19104-4112
www.upenn.edu/pennpress

Printed in the United States of America on acid-free paper
10 9 8 7 6 5 4 3 2 1

Library of Congress Cataloging-in-Publication Data
Names: Adler, William D., author.
Title: Engineering expansion : the U.S. Army and economic development,
1787–1860 / William D. Adler.
Other titles: American governance.
Description: 1st edition. | Philadelphia : University of Pennsylvania Press,
[2021] | Series: American governance : politics, policy, and public law |
Includes bibliographical references and index.
Identifiers: LCCN 2021012580 | ISBN 978-0-8122-5348-1 (hardcover)
Subjects: LCSH: United States. Army—History. | Economic development—
United States—History. | United States—Politics and government—
1783–1865. | United States—History—1783–1865. | United States—
Economic conditions—To 1865.
Classification: LCC HC105 .A55 2021 | DDC 338.973009/034—dc23
LC record available at https://lccn.loc.gov/2021012580
ISBN 978-0-8122-5348-1

To the memory of my father, James Adler

CONTENTS

INTRODUCTION

This book responds to one of the central puzzles of American political development: if the United States had a weak central state in its earliest years, then how did national consolidation and rapid economic development occur? Since sustainable development is difficult without strong public institutions, how did the U.S. economy grow and prosper?[1] Or did the American economy develop in the absence of a strong central state, somehow different from other countries? I answer this puzzle by demonstrating that the early U.S. Army was the instrument of a strong central state that worked to hold the nation together and provided a variety of collective goods well in advance of market-generated demand.

Although parts of this story have been presented in piecemeal fashion by historians, insufficient work in political science has paid attention to the Army's important contributions in early America. Indeed, the field of American political development has traditionally presented the dominant paradigm of the early national state as an underdeveloped "state of courts and parties," in the oft-quoted words of Stephen Skowronek.[2] By common measures of resources and capacities, the early national state certainly qualified as very modest. It generally lacked skilled civilian personnel and reliable bureaucratic structures. Along with a new wave of scholarship on the early American state, however, this book's close examination of the Army paints a very different picture, in which an activist central state promoted specific economic goals and used its power to carry them out, shaping the direction and pattern of economic activity. To state it succinctly, the Army helped build the American economy, and through it the American nation. It spurred the development of a continental economy that by the beginning of the Civil War was poised for a rapid industrial takeoff that would vault the United States into the front rank of industrial nation-states by the late nineteenth century.

It is not surprising that the early Army has escaped close attention. If we divide the national state into the broad categories of economic growth and regulation, social welfare provision, and national security, a national security apparatus seems to come into its own only in the modern period, during and following World War II.[3] The peacetime Army of the early nineteenth century was modest in scale, consisting of no more than a few thousand soldiers scattered across a vast territory. Yet notwithstanding its small size, I argue that the early Army proved to be a powerful instrument for supporting economic expansion and for promoting specific sectors of the economy through policy choices made by politicians as well as actors within the Army itself. Though the U.S. Army was not necessarily always a force for positive economic developments (as policy choices had variable consequences for the economy), the evidence will show that it broadly made positive contributions to economic growth as well as the growth of the American central state—and, crucially, shaped the *patterns* of those developments through those choices. I argue that the Army did so both through its traditional role as a coercive agent and as a socioeconomic actor.[4] Any account of the early American political economy in which the Army does not play a central role is therefore radically incomplete.[5]

Examining the Army also leads me to reconceptualize the early American state as a bifurcated entity—the *periphery*, largely dominated by the Army, and the *center*, in which the Army still played an essential role in economic development but other public institutions also performed key development functions.[6] To understand the Army's crucial role in the economy, we must examine which actors directed it in each of these arenas and how they used the Army to further their development goals. Political control over the Army's activities varied depending on whether soldiers were engaged in the use of force or in promoting the development of an economic infrastructure. Besides partisan leaders, members of Congress, and presidents, two actors emerge as especially important players in shaping the economic development activities of the early Army—secretaries of war and the heads of War Department bureaus, both of whom could be highly entrepreneurial in identifying and seizing opportunities to expand the range of socioeconomic Army operations in both the center and the periphery. External forces, such as sectionalism, as well as endogenous influences, such as the preferences of military bureaucrats, would also shape how the Army molded American economic development.

I argue that the early American state operated in two distinct modes, each with its own characteristics and hierarchies of authority, in two regions of the nation. First, there was the *center*, based in Washington, D.C., and in the established population centers in the East. Within the center the national government made significant contributions to economic development, including continued infrastructure building and improvements, security, the expansion of the Post Office and postal road system, and the ensuring of stable property rights. The Army here was certainly important but was just one among several public actors helping to promote national economic progress, along with the Post Office and state governments. Because this is the region of the country where states were already formed, voters had representation in Congress and a say in choosing the president. Elected officials therefore had a greater incentive to monitor the socioeconomic projects affecting this portion of the nation (though even here oversight could often be lacking).

The second mode was the *periphery*, containing the frontier regions of the nation. In the periphery, no institution came close to the Army's overarching presence. The Army acquired land for white settlement by battling and displacing native tribes, surveyed new lands and directed settlers toward the most fertile and productive regions, protected traders and emigrants heading west, and made certain that a remote frontier region remained attached to the rest of the nation. It is no exaggeration to say that the Army built the emerging American nation through its presence in the periphery. Ironically, despite the scale of the economic development task, this region's lack of elected representation drove politicians to leave many important decisions about its future to unelected officials, such as the secretary of war and Army bureau chiefs. While territorial governors could occasionally be relevant to some policy decisions, they were appointed by national officials and not entirely representative of their territory's interests. In no sense, then, could "courts and parties" have controlled the fate of the periphery.

As the country's territorial boundaries expanded, leading to a continental empire, areas that were once on the periphery (such as the trans-Appalachian region in the early republic) were gradually assimilated into the center. The speed with which this was accomplished indicates that some force pushed these outlying regions into becoming more like the established eastern regions. Without the Army acting as such an important force in the periphery, settlement there would have been slower, connections to the East would have been fewer, and indeed the entire frontier could have easily broken off into its own country. The Army played a key role in assuring that the distant West remained attached to the rest of the Union.

At the same time that we recognize these distinct modes of governance, we should not overemphasize their differences. Both the center and the periphery were ultimately governed under the same constitutional and governmental structure. Also, the boundary between the two was fluid, and no sharp line divided them. Certainly, there is a continuum between the two. Nonetheless, analyzing the disparities between the two can, I believe, produce important insights about the nature of the state in this period and how the Army shaped economic development in the new nation.

American Economic Development and the State

Classic treatments of how the American economy developed often emphasize a laissez-faire narrative that proceeds from Adam Smith's observations regarding the metaphorical "invisible hand" of the marketplace working to distribute goods, seemingly without outside interference.[7] According to this view (still dominant among popular narratives about early American history), while a small American state shied away from intervention in the marketplace, businesses and entrepreneurs were free to amass capital and invest in new technologies that propelled economic growth.[8] Famously, Alexis de Tocqueville noted this seeming absence of the state in his work *Democracy in America*: "What most strikes the European who travels across the United States is the absence of what among us we call government or administration. In America, you see written laws; you see their daily execution; everything is in motion around you, and the motor is nowhere to be seen. The hand that runs the social machine escapes at every moment."[9] Conventional economic studies in this vein often emphasize the importance of the railroads and private entrepreneurs in sparking economic growth and industrialization in nineteenth-century America.[10]

Historians have for many years pointed out the limitations of adopting such a strict approach, as there are numerous examples of the government (at both the national and state levels) either nourishing or actively promoting development and commercialization. Scholars such as economist Gavin Wright and historian Max Edling have noted that the very founding of the U.S. national government in the form of the Constitution was, in Wright's words, "emphatically an exercise in nation building."[11] Oscar and Mary Handlin and Louis Hartz long ago demonstrated how the states of Massachusetts and Pennsylvania, respectively, helped encourage commerce and trade through policies favorable to businesses, while a recent prominent work by William Novak shows the multitude of ways through which local and state governments regulated private enterprises for the benefit of the public welfare.[12] Similarly, economic historians Naomi Lamoreaux and John Joseph Wallis have argued that the states in early America were central to economic growth through their role as purveyors of public goods, especially infrastructural improvements.[13] In the national context, Forest Hill and Carter Goodrich explored the federal government's promotion of canals and railroads as part of the project of internal improvements, with Hill focusing in particular on the role of Army engineers.[14] Laurence Malone's work empirically confirms the federal government's central role in developing the West through its internal improvement policies.[15] The Army's actions in settling, exploring, and mapping the West were impressively explored by Francis Paul Prucha and William Goetzmann.[16] Colleen Dunlavy compared early railroad development in Prussia and the United States and shows that a liberal and fragmented American political system led the way in railroads per capita, while Prussia's more centralized state lagged behind. American state governments were particularly active in promoting railroad development, as Zachary Callen has also argued.[17] While these important works sometimes call attention to the government's specific activities, many focus entirely on the state governments and downplay the importance of national collective goods provisioning. Others have not yet focused sufficiently on the aggregate impact of the Army's actions or worked to analyze the role played by particular political actors and institutions.

More generally, the subject of development has often been studied from the perspective of those interested in the cultural or ideational foundations of economic growth. Adam Smith's discussion of the "invisible hand" proceeded out of his preoccupation with the moral foundations of the market, while Max Weber concerned himself with how religious principles impacted on the work ethic of the Western world.[18] Modern scholarship in this vein discusses what specific sorts of cultural or social arrangements are most likely to lead to capitalistic development and technological progress.[19] Others argue that this view tends to minimize the political and legal foundations of capitalism and gives short shrift to the limitations of markets.[20] The self-regulating marketplace was a myth, according to Karl Polanyi, because all economies are politically imposed.[21] Oliver Williamson demonstrates how institutions reduce transaction costs and thus are essential prerequisites for private business dealings.[22]

In a series of influential works, economist Douglass C. North has argued for an analytical framework that foregrounds the role of both formal and informal institutions in economic performance. North argues that economic development can best take place in an environment characterized by respect for the rule of law and strong property rights. A state that provides these, he says, is therefore "essential for economic growth."[23] North and Barry Weingast have also demonstrated the centrality of credible commitments in the Glorious Revolution in laying the foundation for a thriving economy in seventeenth-century England.[24] Work extending these principles by North, Wallis, and Weingast argues that the state's need to manage violence and ensure the rule of law is at the heart of modern transformations that provide for open economies.[25] Similarly, Margaret Levi has argued that states that successfully promote trust (and are themselves trustworthy) enhance consumer and business confidence and hence lubricate the wheels of exchange.[26] One recent study has empirically confirmed the primacy of institutions in creating the conditions necessary for economic growth.[27] Daron Acemoglu and James Robinson's influential contribution in their book *Why Nations Fail* demonstrates that, across a wide variety of nations and cultures, accountable institutions are a central underpinning of economic success.[28]

For the purposes of this study, I am less interested in the origins of capitalism and the market economy than in how government-sponsored activities impacted various sectors of the economy and how those actions enhanced or retarded development. Like the literature in comparative political economy on the varieties of capitalism, which examines how differing types of market-government interactions lead to varying economic outcomes, I wish to understand how the Army's activities helped to determine the shape of the American economy.[29] North's work is especially useful in this regard, as he argues that political institutions structure the choices available to economic actors. Borrowing from his conception, I argue that the U.S. Army, through choices about which territories to explore or which regions of the nation would receive engineering assistance, structured how the economy could develop.[30] Importantly, these choices were made by a variety of political actors—and those making the choices helped determine what the American economy would look like as a result. One example of this was through resource extraction, a major driver of antebellum economic growth. The Army encouraged mining by conducting surveys that discovered and mapped the minerals, through the War Department's widely publicizing the findings, and then subsequently through the stationing of troops near the mines to protect miners from potentially hostile native tribes. Those surveys were done by the Corps of Topographical Engineers, whose chief, Colonel John J. Abert, would carve out an autonomous spot for his bureau in providing those specialized surveys. Lacking the Army's involvement, lacking the push by the topographical engineers to conduct those surveys, such extraction would have occurred at a later date or at a slower pace. By providing these sorts of goods, the Army was able to enhance economic development in a way that state governments and private actors alone did not.

The Army's Impact and the Early U.S. Economy

The existing literature on the political economy of economic development in the early United States highlights the impact of state-level policies or civilian national institutions such as the Post Office.[31] I argue that the Army often supplied public goods necessary for economic development beyond those that the individual states could provide at a time when private actors lacked the incentive to do so, and that the Army's range of activities contributed in a wider variety of ways than did other national institutions. Simply put, the Army's actions in early America yielded economic growth and a path to industrialization sooner than would have been the case absent an effective national military, and directly shaped development through choices about which economic sectors and regions received assistance. That the American economy developed in the manner it did—based heavily upon westward expansion and opening lands for white settlement[32]—was not foreordained. Conceivably, economic integration and industrialization could have occurred at a slower pace or could have favored different groups or regions.

To better establish the significance of the Army's activities, I briefly describe the economic development tasks the American national state needed to engage in following ratification of the Constitution as well as the shape of the American economy during this period. Independence had established the new republic with its population and economic life concentrated along the Atlantic Seaboard. The economy depended heavily upon agriculture and trade, with raw materials and agricultural commodities shipped abroad in exchange for manufactured goods.[33] The early American economy was damaged by the Revolution and the costs incurred as a result of the war and the break from British rule. According to a recent estimate, "the per capita income loss up to 1790 may have been as large as 30 percent" from where it was prior to independence, almost as terrible an economic catastrophe as the

Great Depression.[34] American leaders had different visions of future economic growth—the Federalists anticipating the emergence of domestic industry while Republicans looked to agriculture and trade—but all conceptions presupposed the westward movement of population and a widening scope for domestic commerce as well as international trade.[35]

Realization of expansionist economic visions required the provision of a number of collective goods. First and foremost among these was collective security. Security concerns had been an important impetus behind the reformulation of governing institutions reflected in the Constitution; the Articles of Confederation were deemed inadequate to the challenges of maintaining domestic order and resisting external threats.[36] Following ratification, the national government would have to establish effective control over the existing states to assure that its authority would be respected and that it would have sufficient revenue to meet even its limited responsibilities. As settlement spread westward, moreover, distance might undermine the integrity of a continental empire by inviting separatist movements. The national government also faced the perpetual risk of conflict with native tribes whose acquiescence or removal would be necessary to permit westward population migration by white Americans. Initially, those natives would receive some support from European powers still seeking to retain their influence over a substantial portion of the North American continent. Even after the European threat had been removed or minimized (effectively by 1820), the challenge of territorial competition with a foreign sovereign (Mexico) and with native tribes would continue.[37]

Besides security, other collective goods would serve to expedite the new republic's economic development. The initial impetus for territorial expansion, including encouraging a significant number of white settlers to populate new land, rested on provision of collective goods (such as mapped trails and way stations with provisions and medical services) in advance of statehood and beyond the very meager resources of territorial governments. The availability of land would also be key—the ability of western settlers to access and safely work on the land would immediately impact how they could both provision themselves and attempt to expand their access to markets.[38] Identification of resources that might be exploited and routes for migration and shipping could also spur local economic development, but were unlikely to yield sufficient short-term returns to justify private investment and so depended upon action by the national state. In addition to collective goods needed on the periphery of the expanding nation, even the more established states required help from a national government. If farmers were to move beyond subsistence production, they would need to be able to ship their crops to larger markets. An interstate inland transportation system would have to be developed, but individual states were limited to infrastructure development within their borders.[39]

Finally, other forms of economic intervention by the national state that did not involve the provision of collective goods would nevertheless accelerate the pace of development. Certain kinds of expertise vital to economic growth, notably engineering, were in short supply in the early republic.[40] The federal government facilitated growth by helping to meet the need for skilled engineers. Those engineers would help to build the new transportation technologies that were to prove so vital to economic development.[41] Also, to spur technological innovation, the government induced manufacturers to introduce new production techniques by requiring that prescribed methods be used to fulfill government orders and rewarding private industries that innovated with a guaranteed market for their output. Accelerative intervention would not be a prerequisite to growth but would result in more rapid industrialization.

In sum, although the early republic enjoyed enormous, widely recognized potential for economic development, whether that potential would be realized depended upon the vitality of the public sector as well as private initiative and, within that public sector, on both the states and the national government. Certain public goods could be provided only by a national state, making it indispensable to the emergence of an integrated continental economy.[42] In other cases, the national state might accelerate the rate of growth or steer its direction, though other forces eventually would have yielded similar outcomes. In fact, after 1800 the U.S. economy grew substantially faster than the economies of western Europe: "fast per capita income growth and even faster population growth quickly made the American economy by 1860 one of the biggest in the Western world"[43] and "no European economy grew so fast for so long as did that of the United States before World War I."[44] Overall, per capita income grew at an average rate of 1.48 percent for the period 1800 to 1860.[45]

To meet the need for essential collective goods and accelerate the pace of economic development, the national government relied upon a variety of institutions, but leaned most heavily upon the U.S. Army. Sustained coercion, including fighting wars and acquiring new territory by force, could not be performed by any institution other than the national Army, since it alone possessed the capacity and authority to engage in protracted, large-scale violence. In addition, when a serious threat to public order or territorial integrity arose, only the Army had the wherewithal to establish and sustain national governing authority.[46] In fulfilling traditional national defense functions, the Army helped provide true public or collective goods.[47] Its only potential substitutes were the state militias, which faced restrictions on where they could operate (only within the nation's borders, and only outside state borders when called into national service) and were often deemed unreliable when facing domestic upheavals. They also relied heavily on the national Army for much of their support apparatus. Beginning from 1808, the federal government budgeted at least $200,000 per year to equip the militias, a program directed by the Ordnance Department (a bureau within the War Department). The militias also received manuals of instruction prepared by the War Department.[48] Even though they were not required to accept this assistance, most states did and gradually became more reliant on federal support for their militias as a result.[49]

Military force supported the assertion of national authority that was a precondition for a national market. The Army expanded and secured the nation's boundaries by waging large-scale military campaigns that created new areas for white settlement and potential resource extraction, building forts (which themselves helped create new markets on the frontier) to defend remote settlers and protect the American fur trade, and battling and removing Native American tribes.[50] It defended against international threats to the country's integrity from British, French, and Spanish intrigues.[51] In addition, showing the national flag at the margins of settlement helped to connect settler populations to the national state, forestalling separatist tendencies that sometimes (as in the case of the Utah Mormons, for example) were quite pronounced.[52] All of these uses of force helped lay the essential groundwork for an integrated, national economic system.

The Army's socioeconomic activities, on the other hand, involved the production of both collective goods and private goods that might have been supplied by sources outside the Army, including other government agencies or private actors. The technical and noncombat branches of the Army—engineers, topographical engineers, ordnance bureaucrats, and supply personnel—provided scarce expertise, built an infrastructure to support a national economy, instigated technological innovation, and introduced new methods of administration for large-scale organizations.

The distinction drawn here between coercive and socioeconomic activities builds on Michael Mann's twin concepts of "despotic power" and "infrastructural power."[53] According to Mann, despotic power is the power exerted over society by the government—the coercive abilities of the state. By contrast, infrastructural power is power through society, the capability of the state to control policy within its defined territorial domain, penetrating society and establishing its legal authority. Infrastructural power is spatial in its application, insofar as it is organized throughout a particular territory, and relational, as it occurs through "organizational networks that [states] coordinate, control, and construct."[54] In the early United States, the Army acted using both modes of power, in varying degrees: coercively, it relied upon the despotic power of the state, while its socioeconomic activities were infrastructural in nature. That infrastructural power was built in fits and starts, sometimes assisted by the coercive actions of the Army. For example, in the Whiskey Rebellion, the Army's coercive force was brought to bear for the purpose of increasing the central state's ability to ensure its fiscal capacity and the reach of the state to tax as it saw fit. As Mann points out, the revenues and expenses of the central state expose to us the infrastructural power of that state.[55] Since coercive and infrastructural state capacity are clearly linked to each other,[56] the early Army's ability to be active in both spheres further highlights its importance to the building of central state capacity.

Nothing in the structure of the early national state assured the automatic generation by the Army of either public or government-sponsored private goods. Political and bureaucratic actors had to decide which to provide and how to distribute them (or not to distribute them, as was sometimes the case)—deciding who would get what, when, and how.[57] To explain political control over Army-supplied goods, I argue that we must build upon the distinction between coercive operations and socioeconomic activities. The former involve the traditional functions of a military (the despotic power, in Mann's conceptualization). As such, the use of force presented issues of control that the architects of the constitutional order anticipated. In the center, both presidents and Congress played a significant role, while the Army's commanding general and the secretary of war were largely subordinate to their constitutional masters. In the periphery, however, factors beyond the text of the Constitution influenced effective operational control over coercive operations. Presidents and secretaries of war were reliant on staff officers and field commanders to carry out their orders at a time when communication was slow and often unreliable, and officers often felt alienated from their civilian masters.[58] As a result, there was at best an attenuated form of civilian control in this era, with significant decisions about developmental policies being left in the hands of unelected officers.

On the other hand, socioeconomic activities (uses of the state's infrastructural power) often fell outside the spare constitutional framework, leaving authority more unsettled than in operations involving the use of force. In contrast to those who have located political direction of the Army's socioeconomic actions in one set of actors or in one external force, I argue that a wide range of political actors worked to control the Army's actions. Even within the center, presidents and Congress lacked the institutional capacity to exercise close oversight over routine socioeconomic functions, though they did demonstrate episodic involvement. A notable exception is in the area of river and harbor improvements, where presidents and Congress were consistently involved in important policy decisions. But for the most part, presidents were hampered by poor staff support[59] and, due to their reliance on the party organization, the absence of an independent political base,[60] while Congress sat for short sessions and committees had to rely on informal (that is, partisan) information sources to monitor government operations.[61]

Into this opening created by constitutional ambiguity and the lack of institutional capacity, I demonstrate, stepped two kinds of policy entrepreneurs.[62] First, the secretary of war often made key choices about Army intervention that influenced the direction and pattern of economic development. The source of that entrepreneurship came from the political autonomy that cabinet officials asserted, itself a product of their political base independent of the president.[63] Second, uniformed officers (the chiefs of staff bureaucracies, commanders of geographic departments, and directors of arsenals) exercised a striking degree of bureaucratic autonomy in directing their domains. Especially in the periphery, officers had considerable discretion over the projects under their immediate command, with bureau chiefs playing a particularly important role.[64] Thus the nonpresidential executive branch, often neglected as an independent policymaking force in the early national period, emerges as a center of influence in the young nation's political economy. Autonomy becomes a factor in explaining policy outcomes much earlier than most studies of national bureaucracy have previously suggested.[65] State capacity then becomes enhanced by this bureaucratic professionalism, as autonomous bureaucracies (or those working toward gaining autonomy) have a greater ability to control the levers of state power to accomplish their goals.[66] To the extent they are successful in doing so, bureaucrats become central policy actors responsible for higher levels of state capacity, in this case increased ability to shape economic development.[67]

External forces such as sectionalism also shaped how the Army contributed to American economic and political development. Competing pressures from southern, western, and northern interests all entered at multiple points throughout the political system, especially in Congress, though executive branch actors were also susceptible.[68] Sectional demands led to occasional regional biases in the selection of which socioeconomic projects were funded.[69] There were also significant instances in which the Army was pressured to apply coercive force in ways that helped specific regional interests. Examples include the War of 1812 (favored by western congressmen),[70] the Mexican War (pressed at least in part by southern interests that desired new slave territory),[71] and multiple wars against native tribes as the nation expanded (usually in the West and the South).[72] Nevertheless, because of the fragmentation of political control over Army activities, these did not respond to a single, consistent set of sectional or partisan priorities.

American Political Development, International Politics, and the Developmental State

This study aims to contribute to several scholarly conversations. First, I will reappraise the American political development literature on the early American state, joining a wave of recent scholarship that has revised Skowronek's "courts and parties" portrait in significant ways. Additionally, while most of this research consistently overlooks the role of the military, I depict the national military as a central actor in the antebellum economy.[73] A conception of a state that focuses on social welfare provision and economic regulation, ignoring its coercive potential, is quite deficient. Another theme taken up in this study is how international influences have shaped American political development. Prominent scholars have called for more attention to the ways in which domestic development has been "shaped by war and trade."[74] I will consider the Army as one such conduit through which international competition was translated into domestic change. Furthermore, I contribute to the literature on the role of the state in economic development by highlighting the aspects of a newly formed state that can either further or hinder growth.

Specifically, I show how a military can provide certain necessary public goods that are not being generated by the private sector or other public actors.

State Building and the Early National State in American Political Development

The common view of the early national state in the United States has long emphasized its very limited presence in the everyday lives of the people. As Stephen Skowronek argued, according to certain measures the early national state was indeed a weak instrument. It had the capacity to perform routine distributive tasks (the particular province of the highly developed mass party system) and to adjudicate economic questions arising from the clash of interests in a market economy (the domain of the courts). Once the demands upon the national state surged in the wake of industrialization, Skowronek asserted, the inadequacies of the existing state became plainly visible. A "new American state" emerged fitfully in the late 19th century as the old "state of courts and parties" faltered in the face of new challenges.[75]

Scholars of American political development questioned Skowronek on many points, but largely did not take exception to his thesis of a weak early national state. Richard Bensel argues that the Civil War led to the first strong, centralized state in America, although he contends that it subsequently disintegrated during the Reconstruction era due to internal contradictions within the Republican coalition that had created it.[76] Theda Skocpol's work demonstrates that the American welfare state originated earlier than previously believed, dating back to Civil War veterans' pensions.[77] Daniel Carpenter shows that the federal bureaucracies that successfully asserted their autonomy in the late nineteenth century (such as the Department of Agriculture) succeeded in their state-building objectives, while those unable to do so (e.g., the Department of the Interior) were thwarted.[78]

Recently, however, scholars have taken another look at the early national state and revised this portrait in significant ways.[79] Brian Balogh's important work *Out of Sight* argues that the national government had significant capacities during the nineteenth century but that they were "out of sight" and largely done in cooperation with private actors.[80] He briefly discusses the Army but focuses more on other institutions of the national government. In a similar vein, Colin Moore demonstrates that the U.S. colonial project at the turn of the twentieth century was carried out through inconspicuous means rather than direct national action.[81] Max Edling argues that the very writing of a new Constitution in 1787 was a defining state-building moment for the young nation, creating the American equivalent of a European fiscal-military state by giving the national government strong powers in the areas of taxation and military force.[82] Laura Jensen challenges the standard view that the early national government eschewed any social welfare function by showing how veterans' pensions and government land sales in the early republic contributed to a nascent welfare system, while Michelle Landis Dauber demonstrates that disaster relief was always a core function of the American state.[83] Stefan Heumann has argued that early national state building was driven by the desire of American policymakers to build an American empire.[84] Sectional interests, according to David Ericson, helped enhance the power of the national state: slave states required federal intervention to recapture fugitive slaves, occasionally support colonization efforts, and protect white southerners from slave rebellions and incursions by Native American tribes.[85] Similarly, Matthew Karp's groundbreaking work on American foreign policy has demonstrated how the Navy became an instrument of slaveholders' interests in the antebellum period.[86] Stephen Rockwell's recent work investigates the importance of Indian affairs in building an administrative apparatus in early America, while William Bergmann demonstrates the centrality of the national state to commerce.[87] Like Rockwell, Andrew Kelly demonstrates that scientific capacity building required the building of significant central state authority.[88] In a number of valuable studies, Jerry Mashaw has demonstrated how administrative law was not a modern creation but in fact existed since the nation's founding.[89] Similarly, Paul Frymer's work on the land office demonstrates the central importance of the national government to territorial expansion in this era.[90] Lindsay Regele's recent study on firearms and textiles shows how national investments in new technologies and diplomatic promotion of those goods abroad helped shape those industries and America's economic trajectory in the early nineteenth century.[91]

While these studies have made incredibly important contributions to how we understand the early American state, there are still significant areas that remain underexplored. Balogh's work has shown the ability of the early national state to act in ways that were, as he says, "out of sight"; but I will demonstrate that much of what the Army did was visible and indeed central to the politics of this period. Like Rockwell, I argue that the national government's role as a key bureaucratic actor in the earliest days of the nation has been too often overlooked. Rockwell focuses on the activities of the Indian Office (later renamed the Bureau of Indian Affairs), however, and downplays the crucial role of the Army in physically conquering territory as well as the ever present coercive threat that the Army's presence meant. Frymer's excellent work *Building an American Empire* emphasizes land policy and the General Land Office's role in expansion. I argue, however, that none of those policies could have occurred without the physical possession and securing of the territory made possible by the Army and its extensive system of forts in far-flung regions of the nation.

In his highly regarded work on the Post Office, Richard John demonstrates how it helped spur innovations in communications and made possible an integrated national market.[92] John has also called more generally for a reexamination of the "courts and parties" framework, maintaining that it does not accurately represent the early American state.[93] Other scholars have also called for a reevaluation of the statelessness theory: political scientists Desmond King and Robert Lieberman point out that a comparative look at the American state can help us better theorize the emergence of state authority,[94] while historians William Novak and Gautham Rao argue that the American state was never truly weak.[95] This study extends this recent reconsideration of the early national state by putting the Army at the center of the early national political economy and analyzing its contributions to the growth of central state capacity. I will demonstrate that there was a central state apparatus in this period which in many ways resembled modern bureaucratic forms—the U.S. Army and the War Department.

The Army in the Early Republic

As part of the reassessment of the early national state, scholars have begun to look anew at the place of the Army in the early republic. Comparative politics specialists have long recognized the importance of wars and military power to state building; however, few have examined these factors in the American context, and the comparative literature has also not explicitly linked armies to economy building.[96] Overlooking the warfare-military-state relationship has led scholars to miss important state-building events that do not fall under the typical social welfare and regulatory studies conducted within American Political Development.[97] Work examining the national security state since World War II is more common,[98] though some studies have looked at earlier periods in American history.

In a provocative exploration, Ira Katznelson uses a comparative state-building framework to examine the various ways in which the Army and the use of force shaped early American political development.[99] The Army before the Civil War, he concludes, possessed the "flexible capacity" that best suited the needs of a liberal state. The Army helped the young nation extend its sovereignty and establish a "physical and legal framework for economic development."[100] Although he stresses the role of the Army in the formation of a liberal polity, he also recognizes that army operations had economic implications. Providing physical security in areas contested by Native Americans and settlers, for example, facilitated more productive agricultural development.

That the American Army made important economic contributions in the early national period has been recognized by several scholars. Specialized monographs have traced the impact of the Army on manufacturing technology,[101] the textile and arms industry,[102] the organization of private enterprises,[103] the improvement of waterway transportation,[104] and the growth of the railroads.[105] Interestingly, none of these Army activities directly involved the use of force. In this vein, it is useful to follow the lead of Christopher McGrory Klyza, who demonstrates that the Army enjoyed broad public support when it used its expertise to provide collective or public goods that would otherwise have been undersupplied by market actors or other government entities.[106] Klyza does not consider, however, which actors or institutions directed these activities or how political control over them affected policy outcomes.

In light of the evidence here of the Army's broad involvement in economic development, questions arise about the distribution of power in the early republic, as *who* controlled these policy choices mattered greatly for understanding *which* policy choices were made, and to *whose* benefit. Who exercised political control over the Army's various coercive and noncoercive activities? Which policymaking institutions, if any, established priorities for economic intervention by the armed forces? Did that intervention correspond to partisan or sectional logic? Or did development-oriented activities advance goals generated from within the organization of the Army itself?

To these questions, the extant literature provides no clear answer. Katznelson asserts without supporting evidence that Congress exercised direction over the Army; Ericson sees the military advancing the interests of the slave states; Klyza depicts presidents and Congress turning to the Army largely by default when other federal departments were found wanting; Robert Angevine argues that partisanship and local commercial considerations were foremost in decisions regarding national railroad policy.[107] Bensel similarly puts parties in the forefront, while Theodore Crackel and Richard Kohn focus on the actions of presidents.[108] Many scholars have focused on Congress and the politics of internal improvements.[109] Some of the literature points to bureaucratic actors—senior staff officers within the army—as key innovators whose preferences had a significant economic impact.[110] Finally, other scholarship blurs the division between exogenous and endogenous factors: the integration of professional officers within the partisan state that took shape in the Jacksonian period raises the possibility that soldiers acted as agents of parties in the implementation of distributive policies.[111] I will reappraise this literature in light of more systematic evidence about the Army's activities.

Methodology

This book proceeds with a descriptive analysis of the Army's broad role in economic development in the years from the writing of the Constitution to the Civil War. I systematically test my claims regarding the Army's central role in the economy through careful scrutiny of both primary and secondary materials. To ameliorate the problem of selecting historical studies that could be biased toward my preconceived hypotheses, I rely on multiple sources.[112]

My thesis rests on the assertion that the Army facilitated economic development through the provision of public goods that neither private actors nor other state actors could produce. To support this claim, I carefully document the many ways in which the Army provided goods and expertise essential to economic development. Much of the secondary literature, which I supplement, already points toward a significant *government* role in this period. Two alternative accounts of the early American political economy must be addressed: first, that other national state institutions supplied essential public goods and, second, that state and territorial governments (including mobilized militias) did so. To establish the centrality of the Army's role, I show that it intervened to generate public goods that other governmental actors failed to provide. The possibility that decision makers responded consistently to sectional or partisan imperatives is also considered. In my analysis of the role of various political and bureaucratic actors, I look for patterns of outcomes that seem to correspond to sectional or partisan interests.

Establishing the importance of the Army in the political economy of development requires the use of different kinds of data. One measure comes from federal budgets and national expenditures on internal improvements as well as on total spending on the army. This helps me calculate the direct and indirect outlays for internal improvements and the proportion of that spending undertaken under the Army's auspices. Comparing national military expenditures with state militia expenditures provides one measure of their relative importance in providing for security. I also argue that central state institutions were crucial in assuring the rule of law and unifying a fragile nation, steps indispensable for economic growth. The contribution of the Army to sustaining national authority and checking tendencies toward fragmentation cannot be measured entirely through quantitative indicators. I examine instances in which national authority and the rule of law were threatened either internally or externally. Here I document my claim that coercion or the threat of coercion by the army was vital to enforce national economic policies (as in the Whiskey Rebellion), suppress secessionist currents or rebellions, and check slave uprisings.

Similarly, I argue that the Army's coercive activities were crucial in expanding the nation's territorial boundaries, opening new regions for settlement and resource extraction, and in connecting remote settler populations to the central state. Here I examine instances of territorial expansion to determine the extent of the Army's importance. Some cases, such as the Mexican War, are clear-cut examples of coercive force being used in the service of expansion. Others, including battles with Native American tribes, are perhaps not as obvious, but no less important. Appropriating land from Native Americans should properly be seen as territorial expansion in the same way as battles with foreign nations that altered U.S. boundaries. The Army also tied remote settlements to national authority. On this point, I examine cases of settler unrest and disaffection from the national state (such as the Mormons) to see how important the Army was in preventing secession or estrangement from national authority.

In examining socioeconomic activities, I argue that the Army made three particular contributions: it helped build a national infrastructure, it supplied scarce engineering expertise to the private sector, and it encouraged standardization and organizational innovations in the private sector. To demonstrate the Army's role in infrastructure building, I identify construction projects ordered and carried out by the Army, or cases where Army assistance was provided to others working on infrastructure enhancement. For engineering expertise, I examine the activities of the Army Corps of Engineers and the Topographical Corps of Engineers to find instances of engineers cooperating closely with or being lent to private businesses. Engineers educated at the West Point military academy who left the Army were another source of engineering knowledge, and I provide evidence of their importance in building and maintaining various projects, such as the railroads. This also highlights the importance of West Point as a crucial element in training those engineers whose future work would be central in propelling economic development. Occasions upon which various branches of the Army bureaucracy, such as the Ordnance Department, encouraged standardization and innovation in the private sector are examined as well.

The other central claim I make is that the distribution of public goods provided by the Army varied according to which political actors directed the Army's activities. I argue that coercive activities were mostly conducted within the framework of the Constitution. To test that assertion, I examine instances where force was used or in which pressure was applied by Congress to use force, including (but not necessarily limited to) multiple battles with Native American tribes, the Quasi-War with France, the War of 1812, the Mexican-American War, confrontations with European nations over border disputes between their colonial lands and the United States, and domestic applications of force to impose national authority and the rule of law. In each case, I analyze which actors pushed to use force and who directed and controlled operations once they were under way.

Socioeconomic activities demonstrate a different pattern of political direction, with a more varied set of actors involved. I expect to find that presidents and Congress intervened irregularly, leaving space for the secretary of war and staff officers heading bureaus within the War Department to act as political entrepreneurs and push forward their own priorities for economic development projects. To test this claim, I examine the full array of noncoercive development activities undertaken by the Army, including internal improvements, the loaning of Army engineers to private companies, and armament policy.

I also argue that several bureaus within the War Department display characteristics of bureaucratic autonomy in their economic development actions. Bureaucratic autonomy here would consist of actors within these agencies, especially the uniformed heads of the bureaus, pushing for activities not at the behest of other actors or institutions but at their own initiative. Here I provide evidence that these bureaucrats advocated development policies when others did not push for the same actions. I will focus on the Ordnance Department, the Army Corps of Engineers, and the topographical engineers, three agencies within the War Department that developed particular forms of technical expertise and advanced bureaucratic structures.

Structure of the Book

Chapter 1 begins the analytical portion of the book, focusing on the Army's coercive activities. The Army used coercion to promote economic development in three particular areas. First, the Army preserved the rule of law and asserted national authority throughout the country, a precondition for successful development. Second, through wars against other nations and native tribes, the Army was the nation's primary instrument of territorial expansion, hence opening new regions to white settlement and resource extraction. Finally, the nationwide system of forts built by the Army expanded the range of land open to white settlement by protecting migrants from threats by native tribes, and also nurtured nascent markets on the periphery. Here the Army was clearly engaged in providing collective goods that other actors were unable to, ranging from large-scale wars against other countries to smaller skirmishes against native tribes, to the suppression of domestic disturbances. Often the Army led the way in staking out new ground that had not previously been settled, for instance by building forts that encouraged migration to the West. Sometimes, however, the Army took actions that could have been provided by the private sector, at least in theory. Protecting mining communities or the fur trade could have been handled by a private security force or state militias, but the Army nonetheless became involved, as no other institution was capable of providing such services. All these activities had a significant impact upon the American economy by encouraging settlement in certain regions of the nation and encouraging resource extraction throughout the West.

Chapter 2 analyzes the Army's socioeconomic role. The Army trained engineers and provided them to the private sector at a time when engineering expertise was extremely rare, allowing for the faster building of infrastructure projects across the nation. Engineers also helped to build roads, canals, and railroads. The topographical engineers surveyed the geography, geology, and mineralogy of lakes, rivers, and newly acquired territories. Western surveys performed by topographers, such as John C. Frémont, advanced the concept of Manifest Destiny in the 1840s and 1850s and spurred many to travel to and settle in peripheral areas. Their maps also helped smooth trade flows across the continent as the nation expanded. Engineers and ordnance officers both encouraged technological and administrative innovations that subsequently spread to the private sector. For instance, the development of manufacturing based on interchangeable parts can be directly traced to the Ordnance Department's armories, which invented the technique to speed the building of armaments. Here the Army provided mostly private goods, although in many cases the needed expertise existed nowhere else except in the Army (as was the case for engineering knowledge in most of this period). Absent the Army's contributions, especially its crucial role in the periphery, the nation's economy would have looked quite different and growth would have occurred significantly later.

The question of which political actors controlled the Army's uses of force is taken up in Chapter 3. It examines the role of presidents, Congress, secretaries of war, bureau chiefs within the War Department, and officers on the ground. Here I argue that presidents and Congress were the primary actors involved in high-level decision making on questions of when and how to use force, as per the powers granted to them by the Constitution. In the center it was relatively easy for presidents and Congress to control the Army. However, in the periphery, due to slow communication and an occasional lack of interest in operational details, the secretary of war, bureau chiefs, and field commanders often made crucial decisions without first consulting constitutional actors. As a result, the periphery saw a highly attenuated form of civilian control, with officers on the ground often making policy decisions contrary to the wishes of their civilian masters—meaning that those officers shaped many of the economic development policies they had been sent to implement.

Chapter 4 explores the politics of the Army's socioeconomic activities. Without any clear constitutional guidance, political actors struggled over control. Presidents and Congress tended to have somewhat less involvement than in coercive activities, though members of Congress did become more involved on high-profile issues such as the building of the Cumberland Road. Instead, secretaries of war and the heads of War Department bureaus exhibited a striking degree of independence in managing and directing the Army's socioeconomic role, especially in the periphery. Bureaucrats heading offices such as the Ordnance Department or the Corps of Topographical Engineers developed a high degree of bureaucratic autonomy far earlier than previous studies have shown. Their independence gave them the ability to press for their desired economic development policies and enhanced state capacity regardless of partisan control of the presidency and Congress, making them the most stable actors in antebellum politics. The topographical engineers, headed by Colonel John J. Abert, became highly influential and were turned to for many of the most important policies of the national state, including surveying western territories and determining the location of the transcontinental railroad. Ultimately, however, their bias toward a southern route helped lead to the corps's demise.

The book concludes 6 with some final thoughts on the role of the Army and international influences in the study of American political development, as well as a reconsideration of the Army's role in economic development. By demonstrating the Army's central role in shaping the new nation's economy, this study joins the recent wave of scholarship that has undermined the traditional perspective of a weak American state in the nineteenth century and draws new attention to the role of the Army in American political development.

CHAPTER 1

Coercion and Economic Development

One of the most important functions any state performs is defending its territory and population from outside attacks, a job generally carried out primarily by the national military. Often overlooked, however, is how this seemingly mundane task also has significant economic implications. In early America, the Army's coercive power was used in a variety of ways that helped to shape the pattern of economic developments and the shape and size of the emerging American nation.

This chapter describes three interconnected areas through which the Army's use of force shaped economic development. First, the Army helped to preserve the rule of law and ensure national authority throughout the country, a precondition for successful economic development, by enforcing national laws and trying to preserve the peace when order was threatened. As Douglass North has argued, a state that can manage violence and ensure the rule of law is essential for economic development.[1] This included large-scale events such as the suppression of the Whiskey Rebellion by President George Washington and the so-called Mormon War of the late 1850s. More subtly, the Army protected slaveholders fearful of slave revolts through its presence at forts scattered throughout the South, thus assisting in the preservation of the southern slave economy. Bruce Porter argues that suppressing domestic revolts was "a critical factor in establishing the authority of the early modern state"[2] in Europe. The same logic can be applied to the United States, as a new central government used coercion (or the threat of coercion) to spread its authority to peripheral regions that remained dissatisfied with the Constitution's creation of a stronger national state.

Second, the Army was the nation's primary instrument of territorial growth. This included major conflicts such as the War of 1812 and the Mexican War, both of which were at least partly driven by a desire for territorial expansion. The Army also enforced order in newly acquired territories such as the Louisiana Purchase, and later in the southwestern territories acquired from Mexico. In addition, frequent skirmishes with native tribes and the Army's consistent pressure on those tribes led to steady acquisitions of territory by the national government on behalf of white settlers. Officers acted as the enforcers of treaties negotiated with tribes by the government's Indian agents (largely under the auspices of the War Department) and the soldiers' mere presence during a negotiation provided a threatening backdrop in case tribal chiefs refused the federal government's demands. The Army was also responsible for implementation of the national policy of Indian removal that began under Andrew Jackson. These actions took place entirely within the periphery.

Third, the nationwide system of forts built by the Army expanded the range of land open to white settlement. The presence of soldiers protected nascent communities in the periphery from perceived or real threats from Indians. Forts often sparked the beginnings of local markets through procurement contracts and the troops' individual purchasing power. The forts were also instrumental in spreading national authority throughout the country by providing security for far-flung settler communities on the periphery.

Politicians and government officials setting up new authority structures in the periphery frequently turned to the Army to enforce the laws, given a lack of other alternatives. No other part of the state had the same potential to use its resources in defense of national authority. Christopher McGrory Klyza argues that in natural resources policies, when the Army had special expertise and acted in support of true public goods, it maintained public support and more effectively carried out its mission. In contrast, when it tried to handle areas it was less competent in and that did not serve a public good, such as mining policy, it failed.[3] Extending this argument, the Army's coercive activities are one policy area where a true collective good was being served (the enforcement of national authority) and the Army held special expertise. Its only potential competitors were the state militias, which were generally either unable to enforce national authority or uninterested in doing so. They also relied largely on the national Army for much of their equipment, including weapons. Beginning in 1808, the federal government spent $200,000 per year to equip the militias, a program directed by the Ordnance Department. The militias also received manuals of instruction prepared by the War Department.[4] States accepted this assistance and eventually became increasingly reliant upon national support for their militias.

Preserving Order, Promoting Development

In this section, I discuss the Army's contributions to development through preserving order and asserting national authority. The new nation was in a state of flux in its early years, with no guarantee that the citizenry would willingly obey laws issued by a new central government. Threats of secession by those dissatisfied with some aspect of national governance were rife and had to be taken seriously.[5] Many Americans viewed the union as "only the means, rather than an end in itself, to the creation of the ideal state."[6] Indeed, there was every expectation that the country could dissolve into several smaller confederacies. Alexander Hamilton took this possibility quite seriously in *Federalist* 6, 7, and 8, remonstrating against those who believed such a breakup to be inevitable and perhaps even beneficial.[7] Trying to scare a population fearful of military might, he argued in *Federalist* number 8 that "standing armies . . . must inevitably result from a dissolution of the Confederacy. Frequent war and constant apprehension, which require a state of as constant preparation, will infallibly produce them. . . . It is of the nature of war to increase the executive at the expense of the legislative authority."[8] He also warned that separate confederacies constantly under threat of invasion from each other would lead to a situation where "the military state becomes elevated above the civil." In contrast, a unified nation would see its army "rarely, if at all, called into activity for interior defense . . . [and] the civil state remains in full vigor."[9]

Although Hamilton denied that Americans would feel the force of the new central state, the Constitution did give the national government significant new military powers with which to enforce the laws. Prior to this, under the Articles of Confederation, the states had retained primary control over the use of force. State militias constituted the bulk of American armed might, reflecting the popular aversion to standing armies.[10] States controlled recruitment for the (small) national force, appointed officers, handled promotions, and occasionally even supplied their own troops.[11] Under the Constitution, by contrast, an effective national army (at least in theory) could be created, without the national government always having to beg states for troops. There was little opposition at the constitutional convention to creating a stronger national military.[12]

The Center

The Army made important contributions to development through its policies of enforcing order in the center, though it was not necessarily involved in every dispute. After the Revolutionary War ended, the Continental Army was almost completely demobilized by Congress, leaving only an eighty-man force.[13] When Shays's Rebellion erupted in western Massachusetts, it took aim at the Springfield Armory, the largest repository of national armaments. Secretary at War (as the position was then called) Henry Knox discovered he could not act decisively to support the established state authorities. He was even unable to order General William Shepard, on the scene, to use the armory's supplies without explicit congressional permission—lacking since Congress did not have a quorum. Knox requested two thousand militia from the states but only Massachusetts and Connecticut responded. Shepard decided to commandeer the armory anyway even without authorization, at which point the rebels finally dispersed.[14] The inability of the national government to sustain order contributed to the movement for fundamental reform of the national state, change that would incorporate significantly greater military capacity at the national level than had existed under the Articles of Confederation.[15] As Richard Kohn notes, "Shays's Rebellion dramatized the military impotence of the United States. . . . The need to suppress insurrection and to guarantee domestic order was injected into the debate over the military powers of the central government."[16]

Importantly, the Constitution gave Congress the power "to provide for calling forth the Militia to execute the Laws of the Union, suppress Insurrections and repel Invasions," and "to provide for organizing, arming, and disciplining, the Militia, and for governing such Part of them as may be employed in the Service of the United States," thus altering the balance of power in military affairs to favor the national government over the states (with states retaining some influence over the militia). The only significant restriction put on Congress's ability to "raise and support" an army was a two-year time limit on any authorization law, requiring regular consideration of the military's place in the American polity. This provision reflected the pervasive fear of standing armies.[17] The Constitution was also vague on whether regular troops could be used to stop domestic disturbances.[18] Henry Knox continued his steady leadership at the helm of the War Department, the only administrative department to maintain its essential structure in the transition from the Articles to the Constitution.[19] In May 1792, using its new powers, Congress passed the Calling Forth Act, giving the president the authority to call out the militia to protect states from invasions and to use military coercion to enforce the laws, if necessary, following a presidential proclamation. Notably, however, regular troops were not allowed to be used in this manner.[20]

An important test of expanded state power arises when those who oppose it find themselves in a position to undo it. In the case of the early national security apparatus, the Democratic-Republican opposition had resisted the expansion of military capacity in the 1790s, seeing it as an instrument of Federalist machinations to retain power and ally the United States with Great Britain.[21] Following Thomas Jefferson's election, the erstwhile opposition found itself in control of the military instruments it had condemned. The Jefferson administration did not hesitate to deploy those instruments.

Although Jefferson reduced the Army to 3,300 troops (Figure 1), much of that cutback had already been made inevitable by the elimination of the New Army at the end of John Adams's term.[22] In fact, the Military Peace Establishment Act of 1802, the law supposedly reorganizing the Army on Jeffersonian principles, did not significantly cut the officer corps. It saved barely $35,000 a year, in comparison to the $500,000 savings that Secretary of War Henry Dearborn had claimed prior to its passage. Eighty-eight of the Army's 230 officers were dismissed, but 20 new positions were created that Jefferson and Dearborn filled with their own appointees. Additionally, before leaving office in early 1801, Adams had added 80 new officers, thus leaving no significant net change in the number of officers, the heart of the regular Army.[23] Jefferson created the military academy at West Point, a Federalist dream that he had long derided as unconstitutional. His unilateral decision to create the academy was later ratified by Congress in the 1802 law.[24]

Working closely with Jefferson, Dearborn took control of military affairs and appointments to both the Army and West Point. From 1802 to 1804, Dearborn proposed appointing 92 specific men to the military academy in his correspondence with Jefferson.[25] Dearborn and Jefferson also rebuilt the Army's administrative structure, eliminating Federalist-dominated regiments and dividing the Army into three geographical departments, each headed by a loyal Republican officer.[26] In the end, Jefferson's Army resembled a streamlined, Republicanized version of the Federalist force; as Kohn notes, "ironi-

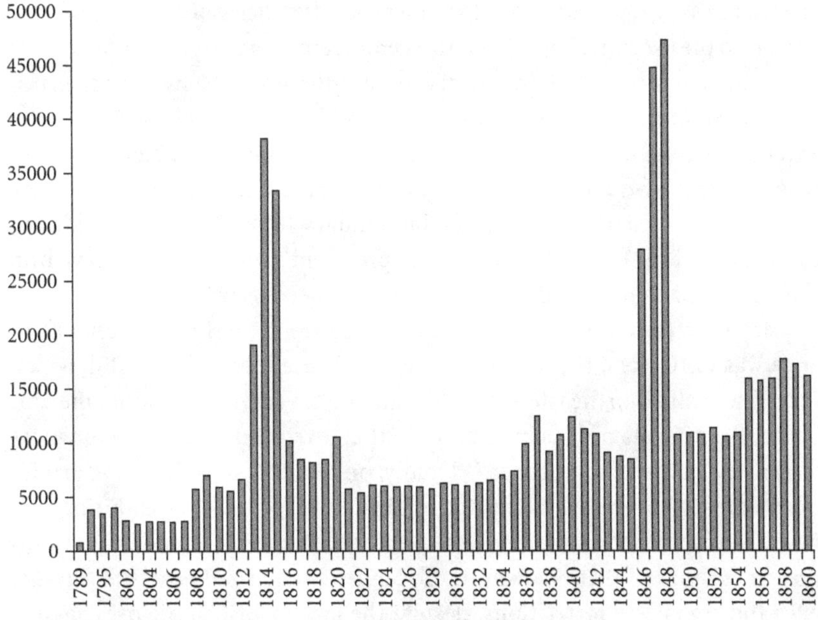

Figure 1. Soldiers Serving in the Army, 1789–1860

cally, Thomas Jefferson completed the nationalist military program of 1783" that the Continental Congress never enacted.[27]

Jefferson soon used the Army to enforce an embargo against trade with Canada and Great Britain. Amid rising tensions with the British after continuing impressments of American sailors and the attack on the American vessel *Chesapeake* in the summer of 1807, war seemed to be inevitable. Jefferson encouraged Congress to first try an embargo as punishment.[28] In sum three embargo laws passed in 1807 and 1808, each progressively harsher than the last, until all forms of trade with the British were outlawed.[29] At the same time, Congress followed Jefferson's goading and in April 1808 increased the total size of the armed forces to over 12,000 men (Figure 1), partly in case of a war, but also intended for use as an enforcement tool instead of the militia, which Jefferson and Secretary of the Treasury Albert Gallatin considered unreliable.[30] This was especially important for the northern border near Vermont and New York, where fierce local resistance nearly erupted into armed insurrection.[31] Apparently most Republicans were no longer as fearful of standing armies as they had been during the days when the Federalists were in charge.

Congress also passed two enforcement acts that delegated significant new powers to the executive branch. The first enforcement act, passed in April 1808, gave Jefferson virtually unlimited discretion, after which Congress adjourned for seven months, leaving the president to decide how to implement it.[32] After extensive smuggling and broad resistance by merchants in New England, where Federalist-dominated states actively tried to undermine the embargo, a second enforcement act was passed in January 1809. This law (also known as the Force Bill) further expanded the president's discretion and gave him the right to call out the militia if he deemed it necessary.[33]

However, the entire edifice of the embargo stood on shaky ground. Defiance was only strengthened by the previously mentioned Force Bill, which served to unify Northeastern Republicans with Federalists against the embargo. Britain was not backing down, either, even though its economy was feeling the pain of the embargo.[34] Finally, on March 1, 1809, Jefferson grudgingly signed a bill ending the embargo.[35] The embargo had little enduring economic impact on the United States, but it did encourage a tendency toward greater feelings of sectionalism in the South. Many southerners fell in line with the embargo's restrictions, despite the lack of British offenses against the South—impressments had primarily hurt trading ships leaving the Northeast. However, southern Republicans later became increasingly hostile toward the North when they felt that northerners did not appreciate their sacrifices made during the embargo period on behalf of northern interests. As historian Brian Schoen has argued, toward the end of the embargo southern spokesmen started to identify their economic interests as separate from those of the nation, beginning a trend that would later culminate in the great tariff debates of the 1820s and 1830s.[36]

The early Jacksonian period saw scattered threats to the rule of law, but few instances of force actually being deployed. Evidently the nation had become somewhat more unified and accustomed to the idea of the Army as the final guarantor of federal authority, though this assumption was not universally shared. The mere suggestion that the Army might get involved often proved enough of an incentive for parties opposing the federal government to back down. Several examples will demonstrate this pattern.

In 1832, Congress approved a new tariff bill that significantly raised the rates on many items. Southern states vigorously protested this action due to its potentially negative effects on exports to Europe, as they had been protesting protective legislation since the so-called Tariff of Abominations in 1828.[37] One state, South Carolina, took its opposition to the extreme when its state legislature voted to nullify the federal law, challenging the very basis of federal authority. Inspired by the recently radicalized vice president, John C. Calhoun, some in the state even proposed secession as a solution.[38] In response to this threat, President Andrew Jackson began preparing to use federal troops based in South Carolina and surrounding states, in case the legislature refused to back down. Jackson had good reason to mobilize forces outside South Carolina as some of the troops there had pro-nullification sympathies and might have been aroused to oppose the federal government.[39]

At first, however, Jackson held out hope for a negotiated solution. He "expected public opinion in South Carolina to compel the nullifiers to desist" until late in 1832.[40] As the crisis continued and the state showed no signs of backing down, the president shifted to a more aggressive strategy involving the use of force.[41] Jackson worked closely with Joel Poinsett, a major pro-Union political figure in South Carolina (who would later become the secretary of war under President Martin Van Buren), to prevent the state from carrying through its threats. He ordered five thousand extra muskets sent to the troops there, dispatched a personal agent to report back intelligence on the situation, and had Secretary of War Lewis Cass send General Winfield Scott to take command.[42] Cass also preemptively strengthened federal forces in Georgia in case any attempt was made there to grab supplies from the federal arsenal in Augusta.[43] On December 10, Jackson issued a presidential proclamation ordering the state not to interfere with the enforcement of federal laws. But South Carolina remained defiant.[44]

Still preparing for a battle but hoping for a compromise, Jackson began working with Congress on two bills. The first would become the Force Bill, giving the president additional tools with which to use force, if necessary; the second was a revised version of the tariff bill, intended to soothe angry southerners. These two elements together compelled South Carolina to back down and grudgingly accept the validity of the federal tariff laws.[45] Although the Army was not actually required to engage in a confrontation, the mere threat of force here worked to undermine South Carolina's position and sustain the legitimacy of federal authority in the realm of economic affairs. Southern separatism would die down for a while afterward, though it continued to bubble beneath the surface.

On at least one occasion, Jackson did agree to send federal troops to intervene to maintain order. This action was spurred by a labor dispute in 1834 during the construction of the Chesapeake and Ohio Canal. The laborers working on construction of the canal, who were largely Irish immigrants, opposed bringing in additional workers to assist for fear that it would reduce their wages. There was a series of riots in early January 1834, as competing groups battled and rioted for control of the construction site. A temporary truce was achieved when the state militia was sent in, but that was short-lived as riots persisted. Finally, on January 28, the state legislature of Maryland voted on a resolution sent to the governor asking that he request military assistance from President Jackson. Governor James Thomas did so that same day, requesting that the president send in forces pursuant to the 1807 Insurrection Act. The next day, Jackson ordered Cass to send at least two companies of regular troops to quell the violence. The troops soon arrived and put an end to this uprising. When later that year it seemed to be bubbling up again, a simple threat to recall the troops ended any movement toward restarting.[46]

Jackson's successor as president, Martin Van Buren, faced a serious crisis over federal authority that was also a major international incident, the so-called Patriot War. Beginning in 1837, Americans sympathetic to the cause of Canadian independence from Great Britain (calling themselves Patriots) organized secret societies and led filibusters into Canadian territory. The Canadian rebellion began in December 1837. After a rebel defeat, some went to the United States and worked with their sympathizers to foment public opinion against the British. On December 29, 1837, as the filibusterers prepared to mount an expedition into Canada, the Canadian militia burned the rebel ship *Caroline* on the American side of the border near Buffalo. One American was killed, and opinion surged against the British and in favor of war. Upon realizing that state militias were unsuited to the task (the New York militia was openly pro-Patriot), Van Buren used the Army to calm the border and attempt to keep the filibusterers out of Canada.[47]

With much of the Army deployed in Florida to fight the Seminole Indians, Van Buren relied instead on several senior officers to stabilize the border. General Winfield Scott was sent to Buffalo in 1839, where he used "rhetoric and diplomacy" more than force.[48] Secretary of War Poinsett instructed him that his job was to ensure that "the supremacy of the laws . . . be asserted and maintained."[49] Army officers worked to restrain the worst impulses of American expansionism through close attention to local prejudices with a minimum of force.[50] Scott did take command of the local militia, however, and also chartered a ship to police the waters between the United States and Canada. Simultaneously, General John E. Wool was sent to Vermont and General Hugh Brady to Michigan. Wool led three companies of militia against

Patriots threatening to cross the border, defeating them easily. Governor Stephen T. Mason of Michigan begged for extra troops, and Brady was reinforced by Colonel William Jenkins Worth. These regular troops battled the Patriots and were largely successful in stopping their activity.[51]

On May 28, the British ship *Sir Robert Peel* was sunk by the Patriots, leading the president to order the Army's commanding general, Alexander Macomb, to the scene, in an attempt to avoid further damage to relations with Great Britain. Macomb ordered artillery moved from the Cherokee frontier to the North to assist in his efforts, and the troops soon caught two members of the gang involved in the attack. Van Buren also successfully requested from Congress an increase in the Army's authorized strength, from 8,069 to 12,379 (though only 8,653 were in service that year [see Figure 1]).[52] The extra troops and the presence of top officers seemed to end the immediate crisis, and although plotting by Patriots continued well into 1841, the worst of the fighting had already ended. Army regulars stayed near the border throughout this period, working with local officials to keep the populace in line with federal policy and opening sufficient space for negotiations with the British to continue.[53] By the time of his annual message to Congress in 1840, Van Buren could report honestly that the United States had "a rigid and persevering abstinence from all interference with the domestic and political relations of other States."[54]

The new administration elected in 1840 soon faced a crisis of its own, the Dorr Rebellion. Rhode Island had been operating under its seventeenth-century colonial charter, which denied voting rights to those who did not own property. At a time of widening democratization in the country this sparked a reform movement, led by Thomas Wilson Dorr, to write a new constitution that would broaden voting rights and create a new governing structure. When the state assembly, controlled by upper-class conservatives, called a constitutional convention in November 1841, the suffragist movement decided to hold its own convention. Two opposing constitutions were soon submitted to the people for a vote: the assembly's version was defeated and the so-called People's Convention triumphed. Both sides then called for elections, with the old government designating the Dorr-led faction a rebellion against the legitimate governing authority of the state.[55]

Governor Samuel King appealed to President John Tyler for federal intervention to ensure that Dorr and his followers would not take over, but Tyler demurred. As a precaution, the War Department placed extra security on its supplies at Fort Adams near Newport, Rhode Island. Each side then held an election of its own, choosing different governments, with Dorr elected as governor by the suffragists. Two more artillery companies were then sent to the state as further security for federal supplies. Governor King's legislature passed a resolution calling the Dorr government an insurrection, and King again asked Tyler for federal help. Tyler again refused. Dorr's forces then seized supplies from a federal armory, and left the state, perhaps preparing for an invasion. King asked a third time for federal help, and Tyler once again refused. However, he did have Secretary of War John C. Spencer send Generals John Wool and Abraham Eustis to the state to gather intelligence and report back. At first, they detected no lingering danger; but by mid-June 1842 the Dorrites had returned. This time, Tyler sent Spencer in right away with a cease-and-desist proclamation, implicitly threatening the use of force if they did not stand down. Tyler privately informed King that he would be prepared to use the Army if necessary to maintain the legitimate state authorities. King declared martial law, and Dorr and his remaining followers fled to Connecticut, ending the rebellion.[56] Although force was not employed in this instance, "the threat of its use clearly played a role in the demise of Dorr's partisans," according to historian Robert Coakley.[57]

On occasion, the Army was involved in stopping slave revolts and returning fugitive slaves to their masters. The southern economy rested firmly on the institution of slavery.[58] Accordingly. the Army's actions in protecting slavery helped to prop up the South and perpetuate slavery as an economic force. Actual slave rebellions were quite rare, but southerners lived in constant fear that one could occur. Therefore, even though state militias were usually used to stop a revolt, "the army served an important psychological function. . . . [T]he presence of the regulars was believed to be a powerful deterrent to any groups contemplating an insurrection."[59] The Army was not used regularly to protect slavery but the few examples of its use do signify an avenue of federal support for the institution of slavery (along with the Navy's use as an instrument of national power to assist slaveholders' interests, as Matthew Karp has shown).[60]

Several examples show the ways that the Army supported the institution of slavery. Troops helped to capture runaway slaves in the Louisiana Territory prior to the formation of distinct states. A slave revolt in January 1811 was only stopped by a combined force of militia and federal troops.[61] In 1831, a slave rebellion in South Hampton, Virginia, was suppressed by five companies of infantry sent out from nearby Fortress Monroe.[62] As settled regions moved farther west, the Army sometimes kept forts in the older locations no longer under direct threat by Indian tribes, simply to guarantee southern peace of mind against potential slave revolts.[63] The Fugitive Slave Law of 1850 strengthened federal powers to capture and return runaway slaves. Though the Army was not mentioned in the law, President Millard Fillmore and his cabinet told a federal judge that regular troops could be used to enforce the law if a marshal or judge determined that their presence was necessary. According to historian Robert Coakley, on at least three occasions in the early 1850s the Army helped to capture a slave who had decamped to the North.[64] These actions weakened the Army's reputation as a neutral arbiter and made it again seem to be a captive of southern interests. The Army's prosouthern actions made it easier for the new Republican Party to portray the federal government as being in the service of the so-called slave power, and Republicans opposed the Army's expansion in the late 1850s as a result.[65]

As this section has shown, the Army was involved in multiple instances of preserving order in the center during this period. The Army was not used frequently, but its uses were targeted toward preserving the rule of law, ensuring national authority, and maintaining stability. Absent the actions of the Army, national authority might have eroded and economic development might have been slower, as instability and uncertainty would have clouded the outlook for investors, consumers, and business.

The Periphery

While uses of force to maintain order in the nation's periphery were not consistent, the cases in which coercion was used proved important as examples of how the national government would enforce national authority when needed. The national government under President Washington soon took advantage of its new powers under the Constitution to tie peripheral regions to the central state, enhancing economic ties across the nation and laying the groundwork for an integrated national economy. Military force played a decisive role during the Whiskey Rebellion, an important moment in establishing national authority that guaranteed the fiscal foundation of the central state and affirmed its power to direct economic development. The basic story is familiar: after Congress, as part of Hamilton's economic program, passed an excise tax on whiskey production in 1791, rebellion simmered in the western Pennsylvania backcountry, the center of American whiskey manufacture. The Pennsylvania legislature denounced the tax, protest meetings formed across the state, and federal tax collectors were harassed, with several instances of violence.[66] As Max Edling and Mark Kaplanoff point out, at the time tax revolts were not uncommon.[67] To acquiesce in the whiskey tax protest, then, would have invited similar resistance elsewhere in a political climate that treated tax revolts as legitimate. Inaction would have compromised the fiscal capacity of the new national government.

Despite this threat to national authority, government officials did not turn immediately to military force, with Secretary of War Henry Knox and President Washington trying for several years to control the situation through easing of the taxes and negotiations. However, when seven thousand to ten thousand men gathered at Braddock's Field in July 1794, Washington tired of conciliatory measures and called out the state militias of Pennsylvania, New Jersey, Maryland, and Virginia. Pennsylvania dragged its feet and Maryland had difficulty due to its own incipient rebellion, but the other states provided the troops requested. Interestingly, regular troops were not used (probably because there were so few at this time—just over seven hundred [see Figure 1]), but it required national authority to bring these disparate forces together. Pennsylvania had hesitated to use its own militia and without federal assistance the crisis could have spun out of control. On October 4, Washington and Hamilton personally came to lead the forces gathered at Carlisle, Pennsylvania. In November and December they marched the troops into the western part of the state, and the rebels quickly dispersed upon learning of the massive force headed their way. Barely two hundred were arrested, and only two were found guilty of treason.[68] The organization of a military response by Washington, with Knox's assistance, and the subsequent collapse of the rebellion without bloodshed thus represented an assertion of the national state's legitimate and superior authority in the realm of economic decision making.[69] Washington's intervention ensured the primacy of national authority by demonstrating the extent of national capabilities: a relatively small government proved strong enough to enforce its laws. Without military intervention, the authority of the central state to enforce its laws and raise revenue through taxation would have been severely compromised.

In 1799, another tax revolt led to a national military response. Relations with France had slowly deteriorated since the ratification of the Jay Treaty in 1795, which gave preferential treatment to the British in trading with the United States.[70] The immediate crisis began in the winter of 1797, the first year of John Adams's presidency. The French Directory, in control at this stage of the French Revolution, issued a directive that essentially allowed French ships to commandeer American ships and sailors. This was especially a problem in the West Indies, as Stanley Elkins and Eric McKitrick point out, because of the increasing trade between the United States and those islands. French actions led to declining economic activity and rising insurance premiums and seriously harmed American traders, causing a degradation of relations between the United States and France.[71] The crisis reached its nadir in the infamous XYZ Affair, when three French diplomats insisted on receiving a bribe for their government before they would deign to negotiate with the American representatives sent by Adams.[72] The so-called Quasi-War began at this point, and a furious Federalist-controlled Congress responded by swiftly building up the nation's armed capacity, including a twelve-thousand-man New Army and a ten-thousand-man Provisional Army to be created at the president's discretion.[73]

This new force, of course, had to be funded. Congress passed a direct tax on land, slaves, and homes designed to raise $2 million. Combined with the repressive Alien and Sedition Acts, these new taxes proved quite unpopular, particularly in southeastern Pennsylvania, where many refused to pay, again underscoring the fragile connection between this region and the new central government.[74] John Fries became the leader of a rebellion consisting of 140 men, largely German immigrants. They harassed tax collectors, and even when the local federal marshal arrested several of them, Fries's followers, armed and willing to fire, forced the marshal to release them. Upon learning of the situation in March 1799, Adams immediately decided to send in regular troops to clamp down. Unlike Washington, Adams did not first attempt to negotiate or call up the state militias as required by the 1792 law (partly because the Army was now significantly larger—over 10,000 troops), partly because of the war fervor). Several weeks later, when the troops arrived in Pennsylvania, Fries's supporters dispersed, but the Army nonetheless proceeded to arrest 60 men while treating the local citizens brutally. Fries and two others were eventually convicted of treason (though they were spared by a last-minute presidential pardon).[75] Although this uprising was never as menacing as the Whiskey Rebellion, national force was again important in stopping this threat to national fiscal authority.

Jefferson and Dearborn first used the Army domestically to thwart a budding secession movement headed by former vice president Aaron Burr. In 1806 Burr was apparently attempting to raise a force in the West loyal to him. He planned to lead it down the Mississippi to seize control of New Orleans, and from there conquer West Florida and Mexico. Jefferson learned about Burr's plans from General James Wilkinson, at which point he issued a cease-and-desist proclamation against Burr and his followers, enjoining them to stop their conspiracy. Dearborn sent copies of the proclamation across the West, authorizing the use of regulars or militia to arrest Burr. Wilkinson was soon able to capture Burr, after making many random arrests of civilians along the way.[76] In response, the Senate passed a bill retroactively suspending habeas corpus for three months, but it was rejected by the House. Instead, a new law authorizing the use of regulars in domestic disorders, based on a proposal made by Jefferson in December 1806, was passed and signed by the president—"positive proof that it was Jefferson, the Republican, who dictated this reversal of the philosophy of 1788" when the Framers had specifically not authorized the use of regulars in domestic disturbances.[77] By ending this secessionist threat, the Army assured national control over the territorial periphery.

As the cross-regional party system that had minimized sectional conflict began to break apart toward the end of the Jacksonian era, sectional concerns rose to prominence again.[78] Conflicts over slavery's role and territorial expansion were exacerbated by the debates surrounding the Mexican War. Now the Army's task in enforcing the rule of law became more complicated as each section of the country pursued its own interests with less regard to national concerns. The Army was soon forced into the role of mediator. Officers who hailed from different regions found themselves more than ever before enforcing policies with which they disagreed, leading to tension within the Army between the goals of enforcing the law and of maintaining a fragile sectional peace. This tension is best illustrated by the increasing number of filibusters attempted by American citizens during the 1850s as well as the lawlessness that often prevailed in the newly acquired western territories.

Following the end of the war against Mexico, American settlement expanded into the newly acquired territories in the Southwest, and popular sentiment in the South favored obtaining even more slavery-friendly lands. Democratic politicians from the South propounded various schemes to get more from Mexico or purchase Cuba from Spain, or sometimes more outlandish plans that envisioned an American slave empire stretching across Latin America.[79] These feelings led to a plethora of unauthorized attempts by private individuals to lead filibusters that would take new territories by force. President Fillmore, who had signed into law the Compromise of 1850, worked hard to extend sectional cooperation by preventing these efforts from succeeding. In 1851, he used the Army to stop expeditions that were trying to grab Cuba and the Sandwich Islands (better known today as Hawaii).[80]

Fillmore also worked to stop filibusters into Mexico, such as those led by Jose Carvajal, who tried to break off part of northern Mexico and form a liberal republic friendly to the United States. The president ordered Brigadier General David E. Twiggs and Colonel Persifor Smith to the border area to stop Carvajal, but despite their efforts trouble continued for several more years.[81]

When Franklin Pierce took over as president he shifted national policy toward expansionism with a southern tinge, leading to the Gadsden Purchase from Mexico and new efforts to acquire Cuba.[82] The Army was also significantly expanded in this period, growing from eleven thousand soldiers to over sixteen thousand, as part of the southern-led push for a stronger military apparatus.[83] Most Army officers were still committed to enforcing the neutrality laws and stopping filibusters, though a distinct minority felt differently and actively aided or did little to stop filibusters.[84] For example, Colonel Ethan Allen Hitchcock, a staunch Whig who commanded the Division of the Pacific, stopped the ship *Arrow* from illegally heading toward northern Mexico out of San Francisco on September 30, 1853. City leaders complained vigorously about the seizure, as did Democratic Senator William Gwin. Within a few days the organizers of the filibuster took advantage of weak security caused by the dispute to grab supplies off the *Arrow* and move them to the *Caroline*, which immediately departed for Mexico. Shortly after this incident Hitchcock, who publicly stated his opposition to filibusters, was replaced by Brigadier General John Wool, a loyal Democrat thought to be more persuadable on the issue.[85] Secretary of War Jefferson Davis stated in his orders to Wool that his post entailed "maintaining our international obligations by preventing unlawful expeditions against the territories of foreign powers. Confidence is felt that you will, to the utmost of your ability, use all proper means to detect the fitting out of armed expeditions against countries with which the United States are at peace, and will zealously cooperate with the civil authorities in maintaining the neutrality laws."[86] It seems that Davis was not entirely serious when he made this statement, however, and that the order was simply routine. In the end Wool also disappointed Davis with his lack of zest for expansion and his continued efforts to reign in filibusters, leading to a series of disputes between the two.[87] The reigning ideology of Manifest Destiny had now divided the Army internally between those committed to its traditional law enforcement mission and those agitating for further southern expansion.

Wool's conflicts with Davis and the Pierce administration seemed to dampen his enthusiasm for using the Army in law enforcement. Still commanding in the West, Wool was on the frontlines as San Francisco was struck with a plague of lawlessness in 1856. After a newspaper editor was shot by a local gambler, a vigilante committee was established that in its rage grabbed two other gamblers from the local prison and executed them. There were six thousand vigilantes running rampant and the local militia seemed powerless to stop them. Governor J. Neely Johnson of California declared the city in a state of insurrection and on June 4 asked Wool for permission to use supplies from the federal arsenal in Benecia. Wool initially seemed supportive, but he quickly changed his mind: he refused the request and told his troops to remain neutral. He told Johnson that only the president had the authority to allow the use of the arsenal. Johnson's subsequent entreaties to Pierce were turned down based on a formalistic interpretation of the 1795 and 1807 laws regulating the use of the Army issued by Attorney General Caleb Cushing. In the end, Secretary of War Davis told Wool to merely protect federal property until the crisis had passed but otherwise keep the Army uninvolved.[88] Davis's concerns about using the Army may have been partly prompted by his worries that an active government role in internal state affairs could later lead to federal meddling in southern slavery, though he also expressed a belief that state militias were better equipped to enforce the rule of law than the Army.[89] (Later, of course, Davis would change his mind about using national force, when he authorized the use of troops during the Bleeding Kansas episode.)

Two challenges at the end of the decade would test the government's newfound reluctance to use troops in preserving the rule of law. The Kansas-Nebraska Act of 1854 opened up the territory of Kansas for settlement and enshrined the principle of popular sovereignty into law: the people of the territory would decide for themselves whether to have slavery. Missouri, next door to Kansas, worked hard to make it a new slave state, and thousands of Missourians poured in. A proslavery legislature and governor were soon voted into power and given strong support by President Pierce. Dedicated free-state forces refused to work with the legislature, instead creating their own shadow government in Topeka and forming a free-state militia. Clashes between the two sides became violent, and Pierce responded by sending in more troops.[90]

The violence temporarily subsided, but events in 1857 and 1858 would rekindle the battles. President James Buchanan and his secretary of war, John Floyd of Virginia, reduced the number of troops in Kansas. The October 1857 elections were won by the proslavery side, which proceeded to write up a constitution allowing slavery and promptly asked for admission into the Union. Buchanan supported the Lecompton Constitution and attempted to have Congress admit Kansas as a slave state. Despite congressional rejection of the effort, it led to further polarization between the two sides. However, the situation remained generally calm, and by June 1858 only six hundred troops were still in the territory. Around this time, radical free-stater James Montgomery started creating new trouble in the southeastern part of the territory, responding to continuing threats against his followers. He believed that the Army was biased toward the proslavery militia, and he attacked regular troops near Fort Scott. The War Department was distracted by trouble in Utah and started pulling out troops, but Governor Thomas Medary convinced the War Department that the threat was too great, and Floyd grudgingly let Medary use the troops to stop Montgomery. Montgomery surrendered on January 18, 1859. When problems seemed to briefly resurface in 1860, troops returned and stopped further difficulties.[91]

Buchanan also had to deal with a separatist threat by the Utah Mormons. Since 1849 the Mormons had been agitating for their own state (to be named Deseret), but leery federal officials denied the request and instead kept it organized as Utah Territory, with Brigham Young as governor. Army officers in the field warned about Mormon tendencies toward separatism and kept a close eye on developments there. Despite occasional clashes the situation remained stable, partially because Democratic officeholders were reluctant to use federal authority against a local institution for fear of setting a precedent that could be used against slavery. However, in the 1856 elections Republicans focused attention on polygamy, so when the Mormon hierarchy forced out three federal judges in early 1857, Buchanan felt compelled to act. In May 1857, he sent twenty-five hundred troops to Utah and suspended mail delivery. The troops, under the command of Colonel Albert S. Johnston, reached the outskirts of Salt Lake City in September. Young ordered his followers not to cooperate and there were several battles between his militia and the Army. However, as winter approached, poor weather made it impossible for the fighting to continue and Johnston remained tied down until the spring.[92]

In the end, a real battle never happened. The War Department sent in extra troops in January 1858, for a total of fifty-six hundred, likely scaring Mormon officials. Buchanan had also appointed a new governor for Utah, Alfred E. Cumming, who worked against Johnston and became somewhat sympathetic to the Mormon position. Cumming was eventually able to negotiate a truce by promising pardons for those responsible for attacks on Army troops in exchange for Mormon submission to federal authority.[93] The Army was again successful in upholding the primacy of federal authority, despite the initial reluctance of Democratic politicians to intervene. In spite of the national dissolution that soon followed during the Civil War, the Army had proven that it could be used as an instrument of national consolidation when asked to do so by political officials. Importantly, politicians from various political parties demonstrated their willingness to use the Army to preserve order on the periphery.

Expanding Borders and Encouraging Settlement

Extending American Sovereignty

The Army helped to expand the nation's borders through battles against native tribes and through its protective function in securing lands for white settlement and development once they had been acquired. In the antebellum years, the Army consistently faced international competition in securing and extending the nation's borders—Britain, France, and Spain jockeyed for position on the North American continent and tried to use native tribes against the Americans.[94] After the Revolutionary War, although the borders of the United States technically extended to the Mississippi River, few Americans lived beyond the Appalachian Mountains, and the reach of national sovereignty over the frontier was limited. Even for those who did live there, the American central state was a distantly removed presence. As Francois Furstenberg has argued, "the danger of a western separation marked U.S. politics of the 1790s to an extent overlooked by most historians."[95] Native tribes dominated the region, and many of them were allied with the British, who still maintained forts there. Extending U.S. sovereignty over what was then termed the West was therefore a slow process that involved a series of confrontations with aboriginal peoples and their foreign backers (Table 1).[96]

As early as 1783, states began requesting help from the national government to deal with native tribes within their borders.[97] However, Congress was in the process of shrinking the Army at the end of the Revolutionary War and as discussed earlier, the Articles of Confederation limited the central state's capability to employ force. In the years that followed, white settlers began pushing farther into frontier regions on land that belonged to native tribes. The Army started constructing forts in the Ohio Valley but did not

Table 1. **Major Conflicts with Native Tribes**

Year	*Tribe(s)*	*Location*
1790–94	Miami, Shawnee	Ohio Valley
1811	Shawnee	Tippecanoe
1813–14	Creek	Georgia
1817–18	Seminole	Florida
1832	Sauks	Illinois, Iowa
1836–37	Creek	Georgia
1835–42	Seminole	Florida
1838	Cherokee	Georgia
1850–59	Navajo, Apache, Sioux, Cheyenne	Far West
1855–58	Seminole	Florida

Sources: Information gathered from Susan B. Carter, Scott Sigmund Gartner, Michael R. Haines, Alan L. Olmstead, Richard Sutch, and Gavin Wright, eds., *Historical Statistics of the United States: Earliest Times to the Present* (Millennial Edition), volume 5 (New York: Cambridge University Press, 2006), 372; Francis Paul Prucha, *The Sword of the Republic: The United States Army on the Frontier, 1783–1846* (Lincoln: University of Nebraska Press, 1969); and John Grenier, *The First Way of War: American War Making on the Frontier* (New York: Cambridge University Press, 2005).

have the capacity to effectively stop squatters from illegally settling on Indian lands. On the contrary, soldiers were involved in negotiations with the native tribes to purchase land and actively assisted settlement by protecting whites who had legally settled the region (while also attempting to remove illegal squatters, although generally with poor results). For example, the Treaty of Fort McIntosh, signed by General Josiah Harmar on January 21, 1785, with the Wyandots, Chippewas, Delawares, and Ottawas, purchased three-quarters of present-day Ohio for the United States.[98] The Army's role was formalized in 1787, when Congress created two Indian departments (northern and southern) and placed them in the War Department.[99]

From 1786 to 1790 whites who were settling in the Ohio Valley consistently pressed the national government for help in battling the native tribes, many of whom were receiving active assistance from the British in the form of arms and logistical support.[100] Knox and Washington were reluctant to use force, preferring diplomacy, but as the situation deteriorated they soon decided they had no choice. Interestingly, troops were only sent to the region north of the Ohio River even though settlers to its south faced similar difficulties.[101] Andrew Cayton argues that the national government's different policies toward the North and South began the process of creating regional identities: "The use of an army became crucial to proving the value of the national government. Nothing else it did was more important in attaching people to the United States, for nothing else was a more visible symbol of the value of the government of the United States. And nothing was more instrumental in alienating people from the national government than the perception that it was using its military power in a discriminatory fashion."[102] As a result, the South began differentiating itself ideologically as a region that did not require and was in fact suspicious of federal power (though in practice it remained wedded to federal power, as in its reliance on the Army to deter slave uprisings).[103]

In mid-June 1790, President Washington ordered General Harmar to prepare for a battle against the Ohio Valley Indians. Harmar's forces met the Indians in October, where the U.S. troops were routed and forced to flee. This shocking defeat prompted Washington to fire Harmar and replace him with Arthur St. Clair, the governor of the Ohio territory. Congress provided more troops, but in November 1791 St. Clair led a three-thousand-man force to yet another defeat. In 1792 Washington and Knox asked Congress to increase the Army to five thousand men in preparation for yet another battle. Southerners were opposed to the deployment, but it passed on the strength of northern and western support. General Anthony Wayne was put in charge, and with Knox's help created a more effective force. Wayne defeated the Indians in mid-1794 at the Battle of Fallen Timbers, during which the British refused to help their erstwhile allies, providing a major strategic victory to the United States in securing the Northwest.[104] American control shattered the Indian economy, which had been dependent on British largesse, while promoting commerce in Ohio and Kentucky.[105] Thus, through the use of force, the national state asserted its authority over an important expanse of territory, allowing for a massive influx of white settlers and setting the stage for the land management and development policies that would follow.

Pressures for expanded white settlement continued in the wake of the Army's triumph. In the East, the beginning of a potential national removal policy was heralded as whites urged that Indians living in their states be forced to relocate west. National officials, however, were not yet prepared to take that step. For example, Governor George Clinton's recommendation in 1801 that the Six Nations living in New York be removed to the west was rejected by Secretary of War Henry Dearborn.[106] Meanwhile, President Jefferson worked to gain new land in the Northwest by other means. Some tribal chiefs were given bribes by Dearborn as an inducement to surrender land.[107] Jefferson also ordered William Henry Harrison, the governor of Indiana Territory, to negotiate new cessions from the Indian tribes there. Harrison essentially forced the Indians to sign treaties giving away land in present-day Indiana, Illinois, Wisconsin, and Michigan by threatening to use the troops under his command if they refused. When Tecumseh formed a confederation of various tribes to stop further cessions, Harrison took to the battlefield and defeated him at the Battle of Tippecanoe.[108] Many of these tribes subsequently allied themselves with the British during the War of 1812. But the Indians lost their ally when the British agreed to give up their remaining forts in the Northwest as part of the Treaty of Ghent, ending the primary challenge to American sovereignty in the region.[109]

In the South, the Spanish had allied with the Creeks against the United States and saw their influence begin to decline as well. General Andrew Jackson battled the Creeks in the course of the war effort, forcing their surrender on strongly pro-American terms in the Treaty of Fort Jackson on August 9, 1814.[110] The Creeks were slow to move out of these lands, however, and the Seminoles in Spanish-controlled Florida also started raiding across the border into Georgia. Georgia pressed the federal government for help in securing the border region. The War Department urged patience but dispatched Jackson to the scene.[111] Jackson decided to go beyond his orders and invaded Florida in his pursuit of the Seminoles (discussed further below).[112]

After Florida was purchased in 1819, despite the Army's occupation of key positions in the territory, officials there soon began relaying their concerns about the Seminoles to national officials.[113] The best land in the territory was occupied by the Seminoles, and they were also protecting runaway slaves who belonged to southerners. In 1823 negotiators forced the Seminoles to sign the Treaty of Moultrie Creek, which obligated them to stay in the center regions of Florida, leaving the most productive lands open for white settlement. The Seminoles were reluctant to move, however, and Secretary of War John C. Calhoun sent reinforcements in January 1824. The troops were instrumental in forcing the Seminoles into Florida's center by 1826.[114]

Many southern states gradually lost their patience with the federal government and started taking the lead to force out Indian tribes. Georgia is the best known example, starting the process of asserting its authority over Creek and Cherokee lands in 1828. Under established precedent, only the federal government could negotiate with tribes over land, but several states were trying to preempt federal authority. Presidents James Monroe and John Quincy

Adams attempted negotiation between the Cherokees and the state of Georgia, including direct meetings between Secretaries of War Calhoun and James Barbour with the tribal leaders. However, these attempts all came to naught.[115] President Jackson, elected in 1828 on a platform of encouraging aggressive white settlement of the frontier, supported Georgia and pushed Congress to pass the Indian Removal Act of 1830, making it official U.S. policy to acquire all the lands of tribes still residing east of the Mississippi River and then remove them to a new Indian territory in the far West.[116] Some tribes, like the Choctaws, moved after feeling just mild pressure—a threat from Secretary of War John Eaton was enough to persuade them to move by 1833 (though Eaton implausibly claimed that "no threat was used; no intimidation attempted").[117] The Creeks and Cherokees resisted the longest. Despite agreeing in 1832 to leave Georgia, the Creeks did not finally move west until forced in 1836 by eleven hundred federal troops under the command of General Winfield Scott.[118] The Cherokees held out until 1838, when they were driven westward in the infamous Trail of Tears that led to the deaths of thousands.[119]

Before removal became official national policy, the Sauks, who lived in present-day Wisconsin and Illinois, had sold much of their land to the United States in a series of treaties they signed right after the War of 1812. They had agreed in 1816 to move westward, but no one had placed any pressure on them and they still occupied the region. In the mid-1820s, whites began to come into the area and demanded the Indians' removal. In 1825, Secretary of War James Barbour and Governor Lewis Cass of Michigan negotiated the Treaty of Prairie du Chien with the Sauks, which required them to surrender their remaining lands east of the Mississippi. One chief by the name of Black Hawk was not a party to the talks, however, and he refused to comply. Over the course of the late 1820s, the governors of Illinois urged the War Department to use force, but only in 1832 was General Henry Atkinson sent in with 220 regulars and 2,600 militiamen. He captured Black Hawk in August of that year, and by the end of the year the Sauks had been forced west of the Mississippi. Black Hawk's defeat dispirited other tribes in the area, such as the Winnebagos and Potawatomies, who gave in shortly thereafter and were also removed under Army escort. With this victory, the Army expunged the Indian presence from Illinois and secured the state for white settlement.[120]

After the passage of the Indian Removal Act, whites in Florida worked to expel the Seminoles and recover runaway slaves whom they were sheltering, with national support in a campaign that required more than two decades.

By 1835, the Army's efforts were failing, and the Seminoles were able to raid and destroy most of Florida's sugar industry. With only 500 troops in Florida at that time, the Army could not match the numbers against them. In early 1836, Winfield Scott led 5,000 men into the heart of the state, the biggest concentration of American force since the War of 1812. Even he could not capture many of the Seminoles, however, and soon it appeared to be another American defeat. This led to a new commander and a new battlefield strategy. Major General Thomas S. Jesup, head of the Quartermaster's Department, was tasked to lead the 9,000 troops in Florida in 1837. Employing harsh new tactics, Jesup rampaged through Seminole lands and by the end of the year quieted the violence to a manageable level. Over the next few years, with General Zachary Taylor in command of 2,000 troops, the Army pressured the Seminoles, gradually capturing and removing them to the west. Final removal dragged out into the 1850s, costing the nation tens of millions of dollars and the lives of thousands of soldiers to completely secure the state for white-led development, while also ending a perceived threat to southern interests.[121] By assisting in the forcible removal of these tribes, the Army expanded the range of land available to white settlement and increased the territories within which the national government's sovereignty extended.

In the late 1820s the War Department decided it needed mounted troops if it wanted to intimidate the Indians on the Great Plains, who were themselves often mounted. Starting in 1829 the secretary of war asked for Congress to authorize a dragoon corps for this purpose.[122] Only in 1832 did Congress supply a mounted force of 600 men, and it was designated for use in the Black Hawk War. When Congress finally authorized a permanent dragoon corps in 1833, Secretary of War Lewis Cass ordered General Henry Leavenworth to lead it against the Comanches and Kiowas, who had been creating problems for American traders headed to Santa Fe. Leavenworth used the dragoons to impress the Indians with American power and "to introduce amiable relations" with them, in Cass's words.[123] The dragoons continued to make their presence felt across the Plains in the 1830s and 1840s, including a yearly tour to remind the various tribes that they would suffer retaliation at the Army's hands if they interfered with trade routes or migrants heading west along the Oregon Trail.[124] In the words of Secretary of War William Marcy, "This exhibition of military force among them is well calculated to impress upon them the belief that we have the power at hand to punish them for their misdeeds."[125] The use of coercion here plainly sought to clear important trade routes and protect American commercial interests.

Following the war against Mexico, the United States found itself in possession of a huge expanse of new territory—territory inhabited by new and mostly unfriendly native tribes. As a result, the Army spent much of the 1850s defending white settlers in New Mexico, California, and Texas against attacks from the Apaches and Navajos. In 1852, for example, the secretary of war reported that of 11,000 men in the Army, 8,000 were in Texas, New Mexico, California, and Oregon, defending the frontier population.[126] The 1850s also saw the Army acting against the Cheyenne and Sioux, stopping them from interfering with traders and emigrants heading to Oregon.[127] Although the Army certainly did not have complete control over the various native tribes within the newly expanded American borders, it was generally successful in forcing them into designated areas and in protecting the economic interests of white Americans.

Wars of Expansion

The Army was the primary institution responsible for expanding the nation's borders through wars of conquest and for securing new territory acquired by purchases or treaties. While this may appear to be an obvious function of any national army, the suspicions that some Americans had of a standing army make its accomplishments more impressive. This section will describe how the new territories gained by the Army shaped the economic future of the United States by providing new areas for settlement, resource extraction, and the expansion of slavery, and by containing the ambitions of European nations trying to restrict American dreams of continental growth.

Jefferson's acquisition of the Louisiana Territory, accomplished through negotiation, was secured with the assistance of the Army. Following its approval of the purchase, Congress delegated to the president the power to use the Army in whatever way he saw fit to control the new territory. General James Wilkinson was told to only use force if necessary, and indeed no confrontations were required, as the French surrendered the territory with minimal resistance and the Spanish decided not to interfere. Forts built in the new territory also helped to protect American interests against British traders still present.[128] The threat of a secessionist movement based in Louisiana headed by Aaron Burr was also stopped by the Army, as discussed earlier.

The War of 1812 was the major instance in this era in which the U.S. military failed to conquer a territory when directed to do so by government officials. Politicians, including the president and members of Congress, believed that Canada would quickly fall to an American invasion and be absorbed into the United States. As a result, President James Madison ordered an attempted invasion in 1813. Hopes for an easy victory were dashed when the forces attempting to cross the border were swiftly defeated by the British.[129] Even toward the war's end, national leaders continued to believe that an invasion could be accomplished with just a few thousand more troops.[130] Despite the thwarting of this potential expansion, the war still had important economic effects. It created a nationalist sense of victory over the British and, as discussed earlier in this chapter, opened up the Old Northwest to further white settlement.[131] At the same time, however, the war "exacerbated sectional tensions" as northerners began to worry that the expansionist rhetoric of southern war hawks such as Henry Clay and Calhoun was merely a cover for perpetuating slavery.[132] This furthering of sectional animus was widespread among many political leaders. Former president Thomas Jefferson, for instance, expressed considerable anger toward New England states for their role in resisting federal efforts during the War of 1812.[133]

Even before the war, American officials were also looking southward to Florida as the next logical step in American expansion. In 1810 President Madison and Congress approved a secret plan to seize West Florida from the Spanish by inciting a rebellion among the local population. The rebellion sparked a brief movement for independence that started a gradual weakening of Spanish control over its colony. As mentioned earlier, General Andrew Jackson invaded Florida during his 1816 campaign against the Creeks and Seminoles. This incident led to no international repercussions, as Madison and the Spanish agreed to ignore Jackson's conduct, and American troops soon left. However, a few years later Jackson essentially conquered Florida. As the situation on the Georgia-Florida border deteriorated, with whites submitting increasing numbers of complaints about Seminole raids, Jackson returned. He argued to President Monroe and Secretary of War John C. Calhoun that the Spanish were protecting the Seminoles and needed to be stopped. Despite receiving orders not to attack the Spanish, Jackson's forces took the fort at St. Marks in mid-1818. Even though Jackson was censured by Congress, the ensuing uproar let a not-particularly-unhappy Monroe administration negotiate the purchase of Florida in the Adams-Onís Treaty of 1819.[134]

The largest expansion of American territory achieved by force happened as a result of the Mexican-American War. Throughout the late 1830s and early 1840s the United States had been slowly progressing toward the annexation of Texas, which had declared its independence from Mexico in 1836. Presidents going back to Andrew Jackson had favored such a step but northerners were reluctant to add another slave state to the union, while others were concerned that annexation could provoke a war with Mexico. France and Great Britain also protested further American expansion. At the end of John Tyler's presidency, with James K. Polk having been elected on a broadly popular proannexation platform, Congress passed a bill annexing Texas.[135] Polk began moving troops toward the Mexico-Texas border in mid-1845. The precise location of the border was disputed, with Mexico placing it at the Nueces River and the United States and Texas claiming it went south to the Rio Grande. When American forces under the command of General Zachary Taylor crossed into the disputed region in early 1846, they were fired upon by Mexican troops. Polk announced that a war had begun, and he swiftly received a declaration of war from Congress.[136]

Over the next two years, tens of thousands of American troops invaded Mexico, conquering Mexico City by the war's end. Mexico was compelled to surrender a vast swath of territory, including California and New Mexico. Victory opened these new lands for white settlement, brought into the nation a new resource-rich territory, secured access to the Gulf of Mexico, and soon made possible the geographic expansion of slavery into the new territories.[137] In addition, the war helped to change international perceptions of American power. As Polk said, "One of the most important results of the war into which we were recently forced with a neighboring nation, is the demonstration it has offered of the military strength of our country. Before the late war with Mexico, European and other foreign powers entertained imperfect and erroneous views of our physical strength as a nation, and of our ability to prosecute war, and especially a war waged out of our own country. . . . The war with Mexico has thus fully developed the capacity of republican governments to prosecute successfully a just and necessary foreign war with all the vigor usually attributed to more arbitrary forms of government."[138]

Zachary Taylor, in his short time as president, helped to maintain order in the Southwest and secure these new lands. In the war's wake, a dispute arose between New Mexico and Texas over the precise location of their border. When New Mexico was preparing to apply for statehood, Texas threatened to invade and seize what it claimed as its rightful territory east of the Rio Grande River. Taylor ordered federal troops to Santa Fe with orders to use whatever force was necessary to keep Texas's forces at bay, and eventually Texas backed down.[139]

Clearly, the Army was a central player in securing new lands through the use of force in this period. Although a potential expansion to Canada was foiled during the War of 1812, the overall record is one of an expanding territory provided through coercion by the U.S. Army. A weaker central state that could not have provided for a strong military, as had been the situation under the Articles of Confederation, would never have been able to expand the nation's borders so rapidly or secure them as easily as it did.

Forts: Security and Markets

The Army constructed a nationwide system of forts in the antebellum period, which had a significant impact on economic development. As the geographic reach of the forts expanded farther west due to national territorial expansion, so too did the Army's capacity to project power and influence that development across the periphery. Forts provided security to local communities and nurtured nascent markets through troops' purchasing power and contracts let by the War Department for supplies.[140] Often forts were placed in sparsely populated areas and thus helped to spur new areas for white settlement. The forts were also instrumental to the Army's previously mentioned activities of preserving order and extending American sovereignty, as they provided the bases from which troops conducted their operations.

Many forts were built early in the nation's history as part of defensive tactics to protect the young republic. When the Army was cut back to only eighty troops in 1784, the tiny force was split between Fort Pitt and West Point. As the Army was expanded during the wars against the native tribes located in the Old Northwest, commanders ordered the building of new forts. General Harmar was perhaps the first to do so when he built Fort Finney in late 1785, at the location of present-day Louisville. Harmar's troops also built Forts Franklin, Steuben, and Harmar, which helped to push frontier settlement farther west under the umbrella of federal protection. These forts were used as the sites for negotiations with the Ohio Valley Indians during the 1780s.[141] General Arthur St. Clair, who succeeded Harmar, also built several forts during his time in the Northwest, including Fort Hamilton and Fort Jefferson.[142] General Wayne ordered the construction of Fort Greeneville, Fort Recovery, and Fort Washington, among others. Fort Washington was instrumental in the growth of nearby Cincinnati, as merchants there became contractors for the Army and the Army's presence spurred new settlement.[143]

The forts were also the center of the "factory system," whereby trading houses were set up at the forts to conduct trade with native tribes as well as other merchants. The concept was to develop a government-sponsored place where traders could freely interact as well as provide diplomatic contacts. The factories were initially established during the Washington administration by Secretary of War Henry Knox. In total, thirty factories were created. However, private interests did not appreciate this interference by the federal government in an area that intruded on their profits. John Jacob Astor's fur company in particular led a concerted lobbying effort to close the factories. Despite support from within the Bureau of Indian Affairs, Congress eventually decided to shutter the factory system in 1822.[144] This was a clear instance of a government failure in the effort to provide a nonpublic good.

Forts were generally not expanded into the Old Northwest until after the region had been fully secured following the War of 1812. The area now consisting of Iowa, Wisconsin, Minnesota, and Illinois was largely undeveloped and unexplored. Posts such as Fort Armstrong, Fort Crawford, and Fort Dearborn helped to establish a white presence far into mostly Indian areas. These forts were instrumental in securing the conditions necessary for negotiating many of the treaties with Indian tribes that led to a gradual reduction of the Indian presence there even before removal became official policy in 1830. Soon white settlement expanded in the Northwest, largely following in the forts' path, as soldiers formed a wedge of security within which whites could live. These forts also became centers of economic activity for their communities. Initially, most supplies had to be shipped to the forts from the East. Slowly settlement would grow around a fort, and these settlers were given contracts for the fort's needs, further encouraging settlement.[145] Later, once these locations were secured and settlement established, many forts would be removed, pushing the line of settlement farther west. Fort Crawford was abandoned in 1849, for instance.[146]

Early on, the War Department was particularly interested in the fur trade, whose "protection was one of the chief reasons for the advance of the military frontier."[147] As just discussed, it established a series of trading factories at the forts, an experiment that began in 1796. This was intended to centralize the trading process and provide direct protection to traders and Indians under Army oversight. It also was supposed to tie Indians more closely to the federal government and gradually bring them under the American orbit, no longer under the sway of British traders. The factories provided manufactured goods to Indians that they would otherwise not have been able to acquire. Competition remained from private traders and the British, however, and supplies were brought in erratically. The program lost money and this intervention in the private sector was ended in 1822.[148]

The forts were also an integral part of the Army's efforts to protect miners and resource extraction across the nation. Locating a fort close to mineral deposits ensured that miners would feel safe to continue their excavations without having to worry about potential Indian attacks. National power was thus used in service of private economic interests. For example, after Governor Lewis Cass of the Michigan Territory discovered copper deposits at Sault Saint Marie in 1820, Secretary of War John C. Calhoun agreed to build Fort Brady there to protect the miners who came.[149] In 1843 the Army still shielded miners there and stopped the local Indians from claiming nearby Isle Royale as their own.[150] Similarly, after the conquest of California, troops there worked to protect the incoming rush of gold miners.[151] New Mexico and Arizona also experienced a wave of miners pouring in after the discovery of deposits there in the 1850s; as Robert Frazer says, "military protection was [often] essential for the uninterrupted operation of the mines" in the Southwest.[152] On some occasions, the Army also worked against the interests of miners by trying to stop incursions into Indian-owned land.[153] Overall, however, the Army favored the exploitation of natural resources.

Another task that forts accomplished was their assistance in the nurturing and protection of mail delivery to the frontier. As Richard John describes in his important work on the early Post Office, mail delivery throughout the nation hastened national economic integration and stimulated the growth of the stagecoach and other businesses.[154] Much of the Post Office's impact, however, would have been negated if not for the Army's umbrella of protection provided to mail delivery in remote regions across the periphery. As early as 1803, Secretary of War Henry Dearborn tried to ensure safe delivery of the mail when he offered a $400 reward to anyone assisting in the capture of robbers who had been assaulting mail carriers on the route from Nashville to Natchez.[155] Mail routes on the frontier developed around the location of key forts, and the first post offices were often located at the fort. Soldiers sometimes carried mail with them when heading to peripheral regions, simultaneously subsidizing and protecting mail delivery.[156] Policymakers consciously located forts where they would be of use in protecting a delivery route. Fort Davis, founded in 1854, was partially designed to protect the San Antonio–El Paso route, for example.[157]

Forts set up along the Oregon Trail provided significant assistance to emigrants heading west, while forts along the Santa Fe Trail protected traders.[158] The War Department recommended creating these posts as early as 1840, though progress was not made on these plans until after the war with Mexico. Fort Kearney was especially useful in providing medical and technical prowess, as well as basic supplies that travelers sometimes lacked such as food. These forts helped to create local communities as well through contracts for supplies, the purchasing power of troops' salaries, and the presence of civilians employed by the forts. Omaha, Nebraska, and Cheyenne, Wyoming, prospered as local depots for the Quartermaster's Department, which provided most of the supplies the forts required.[159] The southwestern region conquered during the Mexican War also benefited economically from the presence of forts. The Army's presence helped to stimulate the economy while transforming it as well. The Army's high demand for goods such as flour spurred innovations in the milling industry, for instance.[160]

Clearly, forts could not continue expanding forever. By 1856, Secretary of War Jefferson Davis asserted that "a new post . . . does not become the nucleus of a settlement" anymore, and that "a limit has, therefore, been reached, beyond which civilization has ceased to follow in the train of advancing military posts." He argued that since so much of the land between the Pacific Ocean and the Mississippi River could not be settled without great expense, the Army should stop placing its forts in far-flung locales where settlers had not yet emigrated, and should instead only provide forts to communities that had already been established.[161] Even if this proposed revision in the War Department's policy had been followed (which it was not), and had settling the remaining interior of the country been left to private individuals, the Army's accomplishments up to that point in encouraging new settlement would still have been of tremendous significance for the nation's economic development. The evidence presented in this section demonstrates the important role that forts played in encouraging and directing white settlement, and then protecting those settlers once they arrived.

Conclusion

Examining the wide range of coercive actions the antebellum U.S. Army engaged in should lead us to reconsider the impact of military force on economic development. From maintaining national order to expanding and protecting settlement, coercion did much more than simply enforce national will—it also shaped the pattern and direction of the country's economic future. Although the Army was not always involved in disputes and despite occasional failures (such as the factory system at the forts), its overall impact was still quite significant. Had the Army not been so deeply involved in economic matters, the United States would have developed in a very different way, perhaps lacking strong central fiscal authority (if the rule of law had not been consistently enforced, as during the Whiskey Rebellion) or confined within a much smaller and less secure territory (lacking the territories conquered during the Mexican War and through battles with native tribes). It is hard to imagine the U.S. economy evolving in the manner it did absent the contributions of the Army, especially in the periphery, where the Army was instrumental in building new markets and maintaining attachments to the central state.

Moreover, the Constitution, by endowing the central government with significant new coercive powers, made possible vast territorial expansion, the extension of national sovereignty over the periphery, and the maintenance of the rule of law and national authority across the continent. Lacking these new powers, the United States would have almost certainly developed in a very different manner, perhaps as a smaller nation (or several smaller nations, the result of multiple secessions) without a national marketplace, ties between the East and the West, or trade flows across the continent. In such a scenario it is easy to imagine an America full of slow-growing republics, less attractive to immigrants, with industrial development delayed until a much later date.

CHAPTER 2

Building the Nation, Building the Economy

The Army's socioeconomic contributions in early America were instrumental in helping to build a stronger economy. In a variety of areas, the Army provided goods ahead of market-generated demand, thereby accelerating the pace of economic growth and fundamentally shaping the nation's economic future.[1] This chapter describes the multiple socioeconomic functions that the Army engaged in during the antebellum period and demonstrates their impact on economic development. I first discuss the Army's actions within the center, and then proceed to its activities in the periphery. Some of the Army's activities crossed the boundaries between the two regions, as I note, as well as crossing the line between the coercive and socioeconomic realms.

In three particular areas the Army promoted economic development as a socioeconomic actor. First, the Army trained engineers and supplied them to the private sector at a time when such expertise was sorely lacking across the nation. These engineers then assisted in the construction of a nationwide infrastructure, including building roads, canals, and railroads, all of which were crucial to the development of the rapidly expanding nation. Although engineering expertise can potentially be provided by the private sector, in early America only the Army could supply these engineering services in sufficient quantities. Second, topographical engineers surveyed the geography, geology, and mineralogy of lakes, rivers, and newly acquired territories. Topographers also built lighthouses to aid navigation, provided maps that helped lead to smoother trade flows across the continent, and encouraged white settlement in the periphery by highlighting new areas ripe for mining and agricultural production. Finally, engineers and ordnance officers encouraged technological and administrative innovations that subsequently spread throughout the private sector, shaping the nation's economic future for decades to come. Some of the Army's activities, such as providing engineers, involved making good serious deficiencies in the private sector, while other activities, such as building infrastructure projects, could have been carried out by private actors, though they likely only would have happened at a much later date without the Army's intervention.

Army supply, led by the Quartermaster General's Office, occurred on a continuum between the center and the periphery. Both regions received roughly equal support from the quartermaster, depending largely on where the Army had its forts located or where it was undertaking a coercive operation. As a result, supply operations in particular linked together the coercive and socioeconomic aspects of the Army. Each major category of military activity, coercive and socioeconomic, depended on the other to some degree: many coercive operations would not have been possible without socioeconomic support, and socioeconomic actions (especially in the periphery) could for the most part only take place once an area had been secured through coercion.

The Center

Within the center, the Army was able to provide many goods and services unavailable from the private sector or from state governments. Chief among these was engineering expertise, then severely lacking. The few engineers that were available from the private sector in early America were essentially skilled craftsmen, largely self-trained and lacking formal scientific education. Until 1824, no school besides the U.S. Military Academy at West Point turned out engineers; and even after Rensselaer was established as a private engineering school that year, it graduated only seven engineers in its first fourteen years of existence.[2] Having skilled engineers was an essential prerequisite for growing the economy because they designed and built a sustainable infrastructure. Only the Army provided engineers in sufficient numbers and with the advanced training that was needed.

Established by presidential fiat under Thomas Jefferson, the military academy at West Point became the nation's first and largest school for training engineers. Presidents Washington and Adams had both pushed for the creation of such an academy, but neither had succeeded in overcoming deeply rooted popular suspicion of any kind of expanded military presence in society. In 1794, a Corps of Artillerists and Engineers was created and stationed at West Point, but it was a far cry from a true academy designed to educate future officers. As the military was expanded during the crisis of the Quasi-War in the late 1790s, Alexander Hamilton and Secretary of War James McHenry urged the creation of a system of academies similar to those in France, but their proposals foundered in Congress.[3] President Jefferson, a longtime opponent of such an institution, ironically ended up creating the academy. His unilateral decision establishing the West Point military academy was later ratified by Congress in 1802.[4] Jefferson intended to create a school that would focus on practical issues relating to civil engineering that could be put to good use across the country, rather than just specializing in military-related engineering problems.[5] Thanks in large part to Jefferson's practical focus, Army engineers became integral to infrastructure development across the country.

Over the following decades, Army engineers trained at West Point were in the vanguard of scientific progress in the United States. They borrowed heavily from established European engineering traditions, especially from France, through foreign travel conducted by officers as well as the influence of French officers who assisted the American military in its early years. Over one hundred trips were made by Army officers to Europe from 1815 to 1861.[6] Sylvanus Thayer, William McRee, and Dennis Hart Mahan, all influential figures and teachers at West Point, studied French engineering methods as part of their overseas travels and actively incorporated those methods into their teachings.[7] French ideas about using central state power for grand economic projects were imported into the United States through the Corps of Engineers, as France was widely considered by American engineers to be the leading scientific nation in the world. Secretary of War William Crawford, for instance, noted to Brigadier General Joseph Swift in 1816 that engineering was more advanced in France than anywhere else in the world, though he argued that England had fallen behind the United States in this regard.[8] At the same time, engineers were not shy about gaining knowledge from anyone they could. Captain G. W. Hughes, for example, visited the copper ore mines in Devon and Cornwall, England, to learn about their mining practices.[9] European engineers were also directly imported into the country. Ferdinand Rudolph Hassler, a Swiss engineer, came to the United States in 1805, and helped launch the U.S. Coast Survey, among other projects.[10] General Simon Bernard of France joined the Corps of Engineers from 1816 through 1831 and helped to guide it in some of its most important work under the General Survey Act (discussed below).[11] General Claudius Crozet of France also taught engineering at West Point for many years.[12]

The corps thus became a hotbed of pro-statist thought, distinctive in its opposition to the prevailing antigovernment sentiments of the time. As historian Todd Shallat notes, the corps's methods in fact "often grated against capitalism."[13] A small seed of state power was thereby planted in the United States through the corps's engagements with other nations. This is not to suggest that the corps succeeded in transforming the broader political culture, which was suspicious of both military power and central state power generally, but it does show that portrayals of the United States as irretrievably antimilitary or antistatist in this period are overstated. Additionally, it is important to recognize that international cooperation and knowledge sharing by the corps represents an important vehicle through which American political and economic development was decisively shaped by nondomestic causes. Contrary to suggestions that the United States was isolated following the War of 1812 and allowed to develop free from international pressures, this indicates that there was never a time at which international influences ceased to be a factor.[14]

Engineers in the center worked on internal improvements through two agencies within the War Department: the Corps of Engineers and the Topographical Bureau, which later became an independent corps. The corps was established in 1779 by the Continental Congress as a military necessity, but was disbanded at the end of the Revolutionary War four years later. As noted, the Corps of Artillerists and Engineers was created in 1794, and in 1802 the engineers were separated into an independent corps as part of Jefferson's military reorganization plan.[15] Geographers were employed briefly during the Revolutionary War, but official status as topographical engineers within the Army was first conferred during the War of 1812 on only eight men. When the organization was dissolved at the war's end, just two men (Isaac Roberdeau and John Anderson) were kept on duty within the corps. Four more were authorized by Congress in 1816, and in 1818 Roberdeau was made the head of a Topographical Bureau consisting of ten engineers.[16] The "topogs," as they were known, were subordinated to regular engineers even after being given independent status. The corps looked down on them and they were "patronized and isolated," according to historian Frank Schubert.[17] Only in 1831 was the Topographical Bureau made completely independent of the corps, until finally in 1838 it was elevated to equal status as the Corps of Topographical Engineers (a development discussed in greater detail in Chapter 4).[18]

Improving the nation's rivers and harbors was one of the Army's top priorities in the center, responding to political demands for them. Many rivers

Table 2. Number of River and Harbor Improvements, 1829–60

Region	*Number of Improvements*	*Percentage of Total*
Northeast	72	59.0
Old Northwest	19	15.6
South	28	23.0
West	3	2.5
TOTAL	122	100

Source: Annual Report of the Secretary of War, 1829–1860, U.S. Serial Set (calculations by author). Improvements to the Mississippi River not categorized. Percentages do not add up to 100 due to rounding.

in this era (roughly 1830–1860) had severe navigability problems, making commerce and transportation quite challenging. As a result, there was political pressure to clear the rivers of hazards, improve their navigability, and improve harbors for the sake of increasing commercial opportunities. Responsibility for these projects was shared by the regular corps and the topographical engineers, with a total of $43 million spent on them during this period, making it one of the national government's largest domestic spending programs.[19] A careful analysis of river and harbor improvements shows a distinct bias toward projects within the center. Table 2 presents a simple breakdown of all the river and harbor projects listed in the official reports of the secretary of war, chief engineer, and chief topographical engineer for the years 1829 through 1860.[20] A total of 122 separate projects were discussed in the reports, of which an overwhelming percentage were focused on the most densely settled portions of the nation—82 percent of the total between the Northeast and South combined. The Old Northwest, the next region to be settled, received less than 16 percent of total projects. The West, settled last, received only three, the westernmost being a project on the Colorado River in Texas.

In one sense, this finding regarding a geographic distribution biased toward the center is not particularly surprising. Congress chose which individual rivers and harbors would be designated for improvement and appropriated the funds for each project accordingly. Since the regions with the most congressional representation were those with the greatest concentration of settlement, they received the most projects. On the other hand, the lack of projects on western rivers or Pacific harbors shows that politicians chose not to invest in building western commerce in the same way as in the East, demonstrating a certain disregard for forward-looking economic development on the periphery. Clearly, socioeconomic Army tasks were not laid out as part of any comprehensive plan for development.

Nonetheless, despite this lack of forethought, the Army's efforts in stimulating the economy through river and harbor improvements have been considered quite successful overall. Historian Paul Paskoff, for instance, has demonstrated that river improvements had a significant and positive impact on economic development, especially by assisting in "the settling and development of the greater Mississippi Valley."[21] Contemporary observers felt similarly about the key contributions made in improving rivers and harbors. Colonel John J. Abert, chief of the topographical corps for the majority of its existence, extolled the beneficial effects of harbor improvements on the Great Lakes by noting that "without these harbors, the number of large towns which embellish the shores of these lakes would not have been built; the immense population upon their borders, and the extensive cultivation of such numerous tracts of land, would not have taken place; the extensive sale of public lands could not have been made, nor the consequent supply and demand have been created, upon which this commerce depends."[22] Abert also supplied data to prove how important these projects were: from 1836 to 1843, exports via the lakes increased from $2.3 million to $32.3 million, and overall trade on the lakes burgeoned from $65 million in 1841 to over $100 million in 1845, supporting nearby communities largely dependent on this business.[23] Similarly, there is evidence demonstrating that the timber and mining industries along the shores of the Great Lakes were partly the product of the topogs' efforts.[24]

The topographical engineers' primary job, however, was surveying. They were mostly involved in surveying far western lands in the periphery, discussed later, but within the center there were plenty of surveying jobs to do as well. Accurate maps of the Atlantic Coast, the Great Lakes, and most of the nation's rivers simply were not available prior to the topogs' efforts in the mid-nineteenth century to create them. More precise mapping led to smoother trade flows.[25] No single state or private institution could have provided these comprehensive maps in this era absent the contributions of the topographical engineers. States were unable to conduct surveys on their own, since they lacked the requisite engineering knowledge contained within the topographical corps, and consequently they were forced to rely on national assistance. Although it is true that states spent more on internal improvements during this era than did the national government, as historian Carter Goodrich demonstrated, a closer look at improvement policy shows that states relied heavily on federal largesse, and especially on Army engineers.[26] Laurence Malone has shown in his work on improvements that Goodrich ignored certain policies, such as proceeds from land sales to new territories and land grants, by which the federal government contributed to state-run projects.[27] Moreover, neither Goodrich nor Malone discusses the role of Army engineers in survey projects, disregarding how their activities helped states as well. For example, in May 1816 Secretary of War William Crawford ordered Major James Kearney to help the state of Virginia survey land that was intended to be used for a new canal.[28] Similarly, Secretary of War John C. Calhoun ordered engineers to help Illinois, Ohio, Virginia, Iowa, Louisiana, Mississippi, Tennessee, Georgia, New York, and Maine with improvement projects during his tenure in office.[29]

The General Survey Act of 1824, passed in the wake of the Supreme Court's decision expanding federal power in *Gibbons v. Ogden*, accelerated this federal-state cooperation, as the law specifically contained a provision allowing states and private companies to request engineering support from the Army for surveying and construction.[30] The law's stated purpose was to authorize the president to assign engineers to "such Roads and Canals as he may deem of national importance, in a commercial or military point of view, or necessary for the transportation of the public mail,"[31] and federally run projects were not necessarily to be given priority. States and cities across the country soon begged the Army for help with their roads and canals. Initially, regular Army engineers worked on many projects, but in 1831 the responsibility for civil projects was shifted entirely to the Topographical Bureau.[32] The topogs responded with an increase in surveying, getting involved in projects ranging from the Chesapeake and Ohio Canal to a road leading from New Orleans to Washington, D.C.[33] In fact, the demand for engineering services was so high that the Army never had enough engineers to fulfill every request it received from states and private companies.[34] Despite the shortage, however, it is clear that the engineers' involvement in state-level and private projects had a significant impact on development. Although civilian geologists were also available to perform surveys in the latter part of the antebellum era, most did not work directly on infrastructure projects and did only occasional consulting work for private corporations.[35]

Surveys focused on developing the railroads proved to be one of the topogs' most enduring legacies. Although surveys for this purpose were not expressly authorized by the General Survey Act, the War Department began lending out engineers for railroad surveys as early as 1827, when Secretary of War James Barbour approved the Baltimore and Ohio Railroad's request for engineering assistance. The Army paid for the engineers in that instance, but in the future the War Department required the company asking for help to pick up the tab. Dozens of railroads received help from the Army in this manner.[36] Private enterprise was thereby nurtured and sustained through a close relationship with this portion of the central state.

The era of Army engineers working on private sector projects did not last very long, however. Opposition from civil engineers intensified as they complained that the Army was stealing their business, while critics within the Army worried about eroding military professionalism. In 1831, the War Department started reducing the number of engineers allowed to go on leave to work on private projects, and in 1838 an Army reorganization law forbade the lending of engineers to the railroad companies. In reaction, hundreds of West Point–trained engineers resigned their commissions and went to work for the railroads.[37] This policy choice removed from the national government the responsibility for railroad design, but ex-Army engineers continued to use their government-sponsored training to assist private corporations. When the national government reentered the realm of railroads, it would be in the periphery.

Army engineers also helped to spread new management practices to the private sector. Early on, the Army created what was perhaps the nation's most impressive bureaucracy at the time. The standard view is expressed by Richard Bensel in his work *Yankee Leviathan*, where he admits that the Army was "the best approximation" to a "statist-bureaucratic element" prior to the Civil War, while arguing that it was nevertheless clearly insufficient to hold the nation together in its moment of crisis.[38] While it is true that the nation fell apart in the run-up to the Civil War, nevertheless this view downplays just how radical even such a relatively small bureaucracy was for the United States. Starting from a very small base with only a tiny staff, the War Department expanded and improved itself through a lengthy process of trial and error, creating a hierarchical structure with accountability, responsibility, and a high degree of specialization, largely especially to the efforts of Secretary of War John C. Calhoun.[39] Given the new republic's ideological resistance to centralized authority of any kind, it is remarkable that the Army became so bureaucratized.[40]

Engineers who went to work for private railroad companies brought their advanced ideas about management and bureaucracy with them. Most

Table 3. Professions of West Point Graduates, 1802–40

Job	*Number*
Officers in state militias	125
Surveyors-general of states/territories	6
State chief engineers	14
Presidents of railroads or other companies	35
Chief engineers for railroads or other public works	48
Superintendents for railroads or other public works	41
Civil engineers	155

Source: George W. Cullum, *Biographical Register of the Officers and Graduates of the U.S. Military Academy at West Point, N.Y., from its Establishment March 16, 1802 to the Army Reorganization of 1866–67*, volume 1, 1802–1840 (New York: D. Van Nostrand, 1868).

important in this regard was Captain William G. McNeill, who worked for several railroads and rewrote many of their internal regulations to parallel the Army's structure.[41] Table 3 shows the various professions that West Point graduates worked in, with many becoming the presidents of railroad companies or serving as their chief engineers. To the extent that the railroads were the first modern corporations, as Alfred Chandler has argued,[42] their positive influence on the rest of the economy is therefore at least in part due to the Army.

The Ordnance Department, a branch of the War Department, made significant contributions to technological progress in the public sector, which then spread to the private sector as well. Ordnance officers were responsible for overseeing the nation's system of armories and arsenals, which had been established even prior to the Ordnance Department's creation in 1812. President Washington and his administration pushed for a bill passed in 1794 that allowed for the creation of four national armories, although none were built until almost the end of the subsequent Adams administration.[43] Before the War of 1812 production of arms was slow and not uniform across the different armories. Secretary of War Henry Dearborn complained that manufacturer Eli Whitney had fallen behind on his promised shipment of ten thousand muskets, for example.[44] Colonel Decius Wadsworth was made head of the new Ordnance Department in 1812, and he and his successor Colonel George Bomford, both schooled in the French pro–state intervention tradition, instituted tight quality control that led to more consistent production. The war itself led to significant improvements in arms manufacturing, both in quantity and quality, carefully overseen by these bureaucrats.[45] They were also instrumental in helping to devise the so-called American system of manufactures, or interchangeable parts, both at the armories and at smaller plants, like Philadelphia's Frankford Arsenal.[46] As historian Lindsay Regele has argued, only the federal government in this era had the resources needed to push for the drive toward interchangeability.[47] Small arms such as the Colt revolver were created using this new technique.[48] In an unanticipated result, other industries starting copying this methodology in the 1840s and 1850s, including "factories making sewing machines, pocket watches, railroad equipment, wagons, and hand tools," according to historian Merritt Roe Smith.[49] The Army's encouragement helped in the proliferation of manufacturing knowledge throughout the center, a key element in fundamentally shifting the base of the American economy by the end of the nineteenth century.[50] Without the Ordnance Department's efforts to improve manufacturing technology, it is likely that industrialization would have only occurred at a later date, when the private sector developed its own new manufacturing techniques.

The Periphery

As in the center, the Army in the periphery supplied goods that were not being provided by the private sector or by state governments. Unlike in the center, however, in the periphery there were no other significant competing national institutions attempting to assist in economic development. Compared to its important role in the center, the Post Office had a relatively small presence on the periphery, and in fact often relied on the Army's protection for mail delivery and transportation.[51] The General Land Office, another potential competitor, was handicapped by the willingness of western migrants to simply settle on any land they desired without official sanction.[52] While it is true, as Paul Frymer argues, that the land office was central to the functioning of territorial expansion, it simply could not provide the same range of public goods that the Army was able to.[53] As a result, the Army filled the vacuum of power with its own presence, taking over many functions carried out elsewhere by other institutions.

Newly acquired territories were placed directly under federal supervision and governed by the Army, beginning with the Northwest Ordinance in

1787.[54] Besides using coercion to subdue Native American tribes, Army officers helped integrate new lands into the nation by governing them in a style consistent with center practices. After Jefferson's purchase of the Louisiana Territory, for instance, Captain Meriwether Lewis was made the territory's governor. In this role he helped to win the allegiance of local elites to the United States by recommending that their sons be admitted to West Point, thereby ensuring their loyalty to the central state.[55] Similarly, after conquering New Mexico during the Mexican-American War, Colonel Stephen Kearney administered the vanquished territory for several years under a code he designed to mimic American laws.[56]

More important in linking the periphery to the center were the Army's efforts in building an infrastructure that could physically knit together the different regions of the country. These ties were vital in propelling the United States toward the development of an integrated national market. Building roads was one way this was accomplished. Table 4 provides a breakdown of all the road construction projects listed in the secretary of war's annual reports from 1829 through 1860. Unlike in the case of river and harbor projects, which as we have seen were concentrated in the center's most populous regions, almost 40 percent of all road projects were in the Old Northwest, demonstrating the central government's early commitment to incorporating that peripheral region into the rest of the nation through physical connections. Of the nineteen projects listed for the South, thirteen were in the state of Florida alone, a territory which had only been conquered by the Army in 1819. The Northeast and the West had only five projects each.

The small number of roads built in the West does not indicate a lack of Army involvement in road building there, however. Rather, the figure reflects the nature of the formal reports: the only roads listed were those paid for by congressional appropriations and worked on by engineers in an official capacity. Many other roads were built by soldiers serving at far-flung forts throughout the nation, usually for expressly military purposes, though they were then also shared by civilians. For instance, the Natchez Trace, an important mail road, was constructed by soldiers with the permission of Secretary of War Henry Dearborn.[57] Similarly, Alexander Macomb was ordered by Secretary of War William Crawford to construct a military road from Detroit to Ohio after the War of 1812.[58] The Northwest received an infusion of soldier-built roads during the conflict with the Ohio Valley tribes during Washington's presidency.[59] In fact, roads were built all across the periphery by soldiers in this manner.[60]

Table 4. Number of Roads Built, 1829–60

Region	*Number of Roads*	*Percentage of Total*
Northeast	5	10.4
Old Northwest	19	39.6
South	19	39.6
West	5	10.4
TOTAL	48	100

Source: Annual Report of the Secretary of War, 1829–1860, U.S. Serial Set (calculations by author).

Perhaps the greatest contribution to economic development made by the Army in the periphery was in the realm of surveying. By providing accurate maps of new territories and by charting the location of important mineral resources, topographical engineers encouraged white settlement and resource extraction in the periphery. Table 5 provides a breakdown of all surveys listed in the secretary of war's annual reports from 1829 through 1860. A plurality were conducted in the Northeast, the nation's most settled region. However, it would be easy to overstate the Northeast's dominance. Fifty-nine of the sixty-four northeastern surveys were conducted under the provisions of the General Survey Act, with only five coming after its effective repeal in 1838. Only four surveys were done in the Old Northwest following 1838. After that point, most surveys were in the South, largely in Florida, or the West. Table 5 also does not include mineralogical and geological investigations, which were constantly being performed by topographers throughout the periphery.[61] Finally, the vast Pacific Railroad surveys, some of the most significant ever conducted, are counted but once for the West in the table.

Inaugurating the Army's explorations in the periphery was the famous Lewis and Clark expedition. The two Army captains supplied the first useful maps of the Louisiana Territory and made initial contact with many Native American tribes.[62] Their expedition was also an effort to secure American control over the farthest western regions of the newly purchased land. Russia, Spain, and England all had designs on the Pacific, and Jefferson intended Lewis and William Clark to stake out the American claim to it as early as possible.[63] Lieutenant Zebulon Pike's expedition to the upper Mississippi region in 1805 was likewise designed to counter the influence of British traders.[64] Without their efforts the region could easily have been claimed by an international competitor, completely reshaping the course of America's

Table 5. Number of Surveys, 1829–60

Region	*Number of Surveys*	*Percentage of Total*
Northeast	64	41.6
Old Northwest	24	15.6
South	45	29.2
West	21	13.6
TOTAL	154	100

Source: Annual Report of the Secretary of War, 1829–1860, U.S. Serial Set (calculations by author). Surveys of the Gallean River, Black River, the Coastal Survey, the lake surveys, military defense surveys, and mineralogical and geological surveys not categorized.

economic future. Similarly, the road to white American settlement in Oregon and California was blazed by Army topographers as early as the 1810s, inducing the long process of farther westward expansion.[65]

On occasion, surveys had a negative effect on development in the periphery. Lieutenant Pike, for example, was also sent out on a mission to the southern plains region in 1806, and the report he submitted upon his return argued that the entire region was simply a large desert, unfit for settlement.[66] Major Stephen H. Long confirmed Pike's judgment during his western survey in 1819.[67] As a result of their official reports, the image of a "Great American Desert" was widely disseminated, temporarily discouraging settlement to the Great Plains. At least for some time, the Army thereby dissuaded those in the East from migrating westward, delaying further expansionist pressures and territorial acquisitions.

Only later did topographers such as John C. Frémont realize the region's potential for settlement. Frémont became the country's most famous topographer following his two expeditions to the West in 1842 and 1843–44. On his first trip, he revised the early portrait of a desert by lavishly praising the trans-Mississippi West as a beautiful region fit for extensive white settlement. His second expedition, to Oregon, California, and Utah, similarly praised that region's potential. The maps he provided in his reports laid out the paths migrants could take, including the exact route for what became the Oregon Trail, along with directions on how to avoid hostile native tribes and where to locate supplies.[68]

Frémont became a public celebrity and persuaded many to head west. Brigham Young, for instance, was inspired by Frémont's description of the Salt Lake area to bring his Mormon followers there. Other topographers later sent to explore the West reported back to the East on the Mormons and their life in Utah, shaping public perceptions of the Mormons that helped stoke the conflicts that led to the Mormon War in the late 1850s. Captain Howard Stansbury wrote a report about the geography and mineral resources of the Great Salt Lake region, while Lieutenant John Williams Gunnison published the first study of the Mormons and their culture. Gunnison did caution against trying to use force to subdue the Mormons, although his warning was ignored.[69] Popular pressure to obtain all of Oregon surged in the wake of Frémont's mission, eventually leading to the treaty defining the Northwest border with Canada.[70] Despite the Army initially deterring settlement, its efforts here ended up later accelerating the integration of peripheral regions into the center by encouraging westward migration and linking the far West to the consciousness of policymakers and citizens in the center.

The most significant, and most politically charged, surveys were the Pacific Railroad Surveys conducted in the 1850s. The idea of a transcontinental railroad was first proposed in 1844 by businessman Asa Whitney, and quickly caught on in the popular imagination as in tune with the spirit of Manifest Destiny.[71] Once the new territories acquired during the war with Mexico made the concept feasible, competition over potential routes became the order of the day. Surveys for this purpose were conducted in the new territories as early as 1849 by topographers.[72] With many options on the table, Congress in 1853 authorized surveys of four routes, each traversing a different section of the country, leaving it to the topographical corps to make a judgment about which one would best serve the nation's needs.[73] All of this was done prior to the existence of any railroad corporation that wanted to build the line, an innovation in railroad surveying, given that previous railroad surveys had been conducted at a firm's request.[74] The surveys, which cost $500,000, produced a massive amount of useful scientific data about the West, including a new map of the trans-Mississippi West, and information on the geology and mineralogy of the new lands. All of this knowledge would be exploited by miners, settlers, and railroad companies in the years to come.[75] In the end, although the topogs recommended a southern route, sectional bickering made it impossible for Congress to approve the idea, and a railroad linking the periphery directly to the center would not be built until the 1860s (these developments are discussed in greater detail in chapter 4).[76] It was a remarkable engineering feat that could not have been accomplished without the Army's provision of these services.

Topographers were also dispatched to the front lines in times of battle to help make maps for soldiers in the field and also to assist in often hasty construction jobs. Good performance in battle promoted the topographers' push for an increased role in civil projects. For instance, eight topogs went to Florida during the Seminole War in the 1830s, where their accomplishments advanced the topogs' efforts to become an independent corps later in the decade.[77] In 1845, as part of the run-up to the Mexican War, topographers were sent to Texas, where they worked on a border survey, providing critical information the Army later used during the war. As the war progressed, topographer William Emory, under the command of General Stephen Kearney, surveyed large portions of the West as the Army conquered them. The topographical reports that resulted brought public attention to bear on the positive qualities of the new region.[78] Topographers were also part of the expeditions against the Utah Mormons and the Sioux in 1857.[79]

The Quartermaster General and Supply

Straddling the line between the center and the periphery, as well as the line between coercive and socioeconomic activities, was the Quartermaster General's Office. Originally established during the Revolutionary War, its primary mission was to supply soldiers and forts wherever they were located. Up through the War of 1812 it was the target of much controversy and often did a poor job, leading to infamous accounts of starving soldiers waiting for supplies to arrive.[80] After reforms instituted in 1818 by Secretary of War John C. Calhoun and the bureau's new chief, Thomas Jesup, quartermasters performed their tasks admirably, with rare instances of mishaps. Occasionally the Quartermaster's Office was involved with internal improvements as well, though this was a secondary assignment.[81]

Following the acquisition of far western territories in the war with Mexico, the Quartermaster's Office became the largest bureau within the War Department, and indeed one of the largest in the entire national government. It spent over $7 million in 1856 alone, the vast majority of that in the West.[82] Mark Wilson contends that the department, led by career Army officers at the regional supply depots, helped introduce "bureaucratic management" in government operations.[83] Perhaps more importantly, this drive led private businesses working with the War Department to adopt many of the same management techniques. Wilson argues that "organizational innovations spurred by the military shaped the emergence of bureaucratic methods in government as well as in business." This reverses the causal relationship that has been posited by advocates of the organizational synthesis, who maintain that corporate innovation preceded the adoption of modern management techniques in the American state.[84]

Conclusion

The evidence detailed in this chapter demonstrates the U.S. Army's impact on economic development through its host of socioeconomic activities. The military academy at West Point trained engineers at a time when the nation had a severe shortage of engineering expertise; those engineers then worked to build infrastructure projects across the nation, including roads, canals, harbors, and railroads. Engineers who left the Army and worked for the private sector helped to bring the Army's hierarchical standards and bureaucratization to private companies, improving their performance through the application of uniform standards, as well as providing them with invaluable technological expertise. The topographical engineers conducted surveys of western territories and later performed the important Pacific Railroad Surveys, which also generated a wealth of scientific information. A nation lacking the Army's engineering expertise would not have built as many roads, canals, or railroads, making it much more difficult for private companies or individuals to trade between states or different regions of the country. Rivers would have been harder to navigate without the Army's dredging program, slowing down the flow of commerce. Railroad companies would have suffered without the strong leadership and technical expertise provided by former Army engineers. Manufacturers would not have created uniform standards nearly as early as they did without the pressure applied by the Ordnance Department through the armories to do so.

The specific provision of these various socioeconomic goods was, however, spread unevenly in a variety of ways. Certain regions of the country benefited more than others, depending on the case: projects to improve rivers and harbors, for instance, were markedly biased toward the center and particularly toward more populous regions in the Northeast. Road building projects, by contrast, were tilted in favor of the Old Northwest region. Additionally, while the General Survey Act of 1824 allowed engineering assistance to be provided to states and the private sector, and even though the assistance provided was quite valuable, that enterprise was ended by the 1838 reorganization act, leading many engineers to resign in protest. Similarly, surveys of the West also had uneven and bumpy effects on economic development: the early western surveys conducted by Zebulon Pike in 1806, for instance, were flawed in their portrayal of the Great Plains as a "Great American Desert," retarding potential settlement in the interior of the country for nearly a generation. Only later, when Frémont's famous expeditions in the 1840s changed this picture, did white settlers begin moving westward in significant numbers. As a result some periphery regions were first settled sparsely and only later, in the 1840s and 1850s, did that shift. The Army did shape the pattern and direction of economic development but, as this chapter shows, sometimes with uneven results.

CHAPTER 3

Who Commands?

The two prior chapters have demonstrated that the Army had a broad impact on the antebellum economy. The question that follows is the political one: who controlled the Army's actions? To understand the Army's impact on the economy, we need to understand *who* controlled it as well as which policy choices those actors made, and therefore to *whose* benefit. The literature on the subject, to the extent this issue is addressed, is divided. Skowronek portrays the early American state as being under the control of "courts and parties," though he pays little attention to this specific period or to the Army's role. Historians such as Richard Kohn in his treatment of the Federalists and Theodore Crackel in his work on the Jeffersonians assume that the president and his top civilian adviser, the secretary of war, managed military affairs, paying little attention to Congress or other forces.[1] Others have focused on congressional debates and appropriations; some on officers; some on partisan or sectional interests. However, there is no broader analysis that puts together all these pieces.

I approach the question of control over the Army in two steps, to distinguish the use of force from socioeconomic activities. This chapter examines the former dimension of military activity, the exercise of coercion. I explore how various actors and institutions interacted, ultimately helping to shape how the use of force contributed to economic development. In Chapter 4 I discuss political influences on Army socioeconomic activities.

To explain which actors controlled the Army's coercive actions, I again rely upon the distinction between the periphery and the center. In the center, since the Army was being used much closer to the central state apparatus in Washington, it was easier for constitutional actors to control the Army. The president and Congress therefore took the lead in this area, with the president taking an especially active role in uses of the Army that focused on enforcing the rule of law. With the exception of the War of 1812, the large-scale use of force was mostly managed by the president in conjunction with his advisers in the executive branch, particularly the secretary of war. The apogee of presidential control was reached by President James Polk during the Mexican-American War, as Polk pushed the nation into the war through his actions and took a highly active role in managing military operations.

In the periphery, by contrast, officers in the field had much more discretion in making decisions about how to use the forces under their command. Since these peripheral regions were so far removed from the center, it was more difficult in an era of poor communication for political actors to control what these wagon-trail bureaucrats were doing.[2] As well, since elected politicians did not have a direct representational stake in many of these territories, they had less incentive to carefully oversee what the Army was doing. While the congressional committees on the territories did oversee the general division of the peripheral regions and appointment of federal officials there, they still could not maintain effective control over day-to-day decisions that were being made on the ground.[3] Partisanship was therefore less of a factor than in the center. On the periphery, unelected officials, chiefly the secretary of war, the commanding general of the Army, territorial governors, and officers on the ground, had a relatively free hand in deciding where to build forts, how to expand the nation's boundaries, and how to control rebellions on the nation's margins.

Furthermore, contrary to most literature on the character of the American state, I argue that a closer analysis of how civilians interacted with the Army reveals a significant lack of civilian control in this era. Popular control over much of what the Army did was lacking, since the ever-expanding nature of U.S. territory and sovereignty made it difficult for civilians based in Washington, D.C., to properly manage operations on the ground. Bureaucrats and officers controlled many of the Army's central activities, raising the possibility that the oft-seen liberal American character (that is to say, a state based on popular rule) was lacking in the antebellum period.

This chapter addresses these issues in the three areas where the Army acted, as delineated in Chapter 1: enforcing the rule of law, territorial expansion, and the nationwide system of forts. First, I lay out how this chapter approaches the issue of civil-military relations. Each subsequent section discusses the political forces at work in both the center and the periphery, and investigates the extent to which there was effective civilian control over a large portion of the American state apparatus.

Presidential Power, Officers, and Civil-Military Relations

The Constitution specifically refers to the military and war-making powers of the president and Congress; other actors, such as officers and cabinet members, are not explicitly mentioned. Congress has the power to "declare war" and create a military, but the president is commander-in-chief of the armed forces of the United States, including the state militias when they are called into national service. The Constitution contains ambiguities over the boundaries of these powers, however, creating an opening into which an active president can step, allowing him to make a claim for greater authority that is hard for Congress to resist.[4] A president deferential to Congress would leave it an opening to demand more control.

Extraconstitutional actors such as the secretary of war and officers also played a central role in determining policy outcomes. The only part of the government that continued from the Articles of Confederation to the new constitutional regime with no substantive changes was the War Department under Henry Knox. This continuity may have contributed to it quickly becoming a center of power, with Indian relations, veterans' benefits, and land sales placed largely under its jurisdiction, in addition to traditional military affairs. Acting as the key conduit between the president and uniformed officers, the secretary of war regularly made judgment calls about operational details in areas where the president was not an expert (such as where to place specific forts). Cabinet officers in this era were much more independent of presidential control than they are nowadays, having an independent political base and often being chosen to satisfy some constituency within the president's party. They often had presidential ambitions of their own.[5] When a president was relatively strong, the secretary of war was the junior partner who acted in service of his president's ideas, as in the case of Henry Knox under President Washington. Weaker presidents gave rise to more powerful and independent secretaries, such as John C. Calhoun under President Monroe.

In 1821 the War Department created the position of commanding general of the Army, held by only a few men in the antebellum period—Winfield Scott being the best known, serving for twenty years under six different presidents.[6] The commanding general often feuded with the heads of War

Department bureaus over questions of who would direct Army operations. He also battled civilian leaders, including territorial governors who also had some responsibility for Army operations on the frontier.[7] The commanding general served as a center of influence removed from the secretary of war—staying in office for so many years gave him independence, and the legal lines of responsibility for each office were not entirely clear.

Officers were sometimes involved in politics—Scott made a run for president as a Whig, and Zachary Taylor was elected president in 1848 after his exploits during the Mexican War. As William Skelton has documented, a disproportionate number of officers were from the South and were Democrats, occasionally tilting their actions in favor of southern priorities. Sometimes officers went rogue and disobeyed orders. Andrew Jackson is perhaps the most famous example, essentially conquering Spanish Florida on two occasions without explicit authorization. But for the most part officers were professional and nonpartisan actors who followed their orders.[8] In contrast to the picture in Skowronek's case study of the Army in the late nineteenth century, which depicts it as well integrated into the partisan state, antebellum officers were more likely than not to envision themselves as professional servants of the state.[9]

For many of the Army's coercive operations, partisan politicians simply were not involved. Congressional debates rarely focused on where to place remote forts or on specific dealings with native tribes on the frontier. Sometimes decisions relating to enforcing the rule of law came to congressional attention, as during the Whiskey Rebellion or the Nullification Crisis of 1832, when presidents requested specific legal authorization to carry out their plans. Overall, however, the regions where the Army was the most active were often territories that lacked any congressional representation, and where communication back to Washington could be slow and unreliable. As a result, the secretary of war, the commanding general, bureaucrats, and officers in the field often had primary control.

The power of nonelected officials, notably in the periphery, leads us to the issue of civil-military relations. If officers and bureaucrats indeed had so much independence from their elected masters based in the center, to what extent was there truly civilian control over the military? The literature on the subject produces a wide variety of expectations about how soldiers and civilians should interact with each other, and the proper role of each in assuring civilian control. Samuel Huntington, in his classic work *The Soldier and the State*, argues that civilian control happened in the United States despite the Constitution, not because of it. He sees true civilian control, which he calls "objective," as arising from military professionalism, which then leads to a non-political military that willingly listens to civilian commands. The Constitution, he argues, actually blends military and civilian roles, just the opposite of objective control, which separates the two as much as possible. As well, due to the separation of powers, there is never a clear line of civilian authority, except under rare circumstances.[10] More recent work on the subject questions Huntington's analysis as well as his normative assumptions about professionalism as an unqualified good. Peter Feaver, for example, has applied a rational choice analysis to the civil-military question, viewing officers as the agents of civilian principals in a strategic game. Soldiers are responsive to civilian leaders, he contends, to the extent that they are punished for lack of response to civilian commands.[11] A historical account offered by Russell Weigley argues that "throughout the nineteenth century, military forces were too small and too peripheral to American politics and society at large to be anything but compliant with civilian control."[12]

I argue that none of these perspectives fully accounts for the actual behavior of the Army in the antebellum period. How officers reacted to civilian command deeply reflected the character of the antebellum American state. Contrary to conventional portrayals of a liberal American polity, a closer examination of civilian control here reveals the disturbing possibility that early America only had, at best, an attenuated form of civilian control.[13] Officers were not yet fully accustomed to obeying civilian commands. Although historian William Skelton has rightly portrayed the Army in this period as being considerably more professional than previous scholarly accounts were willing to admit,[14] there were nevertheless still significant instances in which officers disobeyed orders or attempted to contravene their orders through creative interpretation. This seems to have been especially the case in the periphery, where long distances and poor communication opened up opportunities for officers to disobey. Thus, it may indeed have been the case that civilian control over the Army was lacking in antebellum America.

The Rule of Law: Presidential Command, Congressional Authorization, and Officers

Preserving national order was one of the Army's most important tasks in this era. As described in Chapter 1, the Army was used in a wide variety of situations to uphold the rule of law and assert national authority, and thus undergird the foundations of the emerging national economic order. Across successive administrations, politicians of differing partisan orientations and ideologies found it relatively simple to turn to the Army as a solution when a crisis occurred. Many of these crises took place on the periphery, but even in the center the Army was called on to combat challenges to national integrity.

This section analyzes the Army's activities in securing the rule of law in both the periphery and center, and attempts to identify which political actors controlled military order-sustaining intervention, as well as the extent to which officers were able to direct actions on the ground as "street-level bureaucrats." These activities have been discussed previously in Chapter 1, but here I take an analytical look at which political actors controlled them. In general, I argue that presidents were able to take the upper hand in operations intended to preserve the rule of law, especially in the center. Although they often turned to Congress for authorization prior to taking coercive action, later in the antebellum era presidents became more willing to act without waiting for Congress. In the later antebellum years, too, officers seem to have become somewhat more independent, perhaps related to the longer distances the Army was being called upon to travel as the nation expanded farther to the west and communication became more difficult. As well, officers were regularly called upon to manage the details of operations while on the scene, at a level of detail beyond what could have been expected of political actors far away in Washington.

The Center

As discussed in Chapter 1, the Jefferson administration placed an embargo on imported goods from Canada and Great Britain from 1807 through early 1809. Although the embargo was ultimately a failure, it did provide Jefferson with an opportunity to employ the revamped military establishment in a manner consistent with his own foreign policy goals. Acting as a blockading force, the Army was used to enforce the administration's objective, though not without much struggle to control smuggling across the border. Eventually the embargo was ended when it became clear that it had failed to change Britain's behavior toward the United States and was extremely unpopular.[15]

At first glance, it may appear that Congress was directing policymaking here and that the executive branch took a secondary role. Scott Silverstone, for example, in his work on war making in the early republic, has argued that

Jefferson could have chosen to go to war in 1807, yet deferred to Congress and let it choose an embargo instead. Congress passed the various embargo laws and increases in the Army's size necessary to enforce them.[16] This depiction of Jefferson's presidency as reliant on congressional direction is unsurprising, given theoretical accounts of the presidency that assume presidents in the premodern period were weak and deferential to congressional prerogatives and to their parties in Congress.[17]

Nonetheless, a deeper examination shows that Jefferson in fact took the lead in promoting the embargo and in using the military to enforce it. He first proposed an embargo in a message to Congress.[18] Furthermore, despite divisions within his own party over the issue, Jefferson pushed for an increase in the size of the Army to accompany the embargo policy.[19] In particular, the so-called Old Republicans, strongly opposed to a strong central government or a standing army of any kind, tried to kill Jefferson's embargo plan but were ultimately unsuccessful.[20] One vital piece of evidence that demonstrates Jefferson's leading role in the embargo debates is his push for Army expansion prior to the embargo itself having been put in place. As trouble with Britain began brewing, Jefferson asked Congress to increase the size of the Army from six thousand to nine thousand men, with a coordinate increase in the officer corps from two hundred to five hundred.[21] This policy shift, representing a move toward a more aggressive military posture and away from traditional Republican fears of the Army, makes evident that Jefferson rather than Congress was the key actor in confronting Britain. Similarly, many historians have credited Jefferson with pressing for the embargo as a replacement for war, despite objections from members of his own Cabinet.[22] Robert Coakley has even gone so far as to assert that "it was Jefferson who legitimized the use of regular military forces in domestic disorders," beyond that which the Federalists had been able to accomplish.[23] Jefferson did rely on Congress to authorize his proposals before acting, but he pushed Congress to proceed, not the other way around.

Like Jefferson, Andrew Jackson was quite proactive as president, taking a primary role in resolving the Nullification Crisis. Consistent with his reputation for strong domestic actions as president, which earned him the moniker "King Andrew" from his opponents,[24] Jackson also exercised firm control over use of the Army. Jackson attempted to negotiate with the recalcitrant government of South Carolina, but he was perfectly willing to resort to military force when the negotiations appeared to be failing. Well before Congress began moving toward passage of the Force Bill in January 1833, which authorized the president to use force to stop the implementation of South Carolina's nullification ordinance, Jackson was working on his own to prepare the Army for such a possibility. In concert with Joel Poinsett, a unionist South Carolina politician, Jackson made sure that the local troops remained loyal to the national government. He started increasing troop strength in the area as well, along with sending firearms to Poinsett for use in case fighting became necessary.[25]

Jackson also employed Secretary of War Lewis Cass to assist his efforts at undermining South Carolina's position. Cass wrote to Major General Winfield Scott on November 18, 1832, to order him, by direction of the president, to "immediately" head to Charleston and begin preparing for any eventuality. At the same time, Jackson and Cass did not simply delegate responsibility for the affair's resolution to Scott. His discretion was clearly limited, as Cass warned Scott about the "great delicacy" of his mission and instructed him to wait to take action until the president had decided civilian power was not going to resolve the crisis.[26] Another letter from Cass to Scott in January 1833 again reminded the general to use "moderation" and act carefully.[27] Scott certainly obeyed, making no attempt to provoke a military conflict. In this instance, we can detect no hint of civilian control being threatened. Jackson and Cass remained in charge throughout.

As the crisis continued without resolution, Jackson and Congress moved to add new weight to national demands that South Carolina rescind its nullification ordinance. The Force Bill, eventually passed in January 1833, authorized the president to compel states to enforce the tariff laws, through force if necessary. There is little doubt that the push for this legislation came directly from the White House. The bill's primary sponsor, Senator William Wilkins of Pennsylvania, was a dedicated Jacksonian.[28] Jackson himself had publicly proclaimed his opposition to the Calhoun-defined version of states' rights doctrine and made it clear he would not accept any resolution that allowed South Carolina to maintain its extreme stance on the issue.[29] The Force Bill was eventually passed together with a new compromise tariff, and the crisis soon ended, largely on Jackson's terms.[30]

Unlike Jackson with his activist stance, his successor, Martin Van Buren, let his subordinates control most of the on-the-ground details during the Patriot War. From the years 1837 to 1839, the Army was largely stationed on the northern frontier, preventing so-called Patriots, supporters of Canadian independence, from crossing the border to fight the British. An analysis of Van Buren's annual messages to Congress, an important source of presidential communication in this era, reveals his attempt to deemphasize the matter, despite its seriousness.[31] In 1838, 1839, and 1840, the years of greatest Patriot activity, Van Buren mentioned it near the beginning of each message. His 1838 message framed the dispute as caused by a group of American "gangs" who sought to push the nation into a war not properly declared by Congress. The president also issued a proclamation against the expeditions into Canada, which was attached to his message.[32] By 1839, Van Buren tried to restructure the debate by blaming the continuing troubles on Canadians who fed the fire of the dispute, as if no Americans were involved anymore.[33] Finally, in 1840, he declared that the United States had "a rigid and persevering abstinence from all interference with the domestic and political relations of other States," though he did not single out the Canadian provinces in particular.[34] Van Buren's statements clearly show his desire to play down the dispute and keep it secondary to other concerns. Perhaps this is not surprising, if, following Skowronek, we see Van Buren as an articulator of Jackson's political program.[35] Van Buren tried to hold together a somewhat fragile coalition at a time of domestic upheaval following the Panic of 1837, and he did not want to undermine his party's stability by highlighting an issue that might divide it.

He chose instead to let his subordinates handle the details, especially the secretary of war and officers on the scene. General Winfield Scott was ordered to the northern frontier in 1839 to manage the deteriorating situation there. Secretary of War Poinsett wrote the order to Scott, stating that the president ordered him to the border because "the supremacy of the laws must be asserted and maintained" and in the hope that his personal "influence may do much."[36] While it was not unusual for presidential orders to be carried out through the secretary of war in this manner, the lack of specific detail in the order was outside the norm. Poinsett had given him very broad latitude to determine what course to follow. With the cooperation of local citizens and the New York state militia, Scott quieted the border region based on his own initiatives. Indeed, historian Samuel Watson argues that "army officers were the primary agents of national policy along the border" in stopping a full-fledged war from breaking out.[37] Nevertheless, there is no hint of civilian control being threatened here in any way. Perhaps senior officers had proved themselves trustworthy agents, and therefore civilian principals gave them greater flexibility to carry out their missions.

Another case of strong presidential control is provided by the Dorr Rebellion in Rhode Island in the early 1840s. The administration of John

Tyler was already besieged on all sides due to Tyler's untenable position between the two parties, as a man nominally belonging to the Whigs yet clearly committed to the Democrats.[38] In this instance, Tyler endorsed the standing government of Rhode Island, which was operating under its original antidemocratic colonial charter that limited suffrage to property holders, even while other national Democrats opposed the standing government. After some hesitation, the president eventually announced in mid-1842 that he would, if necessary, resort to military force to back up the existing government. This move took the wind out of the sails of the Dorr movement and led it to back down, with supporters eventually retreating into Connecticut.[39]

Apparently, the president here acted largely on his own, without relying on subordinates to any significant degree. Tyler did use commanders on the ground to provide him with local intelligence, as he sent Generals John Wool and Abraham Eustis to Rhode Island to provide a firsthand account of the situation.[40] At the end of the day, however, he made the decision to threaten the use of force on his own recognizance despite significant political opposition. Thomas Dorr himself went to Washington to lobby Democratic members of Congress, who were quite supportive. Their backing for Dorr stemmed partly from their general inclination toward greater democracy, and partly from the fears southerners had of overweening national executive power being used against their states.[41] However, Dorr's lobbying effort ultimately proved ineffective in overcoming Tyler's threat.

In summary, presidents clearly held the upper hand in enforcing the rule of law in the center. With the exception of Van Buren, all the presidents in the Center took the initiative in using force to protect the rule of law. Even in Van Buren's case, although officers on the scene had a significant share of the decision making, they posed no threat to effective presidential control, as they quickly responded to presidential directives when they were issued.

The Periphery

Army actions in the periphery to uphold the rule of law in the nation's early years were largely controlled by presidents. Later in the antebellum period, officers began to resist civilian control, especially as their tasks took them to far-flung locales where communication with officials in Washington became slow and cumbersome. When presidents, secretaries of war, and the commanding general found themselves responding after officers on the scene already had acted, civilian control was undermined.

In the Whiskey Rebellion, President Washington exercised decisive control throughout. He did not initially turn to force to stop those protesting the new national excise tax on whiskey production that had been imposed in 1791. For several years, he and Secretary of War Henry Knox attempted to negotiate with the resisters. In 1792, although Alexander Hamilton advised using force immediately, the president first issued a cease-and-desist proclamation. In the combination of this restraint with modifications Congress agreed to make to the tax's structure, fears of an all-out rebellion temporarily subsided. Soon, however, the resistance revived.[42] When the state of Pennsylvania hesitated to take on the rebels gathering at Braddock's Field, Washington and Knox put together a ten-thousand-man force capable of stopping the resistance movement. In an exceptional moment, Washington personally led the troops into the field, staking his own prestige and military reputation on the matter. This tremendous show of force led the rebels to mostly disperse before the troops had even arrived on the scene.[43]

Like Washington, John Adams was clearly in control when he used the Army to protect the rule of law. Adams's actions came in response to another tax revolt, this one led by John Fries of Pennsylvania. Fries and his supporters opposed new taxes passed by Congress in an effort to fund the national military buildup during the Quasi-War. Unlike his predecessor, Adams made no attempt to conciliate the rebels or to negotiate with them. Possibly this quick move to coercion was due to the polarized political climate of the times, as High Federalists demanded swift action. Though Jeffersonians agreed that subverting the law was unacceptable, they opposed Adams's move to send troops to the area to end the rebellion. Like Washington, Adams worked closely with his secretary of war, James McHenry, at one point letting McHenry plan operational details during his annual summer vacation at his home in Massachusetts. Still, it seems that Adams maintained effective control of the military throughout this affair.[44]

In the case of the Burr Conspiracy in 1806–7, there was an actual threat to normal civilian control over the military, caused by Burr's own actions. Burr exploited latent Federalist sympathies among many Army officers and tried to woo them to his side. His plan to have part of the Southwest secede from the nation came to naught largely because the top general at the time, James Wilkinson, eventually retreated from his (apparent) inclination to join Burr's forces. Wilkinson, along with other officers, seemed ready to use national military power in a blatant attempt to leave the union. Only at the last moment did he inform the president of Burr's treasonous behavior, at which point Jefferson ordered the general to arrest Burr, which he promptly did. Congress, for the most part, stayed out of the dispute. Its only action was an aborted attempt to retroactively suspend habeas corpus in regard to Wilkinson's random civilian arrests during his pursuit of Burr. Like Washington and Adams before him, Jefferson was clearly in control of this operation, despite its distance from the nation's center.[45]

Later in the antebellum period, as debates over sectional concerns intensified, private citizens began undertaking so-called filibustering expeditions to grab territory for the United States, without official approval from the government. A spate of these incidents in the 1840s and 1850s led to several instances in which the Army was called upon to prevent the filibusterers' seizures. Due to the increasing salience of sectional tensions, however, some officers in the periphery attempted to evade presidential directives or, at the very least, to creatively interpret those orders to reach their own preferred outcomes, which differed from the incumbent administration's. With the cross-regional party system breaking down, presidents had a weaker support base and thus found it increasingly difficult to call upon reserves of political capital in their parties or Congress to sustain their coercive initiatives.[46]

Southern Democrats were especially interested in further expanding the nation's boundaries after the end of the Mexican-American War. They proposed various schemes such as purchasing Cuba from Spain or simply grabbing lands by force throughout Latin America.[47] Though none of these plans came to fruition, they did reflect popular sentiments among many southerners. Not surprisingly, then, some individuals proceeded on their own initiative. Some tried to take Cuba and the Sandwich Islands (now known as Hawaii), leading President Fillmore to issue cease-and-desist proclamations and authorize the use of force against them.[48] Fillmore's intervention prevented both of these situations from deteriorating into full-fledged international incidents.

Under the administrations of Franklin Pierce and James Buchanan, by contrast, national policy toward filibustering took a significant detour. Pierce and Buchanan, both Democrats, supported further expansion toward the south and reduced the national government's emphasis on preserving national authority. This shift in policy led to conflict with some Whig-leaning officers within the Army; at the same time, it did not go far enough to suit other officers who backed more aggressive expansionism. The officer corps became internally fragmented around sectional issues, just like the rest of the nation in the 1850s, making it harder for top-down civilian control to operate in the normal manner.

Colonel Ethan Allen Hitchcock, a committed Whig in charge of the Army's Division of the Pacific, stopped a group of filibusterers in 1853 that was leaving from San Francisco to seize parts of northern Mexico. After loud complaints about his actions from local Democratic leaders, including Senator William Gwin, Hitchcock was soon replaced by Brigadier General John Wool, a Democrat who was thought to be more sympathetic to southern expansionism. After a short time, it became clear that Wool, too, would continue the Army's long-standing policy of stopping filibusters, regardless of what the new national leadership preferred. Secretary of War Jefferson Davis and Wool exchanged a series of harsh letters, eventually leading Wool to back down and minimize future uses of the Army in this manner.[49] Davis seemed particularly concerned about not using the Army domestically more than absolutely necessary, perhaps because of his fear that it could be used against slavery at some future point. Elsewhere, he declared that "the [War] Department conceives that the Army should not be called to aid the civil authority in enforcing the laws of the United States."[50] While most officers acted like Wool, a significant minority were sympathetic to the filibusterers. As Robert May points out, young American men deciding on a career path often chose filibustering over the Army because of the former's promise of excitement and adventure. Even within the Army's ranks, there were several occasions upon which officers helped filibustering rather than trying to stop it.[51]

The problem of resistance to civilian control escalated during the Kansas crisis in the 1850's. Army officers working to stop violence from both proslavery and antislavery forces often flouted presidential orders that they disliked. Colonel Edwin Sumner, for instance, who was the officer in charge at Fort Leavenworth, took his zeal for enforcing the Pierce administration's proslavery leanings much further than Pierce or Secretary of War Jefferson Davis wanted. Pierce and Davis had given him full authority to use force in protection of the existing proslavery territorial government, under the immediate direction of Governor Wilson Shannon. But when Shannon had Sumner's troops forcibly break up a meeting of the free-state legislature, Davis reprimanded the colonel and replaced him with General Persifor Smith.[52] When James Buchanan became president, he decided to maintain an outright proslavery effort in Kansas. His appointee, Colonel William S. Harney, was put in place on the apparent assumption that he would toe the administration's line, but he turned out to be significantly more independent than

Buchanan or Secretary of War John Floyd wanted. Harney pledged upon his arrival in Kansas that he would remain nonpartisan and enforce the rule of law. Simply by keeping an open mind, Harney encouraged free-state supporters, who pushed for a new election. Harney's lack of proslavery enthusiasm led the Buchanan administration to replace the territorial governors repeatedly until they found one, James W. Denver, who was sufficiently opposed to the free-staters.[53]

Similarly, during the Mormon expedition under the Buchanan administration, some officers tried to go further than their orders allowed. Colonel Albert S. Johnston, who was leading troops in the field in Utah, was convinced that force would be required in order to make the Mormons obey federal dictates. Initially, it seemed as if the administration and territorial governor Alfred Cummings agreed, as they pushed Johnston to prepare for a battle. Soon, however, President Buchanan decided to send a peace envoy to negotiate with Brigham Young and the Mormon leadership. Cummings fell in line and sided with the envoy. But Johnston was displeased and continued to threaten a battle, with his troops fully prepared to march at any time. The tug of war between Johnston and Cummings continued through 1858 and 1859, until the president finally and firmly declared that Cummings was in control.[54]

In the periphery, therefore, the latter part of the antebellum period saw looser presidential control over the Army. Although presidents could still ultimately enforce their policy preferences, officers had significant leeway to interpret their orders to give them discretion to act as they wanted, at least in the short run. Long distances from Washington and the increasing divisions within the officer corps over slavery led to escalating conflict between presidents and the Army.

Territorial Expansion: Politicians as Policymakers, Officers as Managers

Presidents and Congress generally took the lead when the Army was used for the purpose of territorial expansion, sketching the broad outlines of policy and enunciating their desired goals. Operational details, however, were often left to the secretary of war, the commanding general of the Army, and officers on the ground. In this area, the division between the center and the periphery was less relevant, as most actions took place strictly in the periphery.

This section analyzes territorial expansion in two categories: first, large wars of expansion, such as the Mexican-American War, and second, conflicts involving the extension of U.S. sovereignty over lands taken from native tribes.

Wars of Expansion

During the antebellum period, the United States fought three wars of expansion: the War of 1812, the Florida wars, and the Mexican-American War. Although all presidents are commander-in-chief of the armed forces under the Constitution, that designation translates into varying degrees of actual control depending on the president's leadership, the partisan context in Congress, and the strength of the military forces at the president's disposal.[55] For the three primary cases of expansionary wars in the antebellum years, as each of those factors varied, so too did the outcome. A more assertive president could exercise command more closely; at the same time, a president whose party in Congress was divided could find it more difficult to achieve his military objectives. Resistance from reluctant or renegade commanders also led to difficulty in some cases.

President James Madison is widely considered to have been an ineffective commander-in-chief during the War of 1812. He was pushed into the war by a faction of his own party in Congress, consisting of westerners like Henry Clay who were angry at British intrusions on their lands and wanted expansion west and north into Canada. These so-called war hawks eventually convinced the president that the threat to national honor was so great that he needed to ask for a declaration of war, which Congress was more than happy to provide. However, the country was not prepared. The national military was too small and inadequately supplied to fight a large-scale war. Government officials were forced to beg states for extra troops.[56] Congress increased the Army to twenty-five thousand, but it was too little, too late. After an unsuccessful push into Canada and the near destruction of the entire federal government when the British burned large portions of the capital, U.S. negotiators sued for peace.[57]

The early stages of the conflict highlighted the deep divisions within the nation, as well as those within the Democratic-Republican Party, all of which made Madison's job much more difficult. Federalists were united in their opposition to the war, with some threatening to secede from the Union. Madison's own party split between New Yorkers favoring war, southern Old

Republicans opposed to any sort of standing army, and western war hawks. Madison found it necessary to attempt to pacify all portions of his party but satisfied no one in the process. Secretary of War John Armstrong, for instance, had advised Madison that no invasion of Washington, DC could occur, and so the capital was virtually undefended when the British arrived. But because Armstrong represented the important New York Republicans in the Cabinet, Madison could not simply fire his war secretary for incompetence, and was instead forced to let him resign on his own terms. Meanwhile, western war hawks were angered by the administration's reluctance to press for a full invasion of Canada, not realizing how poorly equipped the Army was for such a task.[58] Considering the challenges facing Madison's leadership, it is no wonder his record during the war appears so unimpressive.

At the start of the war, the officer corps was also not ready for the large-scale use of force that followed. It consisted largely of undisciplined men whose formal training in military science was quite limited, with few having been educated at the relatively new West Point academy. Many were political appointees brought in due to the extreme shortage of experienced men able to lead a fighting force. The war, however, led to dramatic improvements in the quality and quantity of officers. As historian Samuel Watson notes, some of the Army's top soldiers in the years after the War of 1812 cut their teeth during the war, leading to "the gradual rise of a cadre of capable, experienced senior commanders and staff officers."[59] Younger officers proved their skill as older officers demonstrated their lack of qualifications. This younger set of officers helped rescue a stalemate in the war rather than the outright American defeat that almost occurred.[60] In particular, General Andrew Jackson became a national hero for his role in winning the Battle of New Orleans. Jackson's operational plans were not preauthorized by the president, the War Department, or his superior officers. In fact, Jackson imposed martial law on the city of New Orleans, even going so far as to have a member of the local legislature arrested for complaining.[61]

Jackson's independent conduct in New Orleans proved to be entirely consistent with his usual style. Following the War of 1812, he became one of the prime agitators for annexing Florida, either through treaty with Spain or outright military conquest. Jackson's preferred route was force. On at least three separate occasions, he led expeditions into Florida, against explicit orders from the secretary of war, in an attempt to seize the territory for the United States. The first of these, in 1814, involved the city of Pensacola, which was returned to the Spanish within just a few days.[62] Then in 1816, based on fears that the Spanish seemed to be allying with local Indian tribes, Jackson ordered Brigadier General Edmund Gaines to destroy the so-called Negro Fort in Florida. Secretary of War William Crawford explicitly commanded Jackson on several occasions not to cross into Spanish territory.[63] Nevertheless, Jackson disregarded the normal chain of command. As David Heidler and Jeanne Heidler note, "the War Department remained ignorant of Jackson's extensive preparations for war" until it was too late to do anything about them.[64] Finally, in 1818, Jackson seized Florida in the name of the U.S. government and refused to leave the territory, forcing the Monroe administration to negotiate the Adams-Onís Treaty transferring control to the United States. Once again, Jackson ignored direct orders in the process. As early as 1817, he told officers working under him to ignore instructions from the War Department unless they came through him first. Secretary of War John Calhoun rebuked him, but Jackson remained sanguine.[65] Despite further orders from Calhoun in 1818 not to attack, Jackson went ahead and grabbed the territory.[66]

Much of the disrespect Jackson showed was directly related to political motivations. The secretaries of war with whom Jackson clashed, not to mention Jackson himself, all had their own designs on the presidency. In 1814, James Monroe was the secretary of war; he soon became president. Crawford was one of Jackson's opponents during the election of 1824, and Calhoun ended up becoming Jackson's vice president later on. William Skelton argues that Jackson's actions should be seen as an aberration in the overall view of civil-military relations in the antebellum period; soon officers would regard disobeying orders as completely unacceptable.[67] To a point Skelton is correct, insofar as few officers demonstrated a blatant and routine disregard for the chain of command like Jackson. However, as we have already seen, there were numerous incidents in which officers reread orders to fit their needs, or merely implemented orders differently as conditions on the ground changed.

Unlike Madison, James K. Polk took direct and active control over operations during the Mexican-American War. Not long after the telegraph was invented, Polk used the technology to receive reports directly from the front and send quick messages to his commanders in the field. This innovation greatly eased the problem of presidents overseeing troops located in the periphery, and in combination with Polk's aggressive posture in favor of Manifest Destiny led to a demonstration of strong presidential leadership. Polk claimed to have done nothing to press Mexico into a war, disingenuously asserting that "the United States were the aggrieved nation, Mexico commenced the war."[68] In truth, he ordered General Zachary Taylor to cross into the disputed territory between the Nueces and Rio Grande Rivers. Once there, the Mexicans fired upon Taylor's men, giving Polk the excuse he needed to ask Congress for a declaration of war.[69] Polk had a majority in Congress for most of the war, which allowed him to do most of what he wanted in the conduct of the war. Democrats had some dissenters, but most were strong supporters of the war. The minority Whigs bitterly complained about Polk's methods, from the way he initiated the conflict to his seeming disregard for Whig-leaning officers, but to little effect, and in the end they overwhelmingly voted to fund the troops once fighting had started.[70]

However, even a strong president such as Polk could not control every aspect of the fighting. Reliance on local commanders was still a necessary part of any operation, especially once battles moved deeper into Mexican territory. Even Polk's initial directive to General Taylor to cross into disputed land was extremely vague, not specifying that Taylor should respond with force to any Mexican attack. Historian John Eisenhower notes that the president thus "placed in the hands of a field commander the power to decide whether or not a state of war existed, a remarkable step."[71] Moreover, despite Polk's strength as a wartime president, he could not convince Congress to give him everything he desired. Unhappy with the leadership of General Winfield Scott, Polk sent a bill to Congress that would have authorized him to appoint a new lieutenant general of the Army, ranking above Scott. Polk apparently intended to place Senator Thomas Hart Benton, a loyal supporter of his, in the new position. Even many Democrats demurred and the bill failed in the House.[72]

Those further down on the chain of command sometimes disregarded the wishes of the president or others above them. The most stunning example of this occurred when Captain John C. Frémont, Senator Benton's son-in-law, decided to instigate California's rebellion against the Mexican government. Frémont's mission had originally been another in his line of western surveys, but he soon decided to make it his personal objective to gain California for the United States. Before he had learned that Mexico and the United States were officially at war, he worked with local American settlers to declare California an independent republic, in the so-called Bear Flag Revolt. William Skelton again sees this as a deviation from the norm of officers following their orders, but Frémont's behavior is only an extreme example of what often happened on the periphery.[73] Similarly, the war ended despite the president's wishes when Nicholas Trist, the president's chosen envoy to Mexico, negotiated more generous terms in the Treaty of Guadalupe Hidalgo than Polk preferred. Polk had attempted to recall Trist prior to this, but the order came into Trist's hands after he had already finished the negotiations, and facing a new Whig majority in Congress, Polk was forced to accept Trist's treaty.[74]

Clearly, even when a president was relatively powerful, wars of expansion that took place on the periphery had to be managed and directed at the local level by the officers on the scene. At times, renegade officers decided to ignore or creatively reinterpret their orders to fit their own policy preferences, making it difficult for the chain of command to work in a normal top-down fashion. As a result civilian control was sometimes compromised.

Extending American Sovereignty

Through wars against native tribes, control over territory was gained by the national government (see Table 6). Presidential decision making in this area was mostly limited to policy choices, such as whether to attack a tribe or attempt to negotiate a treaty instead. Few presidents directly engaged in operational details, leaving them to the commanding general, the secretary of war, and officers on the ground. Congress often held hearings after the fact to determine whether national policy should be changed, occasionally passing laws relating to how Indian lands would be governed; but members of Congress were rarely interested in battles that occurred in peripheral regions, outside of those in their own states or the general impulse of the times in favor of expansionism.

In confronting the Ohio Valley tribes in the 1790s, the national government's policy was directed by President Washington and Secretary of War Henry Knox. Washington entrusted Knox with major policy decisions and relied heavily on his advice. Both the president and Knox agreed initially to negotiate with tribes in the region. Knox stated in letters to commanders on the ground that "every effort for peace, should precede coercion" and that they needed to "make every reasonable effort [to negotiate peace], in order to convince a considerable proportion of the citizens of the United States, that the thing is impracticable."[75] The military governor of the region, Arthur St. Clair, was on board with this plan at first. Soon, however, Washington and his administration wearied of negotiations and turned to a policy that relied more on force.[76] Washington convinced Congress to authorize St. Clair and General Josiah Harmar to call out the militia, under the assumption that it was strictly a defensive measure. Defense was not, in fact, its true purpose.

Table 6. Major Conflicts with Native Tribes

Year	*Tribe(s)*	*Location*
1790–94	Miami, Shawnee	Ohio Valley
1811	Shawnee	Tippecanoe
1813–14	Creek	Georgia
1817–18	Seminole	Florida
1832	Sauks	Illinois, Iowa
1836–37	Creek	Georgia
1835–42	Seminole	Florida
1838	Cherokee	Georgia
1850–59	Navajo, Apache, Sioux, Cheyenne	Far West
1855–1858	Seminole	Florida

Sources: Information gathered from Susan B. Carter, Scott Sigmund Gartner, Michael R. Haines, Alan L. Olmstead, Richard Sutch, and Gavin Wright, eds., *Historical Statistics of the United States: Earliest Times to the Present* (Millennial Edition), volume 5 (New York: Cambridge University Press, 2006), 372; Francis Paul Prucha, *The Sword of the Republic: The United States Army on the Frontier, 1783–1846* (Lincoln: University of Nebraska Press, 1969); and John Grenier, *The First Way of War: American War Making on the Frontier* (New York: Cambridge University Press, 2005).

As Richard Kohn notes, "only later, after Washington cited the amendment as authorization for Harmar's campaign, did Congress understand fully that it had given the President permission to wage war on his own authority."[77]

As noted in Chapter 1, Harmar's campaign went poorly, however, and Washington relieved him of command. St. Clair was appointed in Harmar's place to command the Army's next phase of operations, but he too failed to defeat the Indians. Following these defeats, Knox's influence in the cabinet began to decline, with Washington leaning more heavily on advice from Secretary of the Treasury Alexander Hamilton. Congress also shifted some control over the purchase of supplies from War to Treasury, in an attempt to fix organizational difficulties that had hampered Harmar's and St. Clair's missions. Washington's third commander, Anthony Wayne, was eventually successful in defeating the tribes at the Battle of Fallen Timbers in the summer of 1794. Wayne embraced a new strategy, converting the Army into what he called the Legion of the United States. With new training and careful preparation, the soldiers were in a much better position to fight. On one occasion, Wayne did overstep his authority somewhat, when he began building an unauthorized road into the Indian lands. Upon hearing of it, Knox ordered

Wayne to retreat and wait until a final round of negotiations had failed. At the end of the day, however, it is Wayne who must ultimately receive the credit for this victory, as it was his new strategy that proved decisive in the final outcome.[78]

In the early 1810s, commanders on the ground demonstrated a high degree of independence during battles with Indian tribes. William Henry Harrison, governor of the Indiana Territory, was ordered to negotiate land cessions from the Shawnee. When Tecumseh formed a coalition to fight back against the Americans, Harrison led a force that defeated them at the Battle of Tippecanoe, a battle that established his reputation as a brilliant commander.[79] Even more independent was Andrew Jackson, who took on the Creeks in southern Georgia. Jackson led the Tennessee militia, under orders from Secretary of War John Armstrong. After Jackson's forces defeated the Creeks using unusually harsh tactics, Armstrong told him to force the Creeks to cede land to the United States as part of any treaty. Jackson followed orders, but was even more punitive than anyone expected, demanding half of all Creek lands. Under duress, the Creeks signed the Treaty of Fort Jackson, which would lead to recriminations for years to come as some Creeks, angered by its terms, continued to fight.[80]

The Black Hawk War of 1831 and 1832 against the Sauks saw local officers generally obeying civilian command. After the governor of Illinois requested assistance from the national government to move the Sauks off land they had ceded by treaty, Secretary of War Lewis Cass ordered General Edmund Gaines, commander of the Western Department of the Army, to move in. Gaines quickly came with his troops and defeated the tribe, forcing it to sign another treaty promising to end its resistance. When trouble flared up between the Sauks and Menominees, however, General Henry Atkinson was sent in to seize Black Hawk, the leader of the Sauks, to finally break their spirit. Meanwhile, President Jackson was concerned about the potential electoral impact of an ongoing war, so he ordered General Winfield Scott to the scene. Before Scott arrived, however, Atkinson captured Black Hawk at the Battle of Wisconsin Heights. Officers here acted as their superiors desired, simply making on-the-ground decisions as necessary to conform to their orders.[81]

By contrast, in battling the Seminoles in Florida during the late 1830s, officers quarreled with their superiors over the ultimate goals of the fighting, as well as with each other over tactics. After some Seminoles destroyed most of Florida's sugar industry in late 1835, the five hundred troops in the territory found themselves outmatched by a foe who better knew the terrain. In response, the War Department sent in Brigadier General Abraham Eustis and Major General Winfield Scott with reinforcements. General Edmund Gaines also decided to go on his own initiative, ignoring an order to return to his previous post on the Mexican border. Once there, Gaines and Scott could not decide which one of them was really in charge, constantly coming into conflict. Gaines even tried to negotiate a separate peace with the Seminoles, promising them the southern part of Florida if they would leave the white settlers alone in the north. The War Department refused to consider Gaines's agreement, however, and the fighting continued.[82] While President Jackson supported the Army's actions as part of his overall plan of Indian removal, his role in planning the war seems to have been limited, as much of the fighting took place toward the end of his administration.[83]

With Scott seemingly not able to end the fighting, Interim Secretary of War Benjamin Butler placed Major General Thomas S. Jesup, head of the Quartermaster Bureau, in charge of the Army's soldiers in Florida. Butler gave him wide latitude to pursue the war as he saw fit, telling him that he was "liberty to adopt such measures, and to pursue such course in the execution of them, as the means at your disposal may allow, and as you may deem most likely to accomplish the objects of the campaign."[84] Jesup asked for and received an increase in troop strength to almost nine thousand.[85] He used extraordinarily harsh methods to defeat the Seminoles, including capturing and torturing Indians who surrendered under a flag of truce. Soon, however, he realized the futility of attempting total removal of all Seminoles, due to their natural advantage in the harsh terrain. The new secretary of war, Joel Poinsett, disliked Jesup's lack of enthusiasm for the removal mission. Poinsett told Jesup that "to withdraw our forces now, would betray great weakness, and not only tarnish the honor of our arms but violate the sacred obligations of the Government of the United States to protect the persons and property of the citizens of Florida from the savage aggressions of the Indians."[86] Meanwhile, General Gaines again attempted to wrest command away from the War Department, leading to a sharp rebuke from Poinsett, who explicitly instructed him to act only upon receiving orders.[87] Like Jackson, President Martin Van Buren appears to have avoided direct involvement in planning the war, beyond the high-level strategic decision to continue Jackson's removal policy.[88]

During the 1850s, when much of the Army was occupied battling tribes in western Texas and New Mexico, the secretary of war was surprisingly effective in maintaining control over far-flung expeditions. Officers generally followed their orders as they fought the Navajo, Apache, and Sioux.[89] Partly this may be a reflection of the strength of Secretary of War Jefferson Davis, one of the most powerful men to occupy the office. Davis took on those below him without a moment's hesitation when he felt they were unresponsive to his orders. When Winfield Scott, the commanding general of the Army, attempted to subvert Davis's authority, Davis had the attorney general and President Pierce rebuke Scott's interpretation of the relevant laws.[90] One exception to strong civilian control in this period occurred when Brigadier General William S. Harney was dispatched to stop attacks on settlers in the Oregon Territory. Harney was a loyal southern Democrat, and a close confidant of both Presidents Pierce and Buchanan, making it difficult for his superiors along the normal chain of command to control him. Upon arriving in Oregon, Harney sent troops to the disputed San Juan Island and claimed it for the United States. An outraged Great Britain demanded that Harney leave immediately, which he refused to do. Winfield Scott was brought in to negotiate a troop removal, but once he left, Harney again sent troops to the island. Finally, Secretary of War John Floyd ordered Harney to return to Washington, D.C., where he could do no further damage to diplomatic relations with the British.[91]

As we have seen in this section, presidential control over wars with native tribes took place only at the highest level of policymaking, with most of the details run by the secretary of war and the commanding general of the Army. Officers on the frontier vacillated between following orders and ignoring them when it suited their own policy or political preferences. Many officers must be credited with winning battles due to their own actions, such as Anthony Wayne and his innovative strategy that won the Battle of Fallen Timbers. Other times, they had to be reined in when they acted outside their authority, as in the case of Edmund Gaines during the Seminole War.

The Secretary of War, Officers, and Forts

The forts constructed by the Army in the antebellum period gradually spread across the continent, following the nation's westward expansion. Despite their importance, however, forts attracted surprisingly little attention from elected officials, who left most decisions about their placement and stationing to officers within the War Department and the secretary of war. The officers running a fort could make on-the-spot decisions about moving troops around as needed, especially in the latter portion of the antebellum period, as the nation's larger size slowed communication with Washington. On occasion, the president or interested members of Congress might mention fort placement, if the stakes were particularly high, or if the War Department was considering a system-wide reorganization. Even so, the president often merely reflected advice given by the secretary of war. In the late antebellum era, decisions about these issues seem to have become more of a management issue, with specialists in the War Department making many key decisions.

Early in the republic's history, forts were often placed at the remnants of stations that had originally been established by other nations' armed forces or earlier settler communities. Fort Pitt, for instance, one of the most important forts in early America, was built on the site of the French Fort Duquesne, which at the junction of the Allegheny and Monongahela Rivers had been a key trading post with local native tribes. The British too had located a fort on the site, and in the colonial period it was used frequently for contact between Anglos and Indians, a pattern that continued into the new nation.[92] Others were simply located near large population centers or at strategic locations, such as the head of a river or near Indian encampments. General Josiah Harmar, whose mission to fight the Ohio Valley tribes had otherwise largely failed, built several new forts in the region, including Forts Finney, Franklin, Steuben, and Harmar, all of which extended the sovereignty of the United States and helped encourage white settlement.[93] His successor, General Anthony Wayne, built Fort Greeneville, which scared British traders out of the area, and was later used as the location for pressuring the native tribes to sign the Treaty of Fort Greeneville that ceded many of their land rights to the United States. Others that he built included Forts Defiance, Adams, and Deposit, all designed to ensure a line of defense against the tribes as well as encourage trading and commerce.[94]

As the country's population continued to move west and new forts were needed, where to locate them became a question that attracted much attention from the secretary of war, planners in the War Department bureaucracy, and the officers managing the forts' operations. At the outset of the nineteenth century, the War Department began preparing to establish forts in present-day Illinois and Ohio. Secretary of War Henry Dearborn, for instance, was clearly a hands-on manager regarding fort locations. In July 1802, he wrote Captain Daniel Bissell, asking him to survey near the junction of the Ohio and Mississippi Rivers to build a fort at a "convenient Site for a settlement and ultimately for a place of Business, where the Military may have the command of the Mississippi & the Ohio Both [*sic*]."[95] Dearborn also involved himself in the details of a fort on the Cuyahoga River and repairs to the fortifications at New York Harbor, even as he halted improvements to various forts as part of President Jefferson's economizing movement.[96]

The Army often placed forts ahead of the line of settlement, preemptively preparing for further expansion of the existing population. In this respect, the Army seems to have addressed a societal imperative of providing security to white settler populations located in dangerous regions containing native tribes. Yet by building the forts first, the Army took a proactive approach that encouraged the extension of white settlement to the west. As Francis Paul Prucha notes, "when the frontier moved west the army garrisons moved along, usually a jump ahead of the settlers."[97] After the War of 1812 concluded, and the British abandoned their forts in the Old Northwest, Secretaries of war like John C. Calhoun and James Barbour wanted to add forts in remote locations far ahead of where settlers already lived, while consolidating and reducing troop strength in forts near existing population centers as security improved. Posts like Fort Dearborn near Chicago were abandoned as part of this policy, while Fort Leavenworth, in present-day Kansas, was established in 1827.[98]

In the 1830s and 1840s, while the topographical engineers surveyed the expanding western territories of the United States, the War Department tried to plan ahead of settlement. Accordingly, the department sited forts in locales where no one had yet settled or in strategic locations along routes that settlers might use when heading westward. The Army thus helped to make real the promise of Manifest Destiny, which presumed that white settlers would spread across the vast continent. Under the new approach, the Army built forts to protect travelers along westward routes, rather than simply advancing slightly ahead of the line of settlement. In 1840, Secretary of War Joel Poinsett, reflecting the advice of his underlings in the War Department, recommended reorganizing the western forts to protect east-west routes rather than attempt to line up forts along a north-south axis across from existing settled areas; his successor, John C. Spencer, followed Poinsett's suggestion. Three of these forts were built along the Oregon Trail.[99] Interestingly, this policy shift continued from the Democratic presidency of Martin Van Buren to the Whig-controlled administration that took office in 1841, demonstrating a lack of partisanship and a reliance on bureaucratic priorities.[100]

President John Tyler, in his annual message to Congress, echoed Spencer's call for "a chain of military posts from Council Bluffs to some point on the Pacific Ocean. The benefit [is] thereby desired to accrue to our citizens engaged in the fur trade, over that wilderness region."[101] With the Army simultaneously surveying the new western territories, the cumulative effect of this plan was to have the Army in the vanguard, affirmatively inducing the nation to expand.

The manner in which forts were garrisoned and located was driven by the scarcity of resources available to the War Department, and no explicitly political or partisan calculations can be seen in the available data. Forts in the Old Northwest (which included Michigan, Illinois, Wisconsin, and Minnesota) saw a gradual drawdown in troop strength during the middle part of the antebellum period (Figure 2). Fort Winnebago in Wisconsin, for instance, which was established in 1827 to help the Army maintain peace between white settlers and the Winnebago tribe of Indians, was abandoned by 1845. This is despite the fact that just a few years earlier, Secretary of War John Spencer had envisioned Fort Winnebago as one of six or eight forts that would assist in securing the western frontier from hostile native tribes.[102] Apparently, by 1845, the War Department had shifted its position and had started to think ahead to the expanded nation that might result after a potential war with Mexico. Meanwhile, Fort Atkinson in Iowa

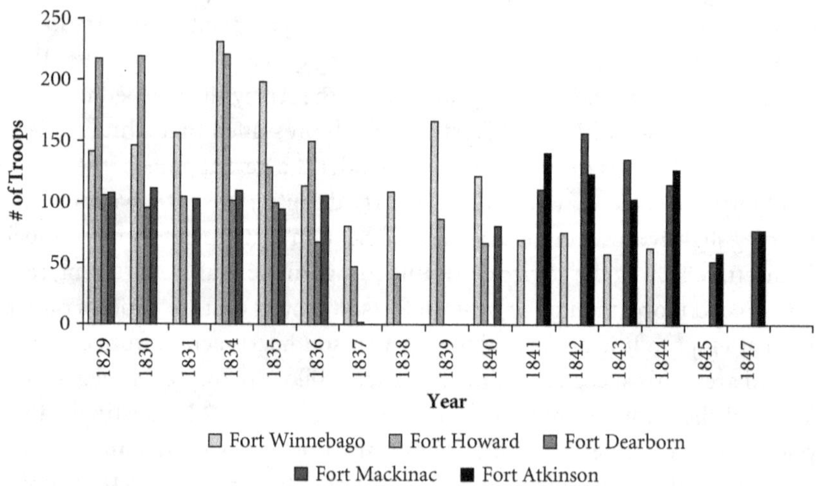

Figure 2. Forts in the Old Northwest

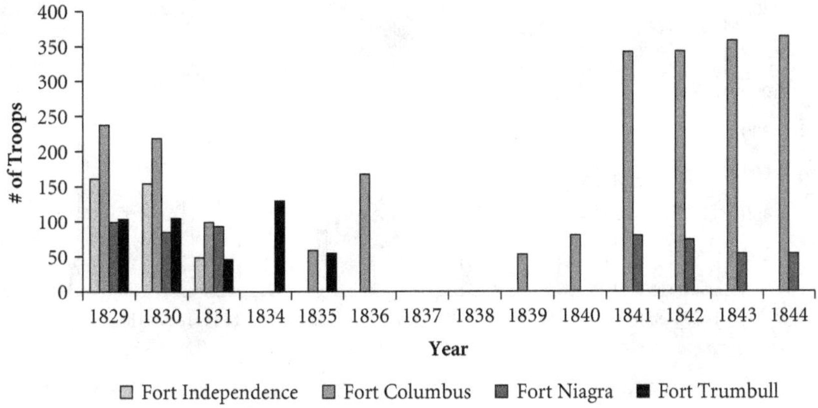

Figure 3. Forts in the Northeast

was built in the early 1840s as the line of settlement moved forward; but it, too, was abandoned by 1849, as the local native tribes were removed farther west and there was no longer an urgent need for a fort in that location.[103] By 1860, almost all posts in the Old Northwest had been removed, with only two remaining.[104]

In the northeastern part of the country, almost all troops were withdrawn from the area's forts from the years 1837 to 1839 (Figure 3). With the Patriot War occurring on the northern frontier, the demand for troops elsewhere was too high to allow the Army to maintain its usual presence in a relatively safe part of the nation such as the Northeast. Posts such as Fort Trumbull and Fort Independence were abandoned afterward, while Fort Columbus (on Governor's Island in New York) became more important as troops were more highly concentrated in fewer posts. In the South, as Figure 4 shows, the pattern was different, as the requirements of the Seminole War saw dramatic shifts in troop strength, especially in Florida. Fort Brooke, one of many posts established in Florida during the antebellum period, is representative, as it was built up during periods of conflict with the Seminoles and then abandoned at other times. Fort Jesup, which had originally been established to help secure the Louisiana Purchase, was built up in 1844 as a staging area for the Mexican War. Its commander in that period was Brigadier General Zachary Taylor, whose mission was to observe the Mexican army and make preparations for war.[105] Although the post had been part of Secretary of War Spencer's plan for a cordon of defense against the native tribes, it too was

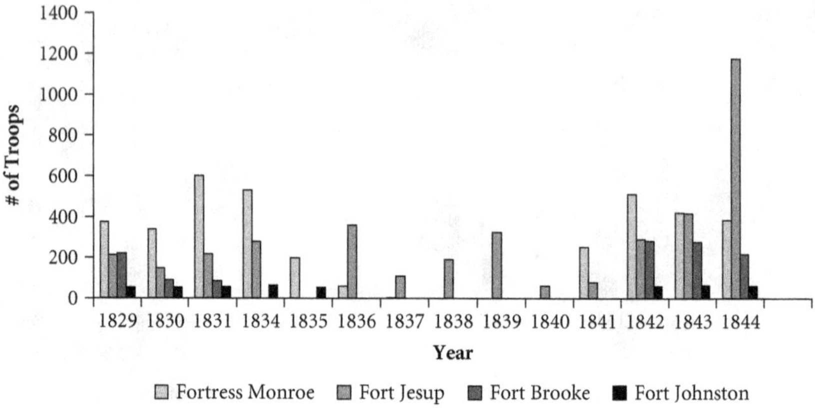

Figure 4. Forts in the South

abandoned in 1846, as troops were presumably shifted to the new western territories.[106]

Figure 5 demonstrates the development of forts in the West, and how fort placement there was driven by security concerns. Fort Leavenworth was the first major western fort. Designated as part of the permanent Indian frontier in 1830, it reached its peak significance in the 1830s as a key base from which the Army could battle native tribes on the western plains. As late as 1841 it was part of Spencer's planned cordon of forts and in the 1850s it was a central component in the Army's strategy to control the violence during Bleeding Kansas.[107] Unusually, given the pattern of forts gradually being abandoned, Leavenworth remains even today an important Army facility. Another post in Kansas, Fort Scott, was established in 1842 to assist in controlling Indians who had been removed from the East. In the pattern to which Leavenworth was the exception, Fort Scott lost troops from a peak of 220 in 1842 to only 72 by 1847.[108] Forts such as Gibson and Towson, in present-day Oklahoma, also lost strength in the course of this period. Clearly, the Army's priorities had shifted toward sending troops out even farther to the west after the end of the Mexican-American War.

Arrangements for new western posts accelerated rapidly after the war's conclusion. Protecting settlers emigrating to the new western lands was one top government priority. President Polk specifically requested the building of new posts in his annual message to Congress in 1848, an unusual

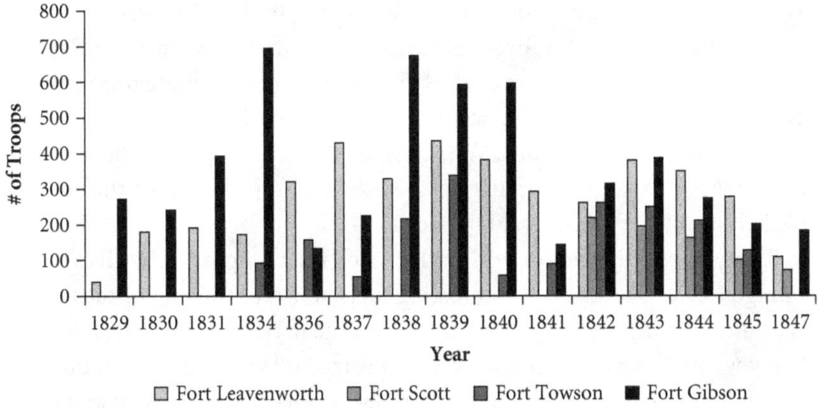

Figure 5. Forts in the West

presidential-level intervention into fort-building policy.[109] Merely taking control of the old Mexican forts in the region proved inadequate to protect the incoming white settlers from native depredations. Frequent complaints from the local population and commanders on the ground are recorded in the secretary of war's official reports from the years 1847 to 1850, directly after annexation. The citizens of Texas, for instance, passed a series of resolutions begging the national government for help. In response, Major General George Brooke informed Secretary of War Charles Conrad that he sent two companies of troops to set up a fort at Corpus Christi, without having received any direct order of the sort from his superiors. Conrad, however, rejects several other requests for new forts, due to a lack of manpower.[110] This type of self-interested behavior on the part of local communities was quite common at the time.[111] Under orders from Conrad, a man with no military experience, Colonel Edwin V. Sumner attempted to stabilize the situation in Texas. On his own initiative, Sumner ordered construction of Fort Defiance deep in Navajo territory, and seized a private fort near the Santa Rita copper deposits, naming it Fort Webster.[112] Commanders on the ground frequently reorganized far western forts during the 1850s in response to changing conditions on the ground and the need to protect new mail routes to the West.[113]

Having examined some of the basics of fort locations and garrison strength, the next question becomes, to what extent did the forts help encourage forward population movement? Though historians going back to Frederick Jackson Turner have argued that forts helped open the way to western settlement and the continued expansion of the frontier, evidence for these propositions has been based primarily on accumulated anecdotal evidence rather than close empirical examinations. To the extent that we can clarify the relationship between forts and population growth, the importance of the Army's role here would be considerably underlined.

The evidence that actors within the Army took it upon themselves to encourage western settlement by erecting forts ahead of the line of settlement is certainly strong. From the earliest days of the nation through the Mexican War, key officials such as the secretary of war and War Department bureaucrats thought of themselves as purposefully encouraging expansion and commerce. J. J. Abert, head of the Corps of Topographical Engineers, stated as much in his 1848 report to Congress: "distant military posts and military roads are the pioneers of civilization and of wealth, by the protection they afford to remote settlements, the value they give to public lands, the encouragement to cultivation by the consumption of produce, and by the intelligent and good habits diffused by such a nucleus of well-informed and orderly persons of both sexes as generally constitute the population of our garrisons."[114] Yet the tide soon started to turn toward allowing settlement to proceed with less central state assistance, partly in an effort to reduce costs. Secretary of War Jefferson Davis argued in 1856 that "a new post . . . does not become the nucleus of a settlement" anymore, and therefore the time had come to stop the policy of placing forts ahead of settlements.[115] Cost considerations may have meant that the end of the antebellum era saw the Army retreating from at least part of its aggressive expansionism.

Starting from the year 1820 and continuing through 1850, I have compiled data that allow us to examine garrison size and the movement of fort locations across time and space.[116] These data are based on the secretary of war's annual report, as well as information publicly available on the website fortwiki.com. A research assistant and I have produced a series of maps that compare the available fort data with population changes at the county level, with population data based on the decennial U.S. census reports.[117] These maps help demonstrate the centrality of forts to population growth and movement in the antebellum era.

Figure 6 depicts fort locations, garrison sizes, and population density as of 1820. Though there are still large concentrations in the Northeast region of the

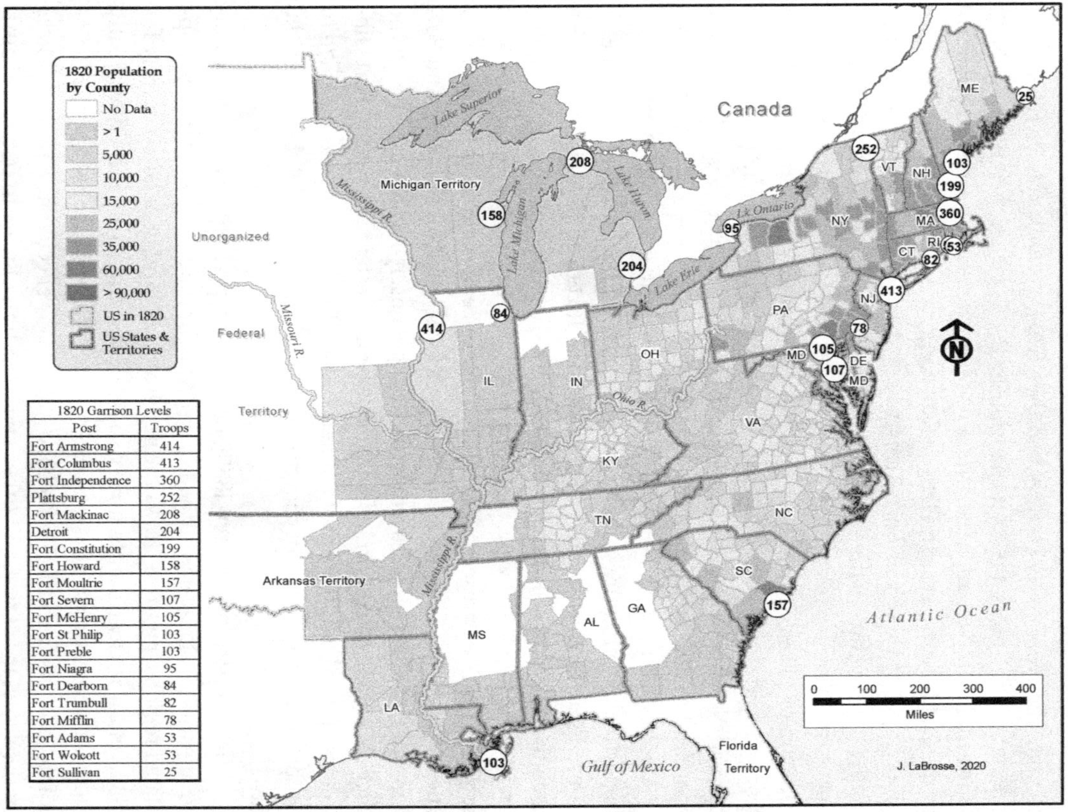

1820 Garrison Levels	
Post	Troops
Fort Armstrong	414
Fort Columbus	413
Fort Independence	360
Plattsburg	252
Fort Mackinac	208
Detroit	204
Fort Constitution	199
Fort Howard	158
Fort Moultrie	157
Fort Severn	107
Fort McHenry	105
Fort St Philip	103
Fort Preble	103
Fort Niagra	95
Fort Dearborn	84
Fort Trumbull	82
Fort Mifflin	78
Fort Adams	53
Fort Wolcott	53
Fort Sullivan	25

United States, note the particular importance of forts in the Old Northwest region. The Northeast certainly had the greatest population, as reflected in the figure, but pressures for expansion to the West were continuing. Forts Howard, Dearborn, and Armstrong were on the leading edge of settlement in the Old Northwest with Detroit also having a substantial troop garrison. The biggest of these was Fort Armstrong, which was central to the Army's ability to carry out its mission in the entire region. Established in 1815 by order of the War Department, this fort was crucial for western defense.[118] Pacification of native tribes and protection of frontier communities all began from the garrison located at Fort Armstrong. Although the population of the Old Northwest was still quite sparse in 1820, the presence of forts would soon lead to new populations moving in.

From 1820 to 1830 the population of the country rose significantly and, in particular, the entire western frontier experienced a surge of new emigration. Figure 7 demonstrates the locations of forts and how the population growth of the era reflected their movement. As settlers began pushing farther and farther to the west, the Army reoriented its strategy for locating forts as well. Here we can see the continued presence of older forts but also new ones such as Fort Leavenworth, Fort Crawford, Jefferson Barracks, and Fort Gibson. Crawford and Leavenworth were purposely located directly on the edge of centers in an effort to further encourage western settlement. Fort Gibson was placed on the edge of the new Indian Territory and was intended to be the primary garrison in charge of policing tribes removed there from the east.

The comparison between 1830 and 1834 is especially instructive in analyzing how fort locations pushed ever farther beyond the boundaries of populated regions. Figure 8 shows the garrison sizes and population density for 1834, and it is clear that in a very short period the Army moved to greatly increase its presence on the far western frontier. Partially this was due to ongoing conflicts with the Winnebago but it also reflected new policy choices by the secretary of war and other commanding officers to purposely push forts toward less populated regions in an effort to induce new settlement.

By 1840 the Army had changed its strategy toward one of concentrating troops at fewer posts and as a result many of the smaller forts no longer appear on the map. However, as can be seen in Figure 9, overall troop strength remained consistent while populations around them surged to greater densities than ever previously. The Northwest region including Wisconsin and

1830 Garrison Levels	
Post	Troops
Jefferson Barracks	591
Fortress Monroe	340
Camp Eaton	286
Fort Gibson	243
Fort Howard	219
Fort Columbus	218
Fort Crawford	196
Hancock Barracks	185
Fort Leavenworth	181
Baton Rouge	180
Fort Snelling	160
Fort Independence	154
Fort Jesup	149
Fort Winnebago	146
Fort Brady	118
Fort Gratiot	114
Fort Mackinac	111
Madison Barracks	108
Buffalo Barracks	107
Fort Trumbull	105
Fort McHenry	105
Fort Dearborn	95
Fort Armstrong	94
Fort Brooke	91
Fort Delaware	89
Fort Moultrie	85
Fort Niagra	84
Fort Pike	60
Fort Preble	59
Bellona Arsenal	57
Fort Wolcott	56
Fort Johnston	54
West Point	53
Fort Sullivan	52
Fort Marion	51
Fort St Philip	48
Fort Severn	48
Fort Constitution	48
Fort Washington	47
Fort Wood	41
Fort Mitchell	39
Augusta Arsenal	21

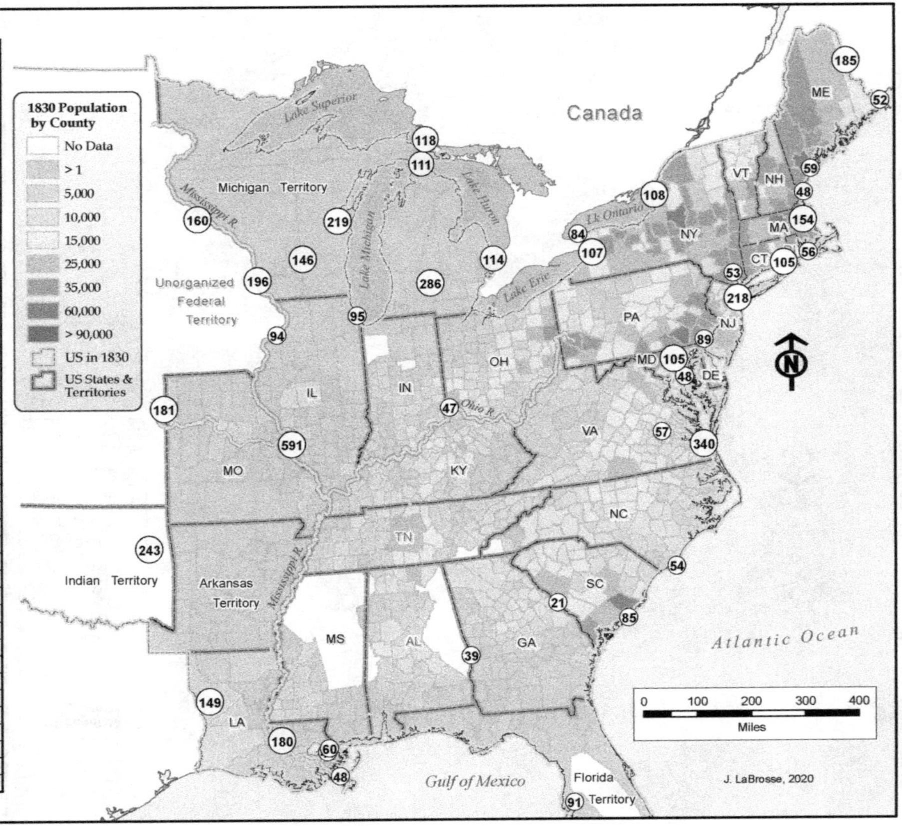

1834 Garrison Levels	
Post	Troops
Fort Gibson	696
Fortress Monroe	533
Jefferson Barracks	417
Fort Jesup	278
Fort Crawford	268
Fort Hamilton	232
Fort Winnebago	231
Fort Howard	220
Hancock Barracks	200
Buffalo Barracks	175
Fort Leavenworth	173
Fort Snelling	165
Baton Rouge	141
Fort Trumbull	129
Fort Moultrie	127
Camp Desmoines	113
Fort Brady	109
Fort Mackinac	109
Fort Dearborn	101
Fort Armstrong	97
Fort Morgan	94
Fort Towson	94
Camp Armistead	92
Fort Gratiot	91
New Orleans	90
Fort Wolcott	66
Fort Marion	65
Fort Johnston NC	65
Augusta Arsenal	64
Fort Macon	64
Washington Arsenal	62
Fort Sullivan	62
Fort Preble	61
Fort Constitution	61
Fort Severn	59
Fort Washington	59
Fort McHenry	58
West Point	52
Ogelthorpe Barracks	46
Fort Mitchell	46
Fort King	45
Fort Key West	44
Fort Coffee	43
Fort Pike	42
Fort Jackson	38
Fort Pickens	30
Fort Wood	22
Madison Barracks	10

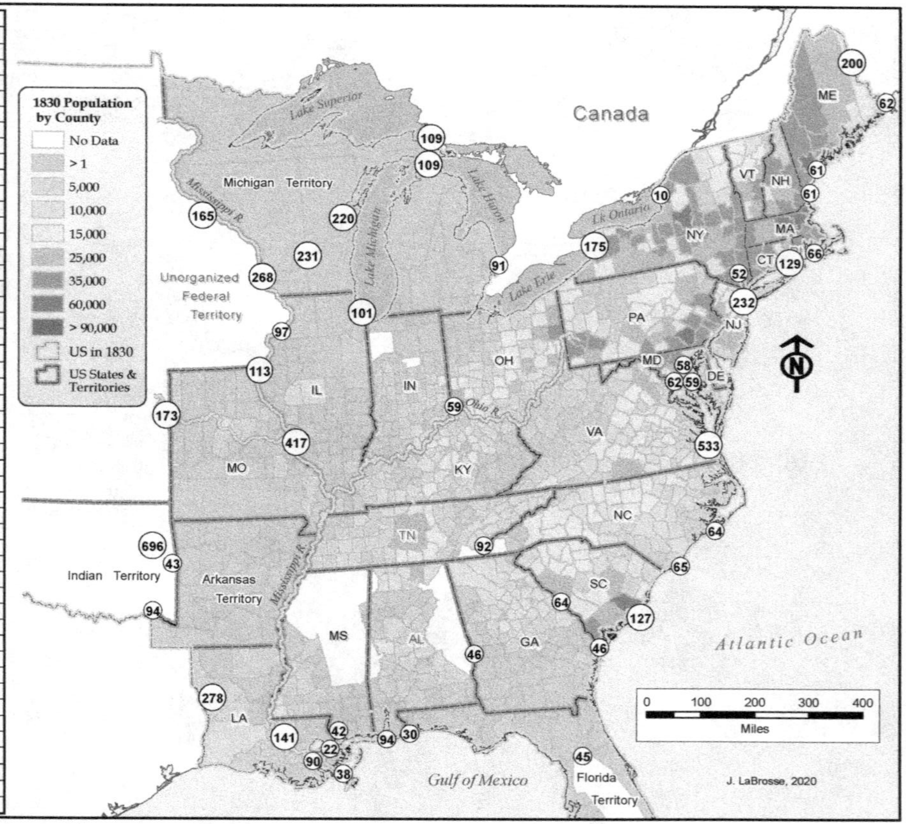

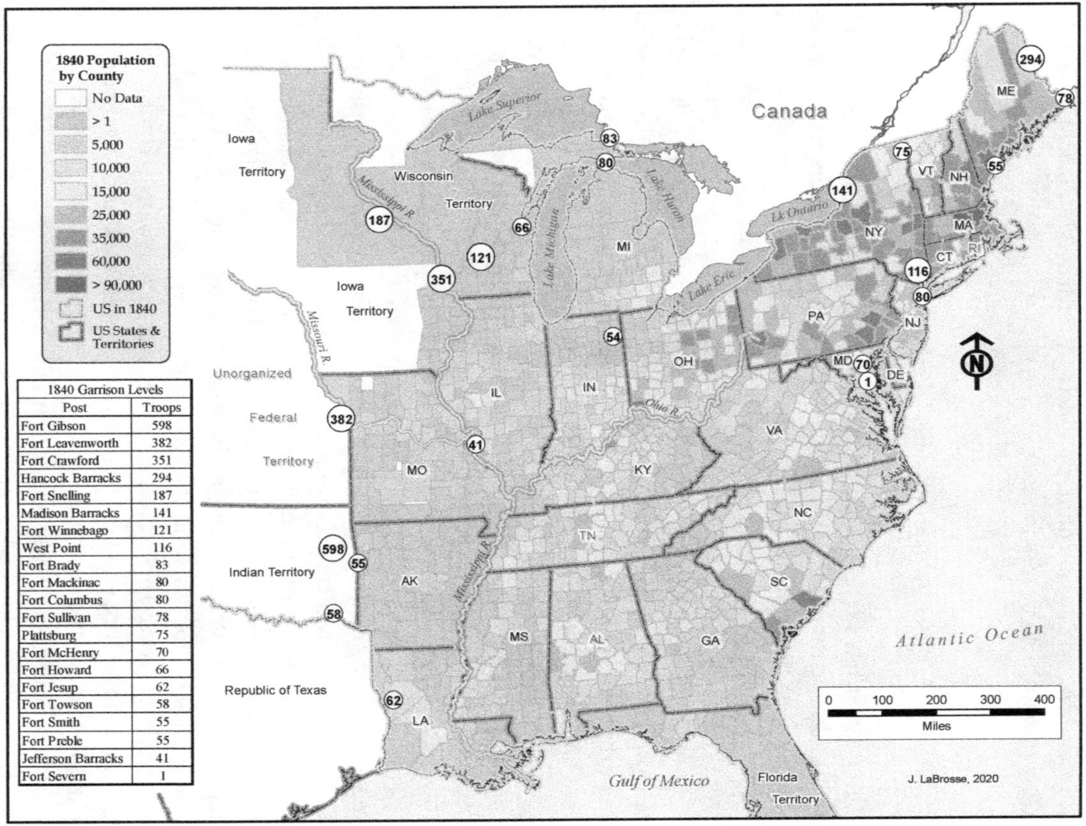

1840 Garrison Levels	
Post	Troops
Fort Gibson	598
Fort Leavenworth	382
Fort Crawford	351
Hancock Barracks	294
Fort Snelling	187
Madison Barracks	141
Fort Winnebago	121
West Point	116
Fort Brady	83
Fort Mackinac	80
Fort Columbus	80
Fort Sullivan	78
Plattsburg	75
Fort McHenry	70
Fort Howard	66
Fort Jesup	62
Fort Towson	58
Fort Smith	55
Fort Preble	55
Jefferson Barracks	41
Fort Severn	1

Illinois demonstrate this quite convincingly with spikes all across them in close proximity to nearby forts.

Conclusion: A Liberal American State?

This chapter has examined which actors controlled the Army's coercive activities during the antebellum period, relying particularly upon the distinction between the center and the periphery. In the center, elected officials were more easily able to control the Army, either through the use of direct orders from civilian superiors (such as the president) or occasionally by congressional oversight. Especially in actions that were designed to enforce the rule of law, presidents had the upper hand and personally directed many of the most important uses of force, such as in the Whiskey Rebellion. Territorial expansion and large-scale wars were also often directed out of the White House, the prime example being James K. Polk's strong actions to push the nation into the Mexican War and his detailed control over its operations. Even when presidents were deeply involved, however, there was always an extent to which they relied upon their subordinates for advice and policy decisions.

In the periphery, by contrast, control by civilian officials was often lacking. Due to long distances from the center of policymaking in Washington, D.C., and the slowness of communication, officers on the ground often had wide latitude to creatively reinterpret their orders or, on occasion, simply make their own policies as they saw fit. Elected officials, who lacked a direct representational stake in many of these far-flung territories, had little incentive to closely monitor what the Army did, except in rare high-profile instances. The executive branch, especially the secretary of war, the commanding general of the Army, and War Department bureaucrats, had a relatively free hand to manage the Army's coercive operations. Partisan control over the Army, therefore, was largely absent from the periphery.

The evidence about who controlled much of what the Army did in the nation's periphery in the early national period suggests that civilian control over the military was, at best, highly attenuated. Since one of the defining characteristics of a liberal polity is popular control over the institutions of government, including the military, this points toward a central state that violated its own liberal premises, at least in part. The great power of the Army for economic development was not always managed by popularly controlled actors. Obscured in the old argument over whether the United States is hopelessly liberal, a debate started long ago by Louis Hartz's work *The Liberal Tradition in America*, is the question of whether state institutions were actually directed by elected officials.[119] A military not subject to popular control that managed much of the nation's economic development planning implies that some of the most important national policies were supervised, directed, and implemented by officials without the responsibility to answer to the citizenry.

CHAPTER 4

Political Entrepreneurs and Institutional Capacity

The important socioeconomic actions described in Chapter 2 that the Army took to enhance economic development did not happen by themselves, nor were they in any sense inevitable. Rather, they were the result of contingent developments, based in part on the decisions of officers, bureaucrats, and politicians operating as policy entrepreneurs—and the decisions those actors made shaped American economic development. This chapter argues that no one institution or set of actors was able to completely control the Army's actions. Indeed, the antebellum Army itself was sometimes internally divided over how to best use its power. Traditional constitutional actors, such as the president and Congress, were limited in their ability to manage the Army's socioeconomic capacities, and as a result much of the decision making in this area fell to those managing and running the military bureaucracy.

As presidents generally lacked the institutional resources to closely monitor routine Army operations and Congress demonstrated only episodic involvement, responsibility for specific socioeconomic projects, especially those in the periphery, fell largely to the secretary of war and the uniformed chiefs of War Department bureaus. Although not entirely independent of traditional constitutional actors, these men were often able to exercise their authority as policy entrepreneurs to either enhance or constrain the Army's capacity to influence economic development. Bureau chiefs played a particularly important role, serving for long stretches of time (often decades) and gaining autonomy much earlier than suggested by previous studies of the federal bureaucracy. The bureaus were thus able to nurture specific types of knowledge that the state called upon as needed, with their uniformed heads making key decisions about the exact ways in which that expertise was subsequently used.

Especially important in this regard is the relationship between the bureaus and the secretary of war. The secretary of war was picked by the president, clearly marking him as a partisan official. At the same time, secretaries were able to carve out a niche for themselves in policymaking that was not strictly defined by presidential commands. As noted earlier, in the antebellum era, cabinet officials were more independent of presidential control, generally having been chosen to satisfy some constituency within the president's party or meet a geographic distribution requirement. This allowed them to maintain their own political agenda and independent base of support.[1] Crucially, the Secretaries of War were often influenced by the preexisting institutional interests of the officers and bureaucrats serving under them. As a result, secretaries frequently endorsed policies that had also been embraced by their predecessors, regardless of shifts in partisan control of the executive branch. Again, unlike in Skowronek's focus on congressional parties,[2] I highlight the strengths of the nonpresidential portion of the executive branch in early America.

State Development and Bureaucratic Capacity in Early America

The literature on the development of the early American state focuses primarily on that state's apparent weaknesses. Scholars have, for the most part, seen the early American state as lacking the fundamental characteristics of a strong state, such as a centralized bureaucracy, a strong executive branch, high spending capacity, strong military power, or the ability to fundamentally shape various segments of American society. More recently, a new wave of scholarship has started to challenge this depiction of central state capacities in early America by pointing to a variety of strengths in the national state.

American political development, as a subfield, has largely accepted the weak state hypothesis. Skowronek, in *Building a New American State*, argues that the state could do a few things well, but he then proceeds to downplay national capacities in early American history relative to the changes wrought by the era of industrial transformation at the end of the nineteenth century. In his words, "the state that evolved in nineteenth-century America scored relatively low on all the basic measures of state organization," particularly national defense, which was "radically decentralized" and primarily "relied upon a militia system of citizen-soldiers organized and controlled by the several states."[3] Richard Bensel similarly argues that, prior to the Civil War, "the national government had no identity apart from that imparted by the sectional forces that occupied the seat of power" in Washington, and that it "contained no statist-bureaucratic element that could prepare for the secession crisis." He admits that the Army was the "best approximation" to a centralized bureaucracy, but sees even that institution as far too weak to contain the sectional crisis from devolving into civil war.[4]

Daniel Carpenter's work on bureaucratic autonomy is particularly relevant to this conversation. While acknowledging recent work that demonstrates strengths of the early national state, he argues that these are merely details that flesh out an existing story of weak institutions lacking independence. He characterizes the pre–Civil War government as a "clerical state" where bureaucrats simply carried out the wishes of elected officials within the government and rarely had the ability to push their own ideas into policy. Due to the twin Jacksonian-era policies of patronage and rotation in office, mezzo-level bureaucrats lacked the ability to develop the network of ties to outside interests and influential members of Congress that would have been necessary to procure their own autonomy. Carpenter thus concludes that "the end result left federal agencies talent-starved."[5] Some recent work has challenged Carpenter's position; Mark Wilson, for instance, sees the origins of bureaucratic autonomy in the Quartermaster General's Office during the Civil War.[6] Wilson even hints at the earlier appearance of autonomy in the War Department when he notes in passing that bureau heads evinced features of autonomy prior to the Civil War.[7] Similarly, Stephen Rockwell has argued that the Indian Office had significant autonomy in the antebellum period.[8]

I argue that a close examination of the early War Department and its bureaus demonstrates that there was ample capacity for carrying out various policies, and furthermore that the bureaus could develop a form of autonomy from elected officials. The captive neither of sectional forces nor of any one group within society, bureaus such as the Corps of Topographical Engineers developed the ability to help shepherd their preferred policies into law or to create new policies on their own initiative when Congress declined to accede to their wishes. The War Department became not merely a close approximation of a centralized bureaucracy but, especially in the nation's periphery, the most significant institutional actor with the greatest amount of power. The autonomy that these bureau chiefs gained came about partially as a result of their long tenures in office, almost entirely unaffected by the norms of patronage and rotation in office prevalent across other areas of the national bureaucracy at the time. Thomas Jesup headed the Quartermaster General's Office from 1818 until 1860, and John J. Abert was the chief topographical engineer from 1829 until 1861, almost the entire life of the topographical corps. Men such as Jesup and Abert developed for their bureaus standing as neutral, professional experts who were providing the best technical advice available to policymakers.[9] Regardless of shifts in partisan control of the presidency, these men stayed in power and regularly influenced successive generations of presidents, secretaries of war, and members of Congress to help implement their desired policies, thus shaping the future of the American economy.

The different manner by which autonomy developed in the early American state, and the circumstances supporting *conditional* autonomy, distinguish it from Carpenter's descriptions of *robust* autonomy. Conditional autonomy is more easily reversible if the circumstances surrounding it change, while robust autonomy is difficult—thought not impossible—to eliminate. Like the bureaucrats studied by Carpenter, officers such as Jesup, George Bomford, and Abert served at the mezzo level of administration, as "durable actors with official authority . . . who maintained stable relations with the oversight and appropriations committees of Congress."[10] However, building their reputations along with a solid network linking themselves to organized interests and experts in the field, as in the case of the Department of Agriculture and Post Office in Carpenter's account, was not the primary method through which their autonomy was attained. There were certainly tentative links to emerging professional organizations and outside interests, but these were preliminary and not sufficient to support the bureaus' autonomy when other conditions underlying that autonomy faltered. The Army was professionalizing at this time, contrary to the assertions of Samuel Huntington's famous survey in *The Soldier and the State*, but this process was just starting and had not yet led to the rise of strong linkages with private interests.[11]

Bureau chiefs in the early Army developed their autonomy due to a combination of several factors: their long tenures in office, perceived organizational and personal expertise, lax congressional oversight, cabinet secretaries who relied heavily on their underlings for knowledge of even basic policy issues, the secretary of war's independence from the president, and little presidential involvement in the details of engineering policy. The mixture of these unique conditions led to an environment in which a short-lived but highly significant form of autonomy could come about. These bureaus became central players in some of the period's most important nation-building projects and thereby shaped the path of economic development. Particularly in early America, which had few countervailing institutions in place, a small degree of autonomy could have an outsized effect. On the nation's periphery, where virtually no other public institutions functioned, this power became especially potent. Paradoxically, however, autonomy exercised in the geographic periphery was simultaneously more tenuous, as the periphery gradually became absorbed into the nation's core and the policies being implemented there became more prominent in the eyes of elected officials.

In principal-agent terms, we might conceive of conditional autonomy as existing when the principal is either ignorant of or chooses not to become involved in agent actions. If the principal relies too heavily on ideas, information, and proposals generated by the agent, then principal control is effectively superseded. To the extent that bureau chiefs shaped the opinions of their supposed principals, then, they exercised a meaningful form of autonomy. The case of the topographical corps thus invites us to rethink how bureaucratic autonomy develops and the circumstances under which civilian authorities control their bureaucratic agents.

Scholars of contemporary bureaucratic politics focus on how Congress and the president manage the bureaucracy and the resources they have to oversee its workings. A large literature has developed exploring these institutional relationships, focusing primarily on congressional control of the bureaucracy. Matthew McCubbins, Roger Noll, and Barry Weingast, for example, explain how Congress can use administrative procedures to control regulatory agencies, while Terry Moe critiques theories that presume congressional dominance of the bureaucracy.[12] These pioneering works have been followed by a long series of studies investigating every aspect of the relationship between Congress and the bureaucracy, usually presented as some variation on classic principal-agent models.[13] A different perspective is offered by historical-institutionalist scholars, who examine historical cases to understand the changing nature of bureaucratic control over time. These studies, in contrast to other work in the field of bureaucracy, interrogate the bureaucracy from a multi-institutional perspective, especially by including the executive branch as a strong, independent force in directing institutional development.[14] Amy Zegart's study of twentieth-century national security bureaucracies is also highly relevant, as she discusses how agencies that deal with foreign policy issues differ from purely domestic agencies.[15]

Here I adopt a historical-institutionalist perspective to analyze the antebellum Army's bureaucratic structure. Influenced by the work of scholars such as Paul Pierson, Karen Orren, and Stephen Skowronek, I argue that the relationship among Congress, the president, and the bureaucracy should properly be characterized as one in which no one institution necessarily predominates.[16] Over time, as coalitions shift and the makeup of the actors within the institutions changes, the balance of power between those institutions shifts as well. Much of the public policy literature assumes that bureaucracies have a limited role in policymaking.[17] Studies in the field of American political development, by contrast, help provide a new perspective on the bureaucracy by analyzing it over a longer period of time. Such an approach opens space for a richer and more dynamic view of institutional change that more fully takes into account the contingent nature of bureaucratic control. As a result, we will see that bureaucrats can sometimes dominate a particular policy arena by becoming more autonomous, if they have been able to build up the necessary resources in relation to elected national officials.[18] Like Zegart, I find that the executive branch often predominates in the politics of a bureaucracy related to national security.[19]

To demonstrate the early development of bureaucratic autonomy in the War Department, I examine a series of key policy decisions made in the antebellum period relating to the Army's socioeconomic activities, especially those involving the Corps of Topographical Engineers. Sustaining a claim of autonomy will require showing where bureaucrats' preferred policy goals originated and the efforts made to convince secretaries of war, presidents, and Congress to pass them. Through careful use of primary sources, including records of congressional debates, messages from the president to Congress, and official documents of the War Department, I show how these bureaus developed, maintained, and then ultimately lost their autonomy when the forces supporting it were undermined.

Setting Priorities: Entrepreneurship and Bureaucratic Autonomy

Although the president in this period always retained his formal authority as commander in chief of the military and chief executive of the government, in practice the absence of presidential staff or other oversight resources prevented most presidents from involving themselves in routine military administration and socioeconomic Army activities, particularly regarding far-away projects located on the periphery.[20] (On two somewhat odd occasions, however, Vice President Aaron Burr was invited by Secretary of War Henry Dearborn to offer advice on improvements to the harbor of New York and on floating batteries.)[21] Only infrequently did a president even focus on the salient topic of internal improvements in his annual message to Congress, an important method of presidential communication in the premodern era.[22] President Jackson mentioned his vetoes of large improvement bills, for example, but otherwise largely ignored the bulk of the Army's efforts.[23]

Congress could supervise more day-to-day economic development activities by the Army than could the president, but here, too, short congressional sessions and limited sources of information hampered congressional control.[24] As Todd Shallat notes with regard to river and harbor improvements, because "public-works committees in Congress knew very little about rivers and harbors . . . the bureaucracy guided internal improvement through power of implementation," despite the fact that Shallat also notes how Congress chose many of the projects to be funded through appropriations.[25] Budgeting was not, however, a particularly efficient method for Congress to use in overseeing the Army. Unlike other parts of the government, military outlays were often appropriated in broad categories, not in line items, leaving discretion on many of the details of spending to the executive branch.[26] Indeed, Congress chose not to involve itself on many occasions, instead deferring action and allowing actors within the executive branch to make important decisions, especially in the periphery.[27] The terms of the General Survey Act of 1824, for instance, handed discretion over to the War Department to pick whichever projects it believed to be of greatest importance. Partisan politicians also had a limited stake in much of what the Army did. Since many of the Army's activities took place in the periphery and offered no distributive rewards to the states represented in Congress, members had little reason to take an interest in them.[28] Therefore, unlike in the argument presented by Stephen Minicucci, who prioritizes legislative affairs in his discussion of internal improvements, I see the executive branch as primary in most of these policies.[29]

Congress's involvement was greatest on highly visible projects in the center, such as the Cumberland Road or other large works. Even then, as Billy Joe Peyton points out, the politicization of the Cumberland Road project led to such poor results that only a takeover by the Army Corps of Engineers saved it from becoming a national disgrace.[30] Smaller appropriations for improvements occurred relatively frequently, depending on the shifting political winds. These bills often responded to logrolling imperatives, sending money to states and districts whose representative were otherwise ideologically opposed to federal spending. Many actors, including presidents, were willing to bend their ideological principles in this manner when it suited their political needs.[31]

Additionally, the structure of government in the early United States made it difficult for presidents to maintain close oversight of the military bureaucracy. As noted earlier, cabinet members such as the secretary of war were chosen based on political considerations, had an independent political base, and were therefore not completely beholden to the president they served.[32] Officers heading War Department bureaus served for long stretches of time across multiple presidential terms, and as a result were relatively isolated from direct presidential control. Similarly, engineers or ordnance officers working on projects remote from the capital, especially those in the periphery, were essentially subject to no direct line of presidential control. To that extent, models of civil-military relations that presume a relatively high degree of civilian control over the military do not seem applicable to the Army's socioeconomic role in this era.[33]

Presidents occasionally staked out positions on high-profile agenda items, such as Madison's veto of the Bonus Bill in early 1817 or Jackson's veto of the Maysville Road bill.[34] But these interventions were clearly not the norm, as presidents rarely exercised the veto in this period generally,[35] and were especially reluctant to use it in opposition to strong congressional majorities favoring improvement bills. As mentioned previously, the president was also unlikely to intervene to stop ongoing Army-led projects. Indeed, the president in this era often seemed to follow bureaucratic priorities, rather than setting a unified agenda for the entire executive branch. In this respect, my argument here is quite similar to that put forward by Daniel Carpenter and Gisela Sin. They show that the Food and Drug Administration played a critical role leading up to the passage of the 1938 Food, Drug and Cosmetic Act, expanding the agency's regulatory profile by preparing years in advance and taking advantage of an opportunity to press their agenda on the secretary of agriculture and the Roosevelt administration.[36] As they contend, "agencies often possess immense informational advantages, particularly when the facts in question are intimately known only by those who administer the specifics of policy."[37] Here as well, War Department bureaus were experts in their arenas and were able to use that expertise to their advantage in advancing their predetermined agendas on the secretary of war, the president, and Congress.

This can be clearly seen, for example, by tracing those positions staked out by bureaucrats or the secretary of war that were then adopted by the president in his annual message to Congress. Beginning in 1831, for example, the Ordnance Department, a War Department bureau under the leadership of George Bomford, requested the building of a national foundry to test and build gunpowder and cannons under strict federal supervision. The secretary of war joined in these requests starting in 1838. Both he and the ordnance chief asked for it annually through 1845, after which they seem to have decided it was hopeless, as no further requests appear in the following years.[38] The first president to specifically ask for a national foundry in his annual message was Martin Van Buren in 1837.[39] Interestingly, these appeals continued from a Democratic administration (Van Buren) to a Whig one (Harrison/Tyler) and then back to Democratic (Polk), while also persisting regardless of the identity of the secretary of war (Lewis Cass, Joel Poinsett, John Spencer, James Porter, William Wilkins, and William L. Marcy all made the same request). As Colleen Dunlavy has argued, Democrats may have opposed improvements in theory, "but in practice they held to this policy only loosely."[40]

Similarly, through its own initiative, the Ordnance Department was able to relinquish control over mining lands in federal possession. Transferred from the Treasury Department in 1821, the national lend-leasing program for mining seemed to be a logical fit with Ordnance's mission of assisting technological progress. However, as Christopher Klyza explains, Ordnance lacked any special expertise in this area and the program was widely viewed within the bureau as an albatross.[41] The process of giving up control over mining lands took Ordnance eleven years, with requests to Congress beginning from 1836.[42] Only in 1845 did President Polk publicly support the idea, with control finally shifting to the Treasury Department in 1847.[43] Ordnance was able to slowly advance its agenda by winning over political actors to its goals. Bureaucratic priorities thus seem to have often had a high level of influence over the secretary of war and the president, more transitory figures compared to long-serving bureau chiefs, who often held their positions for decades.

The secretary of war was also in a position to be a policy entrepreneur, made possible by the political autonomy that Cabinet members possessed in this era.[44] As Table 7 demonstrates, many secretaries of war, even Democrats who supposedly opposed government intervention in the economy, chose to

Table 7. Secretaries of War and Major Socioeconomic Activities, 1789–1860

Secretary	*Tenure*	*Activities*
Henry Knox	1789–94	Corps of Artillerists and Engineers stationed at West Point; pushed Congress to build armories
Timothy Pickering	1795	
James McHenry	1796–1800	Supported western road building and greater practical use of Army engineering talent; supported establishment of a military academy
Samuel Dexter	1800–1801	
Henry Dearborn	1801–9	Helped to found the West Point military academy; authorized use of troops to build the Natchez Trace and other roads; supported the Lewis and Clark expedition and the Pike expedition; stopped the employment of French engineers
William Eustis	1809–13	Resisted West Point expansion; recommended reforms to the Quartermaster General's Office that were passed by Congress; opposed working with John Hall at Harper's Ferry Armory
John Armstrong, Jr.	1813–14	Supported contracting with John Hall at Harper's Ferry Armory
James Monroe	1814–15	Noted the need for more roads on the Atlantic Coast after War of 1812
William Crawford	1815–16	Sent engineer to help a Virginia canal survey; ordered Alexander Macomb to build a military road from Detroit to Ohio; pushed Congress to establish a permanent topographical corps
John C. Calhoun	1817–25	Reformed the War Department's management structure; sent engineers to multiple states to assist infrastructure projects; ordered Stephen Long's western expedition; issued report on improvements that encouraged more reliance on Army engineers; created Office of Indian Affairs; expanded John Hall's role at Harper's Ferry Armory

(Continued)

Table 7. (*Continued*)

Secretary	*Tenure*	*Activities*
James Barbour	1825–28	Approved Baltimore and Ohio Railroad's request for engineering assistance, along with other railroad corporations; asked Congress for more engineers, but opposed a civil engineering corps
Peter Porter	1828–29	Supported building both military and civilian-use roads
John Eaton	1829–31	Asked Congress to finance more Army engineers and topographical engineers; made the Topographical Bureau independent of the Corps of Engineers
Lewis Cass	1831–36	Sent fewer engineers to work on private sector projects; argued that rivers, canals, and railroads should receive priority over fort construction; supported expanding role of the Ordnance Department; requested expansion of the topographical corps; put topographical engineers in charge of lighthouse construction
Joel Poinsett	1837–41	Preferred fort construction; got Congress to end the practice of sending engineers to work on private sector projects while increasing the number of topographical engineers; supported expanding role of the Ordnance Department
John Bell	1841	Gave the Ordnance Department direct control over the national armories and lobbied Congress for a bill to put military superintendents in charge of the armories
John Spencer	1841–43	Supported John Frémont's first two expeditions; preferred fort construction
James Porter	1843–44	
William Wilkins	1844–45	
William L. Marcy	1845–49	Ordered pre–Mexican War western surveys, including Frémont's third expedition

George Crawford	1849–50	Allowed some engineers to work on private sector projects
Charles M. Conrad	1850–53	Asked Colonel John J. Abert to prepare for western railroad surveys; reorganized division of responsibilities between Corps of Engineers and topographical corps
Jefferson Davis	1853–57	Oversaw the Pacific Railroad surveys; after surveys ended, removed western exploration projects from the Corps of Topographical Engineers' jurisdiction; created Pacific Wagon Road Office; preferred national construction projects over local improvements
John Floyd	1857–60	Ordered surveys of military roads in the West; opposed most improvement projects

Sources: William Gardner Bell, *Secretaries of War and Secretaries of the Army: Portraits and Biographical Sketches* (Washington, DC: Center of Military History, 1992); John Lauritz Larson, *Internal Improvement: National Public Works and the Promise of Popular Government in the Early United States* (Chapel Hill: University of North Carolina Press, 2001); Robert G. Angevine, *The Railroad and the State: War, Politics, and Technology in Nineteenth-Century America* (Stanford, CA: Stanford University Press, 2004); James J. Farley, *Making Arms in the Machine Age: Philadelphia's Frankford Arsenal, 1816–1870* (University Park: Pennsylvania State University Press, 1994); Ruth Anne French-Hodson, "New Economics of Organization and Nineteenth-Century Bureaucracies: A Study of the Bureau of Indian Affairs," M.Phil. thesis, Merton College, University of Oxford, 2007; William H. Goetzmann, *Army Exploration in the American West, 1803–1863* (Lincoln: University of Nebraska Press, 1959); Forest G. Hill, *Roads, Rails, and Waterways: The Army Engineers and Early Transportation* (Norman: University of Oklahoma Press, 1957); Christopher McGrory Klyza, "The United States Army, Natural Resources, and Political Development in the Nineteenth Century," *Polity* 35:1 (Fall 2002): 1–28; Erna Risch, *Quartermaster Support of the Army, 1775–1939* (Washington, DC: Center of Military History, 1989); Frank N. Schubert, *The Nation Builders: A Sesquicentennial History of the Corps of Topographical Engineers, 1838–1863* (Fort Belvoir, VA: Office of History, U.S. Army Corps of Engineers, 1988); Todd Shallat, *Structures in the Stream: Water, Science, and the Rise of the U.S. Army Corps of Engineers* (Austin: University of Texas Press, 1994); Merritt Roe Smith, "Army Ordnance and the 'American System' of Manufacturing, 1815–1861," in Smith, ed., *Military Enterprise and Technological Change: Perspectives on the American Experience* (Cambridge, MA: MIT Press, 1985), 39–86; Smith, *Harper's Ferry Armory and the New Technology: The Challenge of Change* (Ithaca, NY: Cornell University Press, 1977).

use their position to promote state-led development policies. Henry Knox, the nation's first secretary of war, began planning for the national armory system in 1793, despite his department's tiny size (Knox and four clerks ran the entire department) and general disorganization.[45] Besides helping to create West Point, the national leader in engineering, Henry Dearborn, secretary of war under Jefferson, was deeply involved in encouraging commercial development. For instance, he closely supervised the production of new artillery at the armories, giving finely detailed instructions on the processes for inspecting, repairing, and supplying new weapons.[46] Dearborn ordered Decius Wadsworth, the first head of the Ordnance Department, to meet with inventor Eli Whitney to discuss his muskets, as Dearborn tracked the progress of this contract quite closely.[47] Similarly, when ordering a survey for the opening of a new fort south of where the Ohio and Mississippi Rivers met, Dearborn specified that it be "a convenient Site [sic] for a settlement and ultimately for a place of Business [*sic*]."[48] Dearborn even ordered Major Daniel Jackson to let the local chamber of commerce use the fort under his command in Boston for signaling to merchants that vessels carrying new products were docking at the port.[49] Following the War of 1812, James Monroe, serving briefly as secretary of war in addition to secretary of state, recommended an expansion of internal improvements, at least in part as a plan for national defense.[50]

Perhaps the most entrepreneurial secretary was John C. Calhoun, who served in the cabinet under President Monroe. Planning a run for president in 1824, Calhoun, who had previously opposed national internal improvements, tried to boost his prospects by supporting a strongly nationalistic improvements program. He approved War Department assistance for canal projects in Illinois, Ohio, and Virginia, and road building in Iowa, Louisiana, Mississippi, Tennessee, Georgia, New York, and Maine.[51] His 1819 report on the benefits of improvements for military defense was one of the impetuses that eventually led to the passage of the General Survey Act.[52] While David Mayhew is surely correct that the War of 1812 itself served as a "generative force" creating momentum for a larger investment in improvements, the war should be seen as an enabling condition rather than a sufficient one. Policy results still require the initiative of political actors.[53] Monroe's and Calhoun's entrepreneurial role in pushing for these projects should not be understated.

In terms of the political control over the Army's noncoercive activities, the policy shifts (both in favor of public-private cooperation and in opposition to it) demonstrate clearly the central role played by the leading political appointee in the War Department. The desire to promote economic development, particularly an advanced transportation infrastructure to capitalize on the emerging railroad technology, led secretaries of war to encourage close cooperation between technical specialists in the Army and the private sector. James Barbour, secretary of war under President John Quincy Adams, lent crucial support to one of the first railroad requests for Army assistance. In 1827, the Baltimore and Ohio Railroad asked the Department of War for the help of topographical engineers in surveying and selecting routes. Barbour, who had previously been an opponent of such assistance, reversed himself and approved the railroad's petition.[54]

Eventually, however, secretaries of war concluded that allowing military engineers to cooperate in the production of what was essentially a private good compromised the capacity of the Army to meet its traditional objectives. Once Army engineers observed the advantages of life in the private sector—including the significantly higher pay and less restrictive work rules—they began to leave the service in significant numbers. Joel Poinsett, Van Buren's secretary of war, decided to stop lending engineers to states or private companies. Following his edict, more than half of the officers working on the railroads resigned their commissions.[55] In opposing Army help to the railroads, both Poinsett and Secretary John C. Spencer, who held office under President Tyler, embraced the official position of the Corps of Engineers that military engineering resources should be used to support construction of defensive forts, while topographical engineers worked exclusively on improvements such as rivers, harbors, and canals.[56]

Administration of the Army's socioeconomic programs also suggests that bureaucratic autonomy may have developed much earlier than shown in previous studies. Daniel Carpenter, in his influential work *The Forging of Bureaucratic Autonomy*, argues that autonomy only came later in the nineteenth century, while in early America "federal officers lacked both a permanent presence in their posts and an enduring statist identification."[57] Some recent work has challenged Carpenter's position; Mark Wilson, for instance, sees the origins of bureaucratic autonomy in the Quartermaster General's Office during the Civil War.[58] Wilson even hints at the earlier appearance of autonomy in the War Department when he notes in passing that bureau heads evinced features of autonomy prior to the Civil War.[59] Carpenter's characterization of early American bureaucracy does not fit well when we look at the Army. As Chapter 2 shows, officers in the engineering corps and topographical

Table 8. Length of Service of War Department Bureau Chiefs

Chief	*Bureau*	*Tenure*
Thomas Jesup	Quartermaster General	1818–60
Isaac Roberdeau	Topographical Bureau	1818–29
John J. Abert	Topographical Bureau/Corps of Topographical Engineers	1829–61
Decius Wadsworth	Ordnance Department	1812–21
George Bomford	Ordnance Department	1821–48
George Talcott	Ordnance Department	1848–51
Henry Craig	Ordnance Department	1851–61
Joseph Swift	Corps of Engineers	1812–18
Walker Armistead	Corps of Engineers	1818–21
Alexander Macomb	Corps of Engineers	1821–28
Charles Gratiot	Corps of Engineers	1828–38
Joseph Totten	Corps of Engineers	1838–64
Joseph Lovell	Surgeon General	1818–36
Thomas Lawson	Surgeon General	1836–61
George Gibson	Commissary General of Subsistence	1818–61

Sources: Merritt Roe Smith, *Harper's Ferry Armory and the New Technology: The Challenge of Change* (Ithaca, NY: Cornell University Press, 1977); http://history.amedd.army.mil/surgeons.html; Erna Risch, *Quartermaster Support of the Army, 1775–1939* (Washington, DC: Center of Military History, 1989); Frank N. Schubert, *The Nation Builders: A Sesquicentennial History of the Corps of Topographical Engineers, 1838–1863* (Fort Belvoir, VA: Office of History, U.S. Army Corps of Engineers, 1988); Todd Shallat, *Structures in the Stream: Water, Science, and the Rise of the U.S. Army Corps of Engineers* (Austin: University of Texas Press, 1994); Theophilus F. Rodenbough and William L. Haskin, *The Army of the United States: Historical Sketches of Staff and Line with Portraits of Generals-in-Chief* (New York: Maynard, Merrill, 1896).

corps thought of themselves as statists in the French mode, while also establishing long careers as civil servants.

The different manner by which autonomy developed in the early Army distinguishes it from that in Carpenter's theory of bureaucratic autonomy. Like the bureaucrats studied by Carpenter, officers such as Thomas Jesup, George Bomford, and John J. Abert served at the mezzo level of administration, as "durable actors with official authority . . . who maintained stable relations with the oversight and appropriations committees of Congress."[60] However, rather than building a solid network linking themselves to organized interests and experts in the field, as in the case of the Department of Agriculture and Post Office in Carpenter's account, bureau chiefs in the early

Army developed their reputations primarily through their long tenures in office and perceived organizational and personal expertise. It was not unusual in this period for Army bureau chiefs to stay in their positions for decades at a time (Table 8). Longevity made them essentially permanent actors in national politics whose positive reputations continued across shifts in partisan control of the presidency and Congress. Using the informal contacts with members of Congress that were prevalent at this time, near-permanent bureau chiefs were often able to press their policies forward and convince Congress, secretaries of war, and presidents to follow their lead.[61]

The topographers' success was not merely due to a surfeit of opposing interests or a lack of partisanship in the antebellum period. Roberdeau and Abert faced opposition to their bureau's mere existence from the very beginning. The Corps of Engineers waged a constant battle to convince Congress and the secretary of war to retain control over the topographers, and every step toward the topographical engineers gaining autonomy met with resistance. After the passage of the General Survey Act of 1824, the War Department established a Board of Engineers for Internal Improvements to determine which projects would receive national assistance. Historian Todd Shallat notes that the board was "dominated" by the regular corps, and engineers Simon Bernard and Joseph Totten worked to keep the topographers in a weak position. When Bernard resigned in 1831, the department shifted surveys to Abert's Topographical Bureau. This bureau was an arm of the regular corps until Abert convinced Congress to give it independence in 1838.[62] Similarly, there was significant partisan disagreement in this era over improvements policies,[63] and many did not wish to see Abert's bureau succeed, as the following section shows. A more likely explanation for the success of the topographical corps is Abert's long tenure in office, his hard-won reputation for expertise, and the informal network he built among important members of Congress, including some men who later became the secretary of war.

One other particularly vivid example of bureaucratic initiative is provided by the Ordnance Department. Founded in 1812, in 1815 the bureau gained statutory control over the nation's armories at Springfield and Harpers Ferry and the right to impose uniform standards on arms manufacturers. The 1815 law giving them this authority was passed after much lobbying of Congress by Colonel Decius Wadsworth, the first chief of ordnance.[64] He and his successor George Bomford, who was chief of ordnance from 1821 until 1842, headed an agency that, according to historian Merritt Roe Smith, helped shepherd the rise of uniform manufacturing throughout the private arms industry.[65] Influenced by the French military tradition, Wadsworth and Bomford imposed uniformity and greater efficiency on private sector companies, both through contracting requirements as well as by insisting that private manufacturers imitate the designs used at federal armories. That policy persisted until contracting for arms ended in the 1840s.[66] They pursued their own independent agenda in a manner similar to that of the late-nineteenth-century mezzo-level bureaucrats Carpenter describes. Unlike Carpenter's bureaucrats, however, Wadsworth and Bomford pursued their initiatives while lacking an outside network of support beyond the nation's capital. No set of interest groups existed to support their agenda beyond the Army itself. Despite this, the ordnance chiefs overcame resistance from the armories themselves, survived a congressional effort to eliminate the bureau, imposed uniform accounting standards and manufacturing practices upon the armories, and supervised artillery research and development.[67] Between 1841 and 1854 the Ordnance Department exercised direct operational control over the various scattered armories. This move, ordered by Secretary of War John Bell, followed Bomford's advice, and contributed directly to the development of a fully functional system of interchangeable parts.[68]

The Corps of Topographical Engineers: A Case of Bureaucratic Autonomy

The Corps of Topographical Engineers provides a useful case study of bureaucratic autonomy and its limits in the antebellum state. The topogs gradually built up support for themselves as independent experts and won important bureaucratic turf wars against the Corps of Engineers. For many years, the topogs were able to create the conditions for a form of bureaucratic autonomy by balancing their independence from civilian officials against the need to convince those same officials to follow their lead on important policy questions. In part they maintained their autonomy through avoiding close oversight: "on a day-to-day basis . . . the Corps tended to elude rigorous scrutiny."[69] Powerful actors, including presidents, secretaries of war, and committee chairs also ended up supporting their efforts. The backing of influential members of Congress was especially important.[70] As a result, when in the 1850s the topogs became embroiled in sectional politics on a high-profile issue of national significance, Congress and the secretary of war became deeply involved in the details of how the proposed transcontinental railroad would be implemented. When several of the conditions supporting their autonomy crumbled, their edifice of support came tumbling down, demonstrating the fragility and conditionality of their hard-won autonomy.

Congress authorized a small group of topographers in 1813 during the war against Great Britain, but they were subsumed within the larger and more well-established Corps of Engineers.[71] As noted in Chapter 2, at the end of the War of 1812, all but two, John Anderson and Isaac Roberdeau, were relieved of duty. In 1816, ten were brought back into service, again under the control of the Corps. In 1818 they were given their own bureau, though the Corps of Engineers still maintained control over it. The bureau was headed in its early years by Roberdeau, a talented engineer who was nevertheless passed over for promotion on several occasions, as regular engineers looked down on topographers.[72] Roberdeau asked for an independent corps as early as 1816, but was refused.[73]

Despite significant opposition, the topogs continued to press for greater autonomy. Roberdeau continually pressed for the expansion of his bureau and for greater autonomy, but he was swimming against the political tide. Initially he did not even handle field reports directly, as they had to go through the Corps of Engineers first.[74] Additionally, the mood within Congress was one of frugality, with Democrats looking to cut federal expenditures wherever possible. In 1821, a bill considered in the House to reduce the size of the Army included a section proposing "that the topographical engineers, and their assistants, shall be discharged from the service of the United States."[75] Not only was this proposition put forward, at one point it commanded a majority of the House, as an amendment to eliminate this section of the bill was voted down.[76] While some supported the topographers, their work was generally viewed with a high degree of skepticism.

Members of Congress used this proposal as an opportunity to debate the broader role of the topogs. Congressman Timothy Fuller of Massachusetts put forward a pro-topog (and generally pro-Army) position.[77] In response, Gideon Tomlinson of Connecticut made a long and impassioned speech opposing the topogs' existence. He argued that the topographers were redundant since their duties "seem not to differ even in name from those required to be performed by the corps of engineers."[78] Furthermore, he replied directly to those who felt that deference to Secretary of War John C. Calhoun required them to support the topographers: "It has, too, been often repeated . . . that the bill before the House is in hostility to the recommendation of the Secretary of the Department of War, and that its adoption may be considered disrespectful to that valuable officer. Sir, I repel the charge, and I improve this occasion to say, that I entertain the highest respect for the distinguished gentleman who presides over the War Department. . . . But great as my respect is for that gentleman, I will not consent to make even his opinions the rule of my own conduct. I act here upon my own responsibility, and shall be directed by the dictates of my own judgment."[79] Although they deferred to Calhoun in certain areas, including the overall organization of the post–War of 1812 Army, and later in the passage of the 1824 General Survey Act, some members seemed to have drawn the line here. For reasons unknown, however, when the bill passed the House the next day, the section eliminating the topogs had disappeared, replaced by wording that "the corps of engineers, as at presently established, be retained in service," and indeed the final version as enacted kept the engineers and topographers "as at presently organized."[80] Perhaps some behind-the-scenes lobbying from Calhoun or other officials influenced this change. Nevertheless, this episode does demonstrate the topogs' early difficulties.

Later years would see the topographers increasing their base of support. During the administration of John Quincy Adams, a strong supporter of internal improvements, Congress agreed to increase the number of engineers and topographers by supplementing their ranks with the top graduates of West Point.[81] Funding for topographical surveys authorized by the General Survey Act came under attack in 1825, as part of the emerging divide between Adams's supporters and Jacksonians. A rancorous debate in the Senate over the issue repeated some of the concerns voiced in the House in 1821, but this time without anyone explicitly opposing the topogs' existence. Senator Nathaniel Macon of North Carolina, a committed supporter of Andrew Jackson, contended that "these Engineers [*sic*] were designed for army purposes. They had no right to divert them from their legitimate duties, by making them Civil Engineers [*sic*]."[82] Even those resisting the surveys no longer questioned the need for topographical engineers. There was significant disagreement, however, over the amount of discretion that the executive should have over how the surveys would be conducted. Josiah Johnston of Louisiana argued that the War Department would be able "to regulate the expenditures . . . [and] seek out the best talents in the country," while Macon and John Holmes of Maine disliked Congress ceding so much authority to the executive branch.[83] Unsurprisingly, there was also continued debate about the constitutionality of conducting the surveys at all. In the end, the Senate voted

Table 9. Senate Vote to Defund Topographical Surveys, 1825

	North	*South*
Yes	13	6
No	9	12
	East	*West*
Yes	17	2
No	7	14

Source: Register of Debates, Senate, 18th Congress, 2nd Session, February 11, 1825. Geographic information on senators for this and subsequent tables is drawn from the *Biographical Dictionary of the United States Congress, 1774–Present*, accessed at http://bioguide.congress.gov/biosearch/biosearch.asp. For this and subsequent tables, states were divided in the following manner: *North*: CT, DE, IA, IL, IN, MA, ME, MI, NH, NJ, NY, OH, PA, RI, VT, WI; *South:* AL, AR, FL, GA, KY, LA, MD, MO, MS, NC, SC, TN, VA; *East:* CT, DE, FL, GA, MA, MD, ME, NC, NH, NJ, NY, PA, RI, SC, VA, VT; *West:* AL, AR, IA, IL, IN, KY, LA, MI, MO, MS, OH, TN, WI.

21–19 not to defund the surveys; though a close vote, it shows some increase in support for the topographers' new mission.[84] Table 9 demonstrates the geographic breakdown of the vote. Northern senators were somewhat more likely to oppose surveys than southerners. When we compare East and West, however, the results are more dramatic: only two western senators supported ending the topographic surveys, while over 70 percent of eastern senators wanted to defund them. Peripheral support for the topographers' mission was quite strong. The opposition to the surveys may have also been based, in part, on the fact that some still opposed improvements as a matter of course, even though Jackson himself would later prove to be a strong supporter of many improvement projects.[85]

In 1825 and 1826, Secretary of War James Barbour, in his annual report, requested increases in the size of the engineering corps, specifically including the topographers.[86] As mentioned previously, Congress in 1825 agreed to supplement the ranks of engineers with new graduates of West Point, although it did not approve an increase as large as Barbour had wanted. Chief Engineer Alexander Macomb echoed this request and called particularly for the passage of a congressional bill designed to augment his ranks.[87] Some members of Congress eagerly followed Barbour and Macomb's lead. James Hamilton Jr., chairman of the House Committee on Military Affairs, reported a bill in early 1826 that followed Barbour's request almost to the letter.

Hamilton simply asserted that the members of the committee "deem it unnecessary to indulge at present in any argument to show the necessity of the passage of the accompanying bill, as the whole view of this subject is so fully and ably presented in the annexed letter of the secretary of war, to which they earnestly and confidently refer."[88] The letter he refers to was sent by Barbour to Hamilton six days earlier, which presented a comprehensive argument favoring an expanded engineering corps.[89] Hamilton followed the lead of the nationalistic Adams administration in this matter, despite being well known as a committed Jackson supporter and later forcefully advocating nullification during the crisis of 1832.[90]

Intriguingly, the bill itself includes one provision that neither Barbour nor Macomb specifically asked for, namely a proposal to separate the topographical engineers into an independent entity, "as soon as the President of the United States shall deem it expedient."[91] It is unclear where this idea originated. Historians who have studied the topographical engineering corps seem to have missed this episode in its development.[92] Circumstantial evidence, however, suggests that the topogs themselves may have been undertaking a cunning campaign to win their independence. After the measure failed in 1826, Major John J. Abert, who would later head the topographers for many years, wrote a letter to the House in 1827 asking not only for more topographers but also for independent bureaucratic standing within the War Department distinct from the Corps of Engineers. Abert said he thought a separate topographical office was a good idea, but "not that we have any feeling adverse to the increase of the engineers of fortifications. We know it to be a corps of scientific men, and believe it to deserve the patronage of government. But we are of the opinion that there does not exist a strong disposition for the increase of both corps, and that by the uniting of them in one bill would certainly occasion a failure in the increase of either."[93] Abert continued his sales pitch by noting that it was no slight to the Corps of Engineers if the topogs were given an increase that year; rather it would simply indicate Congress's desire not to increase both services at the same time. He also insisted that the proposed law would not change the topogs' status, since "it contains no innovations upon our own established customs."[94]

An attached document written from the topographers to Secretary of War Barbour argued more directly for an independent corps of topographical engineers. This unsigned letter concludes by thanking Barbour, the former chair of the Senate Committee on Military Affairs, for his support of their organization: "The topographical engineers have been in the habit of considering you as the patron of their establishment, and that to your efforts when in the Senate of the United States they are principally indebted for their present existence."[95] Clearly, the topogs were working every angle available as part of their campaign for greater independence. They must have made an impact, as three days later a bill was introduced to create an independent topographical corps, no longer at the president's discretion as in the previous year's bill.[96] A symbiotic relationship was developing between the relevant congressional committees, the topographical corps, and the secretary of war, all of whom were working toward a common goal.

The topogs also received support outside Washington in the form of favorable news coverage. *Niles' Weekly Register*, a nationally circulated periodical, repeatedly provided positive reports about the topographers' activities. One story intentionally highlighted the need to familiarize the public with these important works, "so as to give the country the greatest possible advantage which can be derived from [the topogs'] skill and activity" despite the "limited strength of this branch of our military system."[97] Another heralded the topogs' shift to civil engineering projects as a "delightful *linking* of the various parts of our extensive country together, to *consolidate* the good wishes and feelings of the whole people, and yet not interfering with the 'rights of the states.'"[98] The *Literary Casket* and the *North American*, both apparently short-lived journals, published stories about improvements made to the locomotive engine by Major Stephen H. Long of the topographical engineers and the survey of a planned route for the Baltimore and Ohio Railroad.[99]

Roberdeau died in 1829 and control of the bureau shifted to Abert.[100] Abert proved to be quite proficient at maneuvering the thicket of Washington politics and turning his priorities into the goals of those above him, even during the new anti-improvement Jackson administration. Abert asserted that he did not want to be just "a mere keeper of pictures, without any knowledge of my own corps . . . of no more account than an automaton,"[101] and he immediately went to work on expanding the topogs' numbers and autonomy. Proposals to make the topogs into a corps continued to fail in 1830 and 1831, despite the support of Secretary of War John Eaton.[102] However, although he faced strong opposition from Chief Engineer Charles Gratiot and lacked an external support network, Abert convinced acting Secretary of War Philip G. Randolph to give the Topographical Bureau independent standing within the War Department in 1831, though it was not yet a corps.[103] At the same time the topographers were given complete control over surveying, taking away a valuable piece of bureaucratic turf from the Corps of Engineers.[104] Their fight for independence had made great strides.

Abert immediately began a campaign to further expand his bureau and its mission, but the topogs still faced some resistance in Congress from those unhappy with its expanded portfolio. In 1832, for example, when the Senate was debating a bill to create a corps of topographical engineers, Senator Robert Hayne of South Carolina questioned the need for such a proposal, since "there was an engineer corps in the service of the Government [sic]."[105] Senator Thomas Hart Benton of Missouri, chair of the Committee on Military Affairs, defended the bill, but it was nevertheless set aside.[106] Abert did successfully lobby for an expansion in the number of topographers from six to ten in 1834, despite the putative resistance of Jacksonians who supposedly opposed internal improvements.[107] Congressman Richard M. Johnson of Kentucky, chairman of the House Military Affairs Committee, closely tracked Abert's arguments when he introduced a bill to provide for the corps' independence. He argued that "there is no part of the army as defective in its organization as [the corps of topographical engineers], and subject, in consequence, to as great inconveniences in the execution of its duties."[108] Benton and Johnson were both strong supporters of the topogs, and it is worth noting that both represented states on the nation's periphery. Despite this backing from key members of both houses, however, a broader plan to create an independent corps failed to pass.[109]

Still not satisfied, Abert continued pressing for more topographers and a reorganization that would make the bureau into a corps on an equal footing with the regular engineers. Though Abert's objectives were seemingly in tune with Whig politician Henry Clay's controversial American system, he was able to win support from both parties for his plans.[110] The Senate did approve a bill for an independent corps in 1836 and 1837, but it failed in the House.[111] Tables 10 and 11 provide geographic breakdowns for Senate votes on the bill. Though this is not a perfect indicator of support for the topographers, passage of the final bill would have marked a significant triumph for the topogs and for supporters of the Army more broadly. Western support both times remained quite strong, with only a few senators from that region opposing the bill. This is not surprising, as spending on improvements for the West surged during the 1830s.[112] Southern senators were more likely to oppose the 1837 version of the bill, for reasons that are unclear. In the 1837 debate, John C. Calhoun asserted that "there never was a time when so little necessity existed for an increase of the army," whereas in 1836 he "thought that there ought to

Table 10. Senate Vote on Passage of Army Reorganization Act, 1836

	North	South
Yes	11	15
No	5	3
	East	*West*
Yes	15	11
No	6	2

Source: *Register of Debates*, Senate, 24th Congress, 1st Session, June 20, 1836.

Table 11. Senate Vote on Passage of Army Reorganization Act, 1837

	North	South
Yes	12	14
No	7	6
	East	*West*
Yes	12	14
No	9	4

Source: *Congressional Globe*, Senate, 24th Congress, 2nd Session, February 16, 1837.

be an increase of the army . . . only in reference to our Indian relations."[113] The strongest measure of opposition to the legislation seems to have been partisan affiliation, as almost every vote opposing the bill in both instances came from Whigs or other anti-Jacksonians. Calhoun's opposition to internal improvements, along with that of certain other southerners, may have solidified after the election of Van Buren to the presidency.

Abert's congressional supporters tried to grease the wheels of the legislative process by adding a new provision to the bill in 1836 that would repeal the section of the General Survey Act allowing the employment of civil engineers, a program many Democrats had long opposed.[114] Again, however, it seems that Abert was working closely with the congressional committees on this matter, and may have even given them this idea. On the day the House version of the bill was introduced, Abert wrote a letter to Congressman Johnson, arguing that civil engineers were not as capable as topographers.[115] This position reversed long-standing policies within the War Department that had encouraged the use of civil engineers. Abert had already won the support of Secretary of War Lewis Cass for this shift.[116] It appears that Abert initiated this proposal in order to win support for the topogs' independence, a clear instance of the agent influencing the actions principals were taking.

Democrats opposed to internal improvements were apparently somewhat placated by this new proviso. With the civil engineering prohibition attached, Congress finally granted Abert's wish as part of the Army Reorganization Act of 1838. The bill passed in the House by a vote of 112–80, though there seems to be no record of how each member voted.[117] The law enlarged Abert's staff and increased the number of topographers to thirty-six.[118] It directly followed language proposed by Abert in his annual report to Secretary of War Joel Poinsett, yet another indication of how the topogs were leading from behind and convincing others to enact their preferred goals.[119] The topographers were now on equal bureaucratic footing to the Corps of Engineers, and in fact became more important as they took charge of all civil engineering projects, while the regular engineers focused all their attention on military fortifications.[120]

Outside the nation's capital, at least one newspaper did seem to take a special interest in the ongoing debate over increasing the size of the Army, and specifically in the role of the topographical engineers. The *Baltimore Sun* published several stories relating to the impending bill to increase the size of both engineering corps and how important the paper believed this to be for national well-being. On December 20, 1837, the *Sun* reported that the bill "must be a source of gratification to every man of judgment and reflection, to know that a measure so well calculated to advance the prosperity of the country . . . is about to be carried into effect. If any measure can properly advance the real importance of our being possessed of an immense and valuable territory, it must be the correctly and topographically knowing the various advantages of which that territory is susceptible."[121] In July 1838, after the bill had become law, the paper recorded some of the details of how many new engineers had been appointed, the overall increase in the size of the Army, and some new regulations. The article concluded by asserting that "these additions and improvements will make this arm of the national defence [*sic*] much more respectable."[122] One of the War Department–supported service journals, the *Army and Navy Chronicle*, celebrated the success of

Secretary of War Poinsett in convincing Congress to pass this bill, noting how his report "became the foundation of the legislation" and that "to MR. POINSETT is then justly due the reputation of having brought this corps to increased usefulness."[123]

The 1840s were lean years for proponents of nationally funded improvements, with vetoes of many appropriations bills by Presidents Tyler and Polk. Even popular river and harbor improvements received less funding.[124] In response, the topographical corps subtly shifted its aims and thereby promoted and maintained its autonomy. Surveys of little-explored western territories now became its bailiwick, without any specific authorization to this effect from Congress, the secretary of war, or the president. Topographers such as John C. Frémont conducted important explorations in this decade that propelled the nationalistic concept of Manifest Destiny by encouraging citizens to settle in the far West. Frémont gained influence partly due to his powerful father-in-law, Senator Thomas Hart Benton. Benton pressed Abert to give important missions to Frémont, a request Abert fulfilled, though he also attached his own conditions of employment. Interestingly, Abert funded Frémont's first western survey to Oregon with $30,000 of previously appropriated funds, despite the opposition of President Tyler and Secretary of War John Spencer to encouraging immigration there. This shifting of funds represents a clear use of Abert's autonomy. Although Frémont occasionally took actions that went beyond some of his orders, Abert could not have been particularly unhappy with the results: Frémont became a national celebrity, with copies of his surveying reports selling thousands of copies across the country. Surveying became associated in the popular mind with Manifest Destiny, making it and the topographers politically powerful.[125]

The 1840s also saw a triumph for the topographical corps in taking away a valuable piece of bureaucratic turf from another agency. For decades the Coast Survey, run out of the Treasury Department, had been in charge of all surveying of the Atlantic Coast, along with most lighthouse construction and maintenance. Going back to 1807, when Congress passed the initial funding, the Coast Survey and the topographers competed fiercely with each other over this issue. Since the topographers were relatively weak, however, they lost these early battles.[126] In 1834, Secretary of War Lewis Cass put the topographers in charge of construction for lighthouses but they were not given full responsibility for their design and implementation.[127] By the 1840s the issue still had not been resolved. The Coast Survey continually requested that topographers be detailed to its service to continue works on lighthouses. In 1847, however, Abert convinced Congress to give all further lighthouse construction to the Topographical Corps.[128]

In view of the topographical corps's newfound political importance and surveying expertise, it is no surprise that the Pacific Railroad Surveys were placed under its control. Congress in the early 1850s deadlocked on the question of where precisely to place a route for a proposed transcontinental railroad. The debate largely followed sectional lines, with congressmen from the North preferring a route that ran westward from St. Louis or Omaha, and southerners wanting the line to run along the thirty-second parallel. As discussed in Chapter 2, in an effort to end the impasse, Congress in 1853 approved a compromise bill that ordered the Corps to conduct four surveys traversing the nation's various sections, leaving it to the topographers to pick the best one.[129] In truth, the topographers had been preparing for this for several years. In 1850, Secretary of War Charles Conrad and Abert began planning for railroad surveys, after Asa Whitney's 1849 proposal for a transcontinental route had entered into the popular imagination.[130] In combination with topogs' perceived expertise, these bureaucratic preparations made the topographical corps the natural choice to conduct these important surveys. The topographers had the opportunity to provide scientific advice to Congress and the president on the future of the nation's railroads. Their findings would be widely publicized, not just for Congress and national officials but also reaching professionals and the public interested in the subject of railroads. Results of the expeditions as well as surveys in progress were reported on both in newspapers, including the *Baltimore Sun* and the *New York Daily Times*, and professional publications, such as the *American Railway Times*.[131]

Early on, Abert had argued in favor of a southern route, believing it to be the cheapest and most technically feasible.[132] His involvement soon impacted the process. The supposedly nonpartisan surveys quickly became politicized, as members of Congress from both sections pushed for their favored routes. Abert and Secretary of War Jefferson Davis of Mississippi then picked the southernmost route despite contrary evidence indicating that northern routes were also potentially viable.[133] As Matthew Karp has argued, Davis and other "proslavery southerners" were some of the "most aggressive advocates of centralized state power" in this era.[134] However, by siding with Davis and the South, Abert lost one of the most important conditions underpinning the topographical corps' autonomy, its ability to influence its civilian principals. Key members of Congress from the North and West were outraged by Abert's choice, and their backing of the topogs ceased almost immediately. Since the topogs were no longer merely involved in an issue relegated to the nation's periphery, Congress had become deeply immersed in the process and important members stepped up their criticism of the corps. The loss of the secretary of war's support was also crucial. With virtually no protest, Davis was able to simply move western surveys into a newly created Office of Western Exploration, while also recommending the reabsorption of the topographical corps by the regular engineering corps.[135] Davis, who had long been an opponent of internal improvements and both of the engineering corps, had already decided that the topographical corps did not need to be independent from the regular engineers anymore, and he had merely been waiting for the right opportunity to present itself.[136] The autonomy that Abert had so painstakingly built up over decades vanished once the topographers became caught up in the sectional politics of the 1850s. In 1861 Abert retired, and in 1863 a northern-oriented Republican administration folded the topographical corps back into the Corps of Engineers.[137]

Comparing the topographers' experience to the Quartermaster General's Office is instructive about the development and maintenance of bureaucratic autonomy. As Mark Wilson has demonstrated, Thomas Jesup and his bureau gradually gained a reputation for improved administration of supply in the antebellum years, which helped him to build his office into a behemoth during the Civil War.[138] Over $1 billion of spending came through the Quartermaster's Bureau during the war, with top officials of the bureau making decisions about how and where to spend the money independently from partisan influences.[139] By avoiding entanglement in sectional and partisan politics prior to the war, Jesup preserved his bureau's autonomy. Along with the Ordnance Department, his bureau grew in prestige during the war and became more involved than ever in promoting economic development across the nation.[140]

Conclusion

Scholars who have examined national improvements policy in the antebellum period have largely focused on sectionalism and slavery as driving factors in its eventual demise.[141] They have not, however, sufficiently emphasized the central role that officials in the Army and War Department played in pushing for those policies and, eventually, destabilizing their support base. When those officials began allying themselves with particular sides in the sectional conflict, they undercut their independence. This is illustrated by the topographical engineers' selection of the southernmost route for the transcontinental railroad, which weakened the previously strong position of bureaucrats and helped to cost them the autonomy that they had so painstakingly built up over many years.

Focusing our attention on the War Department's bureaucratic structure, bureau chiefs, and the secretary of war reveals the limits of any attempt to neatly categorize the antebellum state using a grand historical explanation. The "state of courts and parties"[142] characterization cannot apply, as Army officials, particularly mezzo-level bureaucrats such as John J. Abert, were deeply involved in pushing for an agenda that rose above partisanship and continued across administrations of differing partisan control. Congress was only occasionally involved in socioeconomic policymaking, and on many key questions deferred to the preferences of bureaucrats. Similarly, Richard Bensel's view that sectional politics dominated this period is only partially correct: until the early 1850s, most War Department officials kept their agendas separate from sectionally based politics.[143] Rather, we need to consider the state in all of its complexity and closely examine the actual policies pursued by the national government.

In examining the topographers' actions in particular, it becomes apparent that their greatest impact came on the periphery of the nation, in what may be considered "the State of the West."[144] With few other public or private institutions in place, the West became the central locus of operations for the topographical corps, and for the entire national military apparatus more generally. As Senator Thomas Hart Benton of Missouri said when he introduced the bill that became the Army Reorganization Act of 1838, "this was a measure of western origin . . . this augmentation was a WESTERN measure, called for by WESTERN voices, and due to the state and condition of that section of the Union."[145] The triumphs of the topographers and the Army were celebrated by the West because they most advanced the interests of those living in the nation's periphery. However, while the topographers enjoyed their greatest achievements in the State of the West, their position was gradually (if not inevitably) being whittled away as the periphery came to be absorbed into the nation's core. Territories that had been largely outside the purview of elected officials became increasingly visible, and therefore the policies implemented there became more contentious too. Paradoxically, then, the corps's success in accelerating economic development in the West, which led to further population growth and its ultimate absorption into the core, eventually helped instigate the loss of the corps's autonomy.

CONCLUSION

The Army and American Political Development

This book has detailed the host of ways in which the U.S. Army impacted economic development in the period from the writing of the Constitution to the eve of the Civil War, and has analyzed the political forces behind the Army's actions. The Army's promotion of science and technology, its assistance in building infrastructure across the nation, its opening of new regions for white settlement through wars against native tribes and foreign nations, and its unifying of the nation by enforcing central state policies all propelled economic growth and helped launch the United States into a new era of commercial and industrial expansion at the end of the nineteenth century. Despite its small size, the Army was an actor of immense significance to the development of the American economy, as well as to the development of central state capacity.

This work joins a growing literature in American political development (APD) and the related field of policy history that challenges the idea that the early American state was a weak one.[1] In fact, as scholars are now realizing, the early American state was not stereotypically weak. Rather, when measured by the functions it was capable of performing, the early American state had many strengths. The Army, as I have shown, was instrumental in shaping the pattern and direction of economic development in the period from the founding to the eve of the Civil War.

In analyzing the various uses of the Army as an instrument of central state power, this study has also touched on a series of related issues that are of vital importance to understanding early American political life and the development of the country's national institutions. Presidential power, cabinet secretaries, bureaucracies, Congress, and Army officers all played a role in shaping the Army's policies that impacted development. Of particular note was the question raised in Chapter 3 of civil-military relations and the extent to which the antebellum period saw a form of attenuated civilian control over the peripheral regions of the nation. In a somewhat similar vein, Chapter 4 investigated the role of bureaucratic actors in effecting the Army's socioeconomic policies, and showed how long-serving entrepreneurial bureaucrats were able to shift the debate toward their favored policies and control many significant policy outcomes. In other words, some of the government's most important economic development policies in the young nation were proposed, managed, and largely controlled by unelected officials. This study therefore adds to the existing literature on the early American state and the field of American political development by establishing the Army's central importance to the political economy of the early state and demonstrating how elected officials often deferred to unelected officials in their pursuit of these policies.

This work also contributes to the literature on the role of the state in economic development by demonstrating the importance of the military to that process through its provision of public goods. My examination of the antebellum Army goes beyond some accounts that treat the military's economic consequences as mere externalities that result from its purchasing power or its own internal research and development programs.[2] Although both of those are certainly ways in which the military can impact the economy, this study has also provided numerous examples in which the Army itself, either through the agency of War Department bureaucrats or Army officers, purposefully worked to create applications of their work in nonmilitary settings. The Army's prodigious contribution to the railroads or the Ordnance Department's long-term interest in the promotion of private sector technological progress went beyond military necessity to show deep concern with the nation's economic progress as a whole. The military should therefore be seen as an actor in its own right deeply involved in economic and political development.

The tremendous economic expansion realized in early America would not have occurred without the involvement of the U.S. Army. No other institution at either the national or state level was able to offer the wide range of public goods that the Army provided. While some have argued that the actions of the states were primary in leading to economic development, this book has demonstrated the myriad economic effects of the Army beyond that of any single state acting alone. Similarly, no other civilian national institution had the wide range of impact that the Army did—the Post Office relied upon the Army for securing its routes and expanding its physical infrastructure, and the Land Office's important actions could not have taken place without the Army first conquering and possessing the territory as well as protecting the white settlers who moved there.

Finally, when the Army's actions are looked at with a broader lens, it becomes clear that its impact was not limited only to economics. What the Army did (or did not) do also made a deep impression upon national cohesion and the character of the young nation. Many at the time of the Constitution's writing had predicted that the new national government would help unify a far-flung citizenry into a cohesive whole. James Madison, for instance, spoke in *Federalist* 14 of how the "cords of affection" that tied Americans together would only be enhanced by the likelihood of central state policies that would help build a national infrastructure.[3] Although Madison did not refer explicitly to the Army, it carried out many of the policies he described. But despite Madison's confident forecast of a more cohesive union, internal tensions within the polity drove the nation apart only seven decades after the Constitution's ratification. The Army, which was the institution primarily responsible for building a national infrastructure, was not able to strengthen loyalties to the central state. This failure did not stem merely from external forces, such as sectionalism and slavery, but can partly be traced to the Army's own choices about developmental projects. Many Army-led projects favored particular regions. This is most especially the case when looking at the transcontinental railroad, when the topographical engineers attempted to select a southern route, damaging the corps's reputation for independence and further weakening national cohesion. The Army's choices ultimately served to further divide the union.

In this conclusion, I connect my findings on the Army to the study of American political development. I begin with a summary of the Army's role in economic development and the political actors behind its actions, focusing particularly on how this work changes our understanding of the development of civilian control. Then I argue that my work shows how the field of American political development needs to refocus its attention on the military. Too often we have ignored it and emphasized other activities of the state, such as regulation or social welfare provision. As the primary coercive actor in political life, the military must be seen as being at the heart of the American state.

The Army, Economic Development, and Early American Politics

As I have shown, the Army was central to the young nation's economic development. Both in terms of its traditional role as a coercive actor and through its socioeconomic activities, what the Army did fundamentally shaped the course of the nation's economic future. This was especially true for the peripheral regions of the country, which were gradually integrated over time into the rest of the nation. Military bureaucrats were the primary agents behind the transformation of the periphery, as no other institution, private or public, could match its influence there. Through their efforts, a continental marketplace emerged and industrialization occurred much sooner than would otherwise have been possible. No other institutions were capable of as wide an impact either at the national level or at the state level.

The Army shaped the pattern and direction of economic activity by providing public goods, unavailable from any other national institution, as well as some private goods in advance of market-generated demand. By choosing certain economic sectors as priorities, the Army structured the direction of economic development, thereby setting the path on which the country's economy would progress. No other public institution, either at the state or national level, was able to supply public goods in sufficient quantities to have seen such impressive economic expansion, and no private institution was capable of doing much of what the Army did across the nation. Scholars who have focused on private actors or the state governments' role in building internal improvements projects are not so much wrong as they have missed the mark, since the vital contributions to those efforts by the Army (by enhancing national stability, conquering that territory for white settlement, or providing engineering expertise, for instance) made them possible in the first place.

The Army's vital activities could not have all been accomplished by any other institution. Consider resource extraction: topographers surveying new territories mapped out the location of mineral deposits, information that was spread to the private sector through publication of maps and official reports; soldiers then protected miners as they traveled to the West along emigrant routes, and again at the mining location. In theory, another institution or private entity could have provided both the knowledge necessary to locate resources as well as the security needed to allow the extraction to progress; but in practice, only the Army had the wherewithal to do both successfully. Similarly, engineering expertise, a vital skill needed for economic expansion but in very short supply, was largely supplied by the Army. Indeed, until 1824, there were no engineering schools in the nation besides West Point, and even after then most skilled engineers were supplied by the military academy. Engineers and ordnance officers both contributed to technological and managerial innovations in the private sector well ahead of market-generated demand for them.

The Army also supplied pure public goods. Sustained coercion, such as fighting large-scale wars and waging protracted campaigns against native tribes, could only be applied by the Army. Although it is true that the state militias were often engaged in these conflicts, their reach was limited and could not extend across the entire nation. Additionally, the militias were weak and relied on the national government for much of their support apparatus. National military figures largely saw the militias as disorganized and incompetent to defeat an enemy without significant assistance. Militias received $200,000 a year from the national government for arms and equipment, and relied upon manuals of instruction prepared by the War Department.

National coercive force kept the country unified at a time of great fragility. With constant threats of secession as well as intrigues by the Spanish, French, and British against the young republic, the risk of the United States dissolving into several smaller confederacies was quite real. The Army was the key actor involved in protecting the nation's borders and preserving national sovereignty over peripheral regions that otherwise could have been lost to a foreign nation. In addition, the Army was used on multiple occasions to forestall separatist or rebellious movements that could have led to far-flung settler populations becoming independent of the central state. Notable instances of this use of the Army include Washington heading a ten-thousand-man force to stop the Whiskey Rebellion in 1794 and the Mormon War of the 1850s.

In addition, the Army was the central actor responsible for the westward removal of hundreds of thousands of native Indians. Many, if not most, uses of coercion in this period were as a result of the Indian removal policy that began officially in 1830 and unofficially much earlier. Because of these actions, millions of acres were cleared for white settlement as well as resource extraction. No other institution—not a single state or a private actor—could have carried out such a far-ranging coercive policy.

Examining these notable economic development activities also leads me to a reconsideration of politics in early America. In particular, the young nation's polity was characterized by the emergence of two different states: the center, in which the Army was one of several important institutional actors, and the periphery, where the Army dominated. While the Army's impact was felt across the nation, its contributions to the peripheral regions were especially important, insofar as the Army's actions kept the nation together and gradually integrated the periphery into the nation. Accordingly, it is most important that the Army's actions in the periphery were not directed primarily by elected officials, such as members of Congress or presidents, but rather were largely under the control of unelected officials, such as the secretary of war, officers in the field, or the heads of War Department bureaus. The nonpresidential executive branch thus emerged as a key actor in the new nation, far more important than previous studies have shown.

Much of what the Army did reflected the efforts of policy entrepreneurs. The secretary of war often acted in an entrepreneurial manner by deliberately choosing policies that would encourage development in particular ways. Some secretaries, especially proslavery southerners John C. Calhoun and Jefferson Davis, played especially prominent roles in determining the various directions that economic policies took.[4] Calhoun fundamentally reorganized the Army and encouraged development projects under the Army's direction across the country, and his report on improvements led directly to the passage of the General Survey Act of 1824, one of the most important pro-growth tools of the era, which provided national assistance to states and private corporations from the Army. Davis promoted the Pacific Railroad Surveys that were instrumental in laying the foundation for a transcontinental railroad, and thereafter decided to transfer responsibility for many projects away from the Corps of Topographical Engineers, changing the authority structure for a fundamental set of national development policies.

Bureaucrats, especially the chiefs of War Department bureaus, played a central role in shaping the Army's development activities. Key policy choices were directly shaped by the preferences of bureaucrats, independently of partisan control of the rest of government. Ordnance officers, for instance, promoted technological innovations at the national armories for decades, across different administrations and regardless of the partisan composition of Congress. Additionally, the president and his top advisers often deferred to bureaucrats in their declarations regarding important policies, as was demonstrated in Chapter 4. As a result of the unique expertise and positive reputations enjoyed by many engineers, topographers, and ordnance officers, and the long terms in office enjoyed by bureau chiefs, bureaucratic autonomy came into being much earlier than other APD scholars have suggested. Of particular note was the Corps of Topographical Engineers and its long-serving head, John J. Abert. Through his creation of a neutral reputation for expertise among both parties, Abert convinced decades of policymakers to increase his agency's size, fund its activities largely based on his preferences, defer to its expertise on important projects, and pass revisions to laws that suited the topographers' needs. However, when Abert and his agency selected a southern route for the proposed transcontinental railroad, they undermined their reputation and allowed Secretary of War Jefferson Davis to undercut their authority, leading within a short time to the agency's demise. Autonomy here was hard won but easily lost, since it was built on a foundation that crumbled once the key piece, a neutral reputation, was removed.

Civilian Control of the Military in the United States

One noteworthy issue that APD scholars have not engaged in a sustained manner is the relationship between the military and civilian leadership. Political scientists have long studied civil-military relations, from Samuel Huntington's classic *The Soldier and the State* to recent work by Peter Feaver updating and refining Huntington's theory, to the opposing perspective explicated by Eliot Cohen.[5] However, this interesting literature leaves open several unexplored avenues of research that APD scholars are well prepared to begin answering. First, although civilian control of the military is widely assumed to be in the Constitution, no explicit mention of the principle can be located in the document itself. How, then, did this idea became so prevalent, and what have been the challenges to civilian control?

Since the nation's founding, disputes over the proper role of military power in a free society have been a central part of political discourse. In the wake of Shays's Rebellion, the problem of centralized military power was one of the key issues leading to the Constitutional Convention in 1787. James Madison, for example, wrote about the "Vices of the Political System of the United States," which included the states not paying their requisitions to the federal government and not following the national government's orders, encroachments by the states on federal authority, and the inability of the federal government to ensure to the states a secure form of government free from violence.[6] Central to the debates over whether states should ratify the new Constitution were the proposed national government's military powers. The fears of many Anti-Federalists were encapsulated in rhetoric that highlighted the Constitution's grant of expanded powers to the national government and the creation of a standing army that they believed would inevitably result.[7] Not only were they concerned about a centralized army, but the Constitution also granted the national government the ability to regulate the state militias, a significant move toward national control of the country's armed citizenry, leading to heightened awareness of federal intrusion in state affairs.[8] One writer went so far as to warn that, if the people of his state of Maryland refused to assent to direct national taxes, the new government "can, and I have not a doubt but they will, send the militia of Pennsylvania, Boston, or any other state or place, to cut your throats, ravage and destroy your plantations, drive away your cattle and horses, abuse your wives, kill your infants, and ravish your daughters, and live in free quarters, until you get into a good humor, and pay all that they may think proper to ask of you, and you become good and faithful servants and slaves."[9] Most were not quite so extreme in their rhetorical opposition, but the overall sentiment was widely shared among Anti-Federalists: too much coercive power was being given to the national government under the Constitution.

Federalists started from the opposite assumption: too little coercive power at the national level meant that there was not sufficient centralized authority to keep order and stability throughout the country. Typical were the views of Alexander Hamilton. In a letter written to George Clinton in February 1778, well in advance of any prevailing notion that a stronger central government was needed, Hamilton discussed how poorly Congress was treating the Continental Army. He complained that a "deficiency of energy, dignity and extensiveness of views" in the representatives had led to this sorry state of affairs in which "the nations of Europe have no confidence in the wisdom and vigor, of the great Continental Government," as the Army was barely scratching out a meager existence without sufficient supplies.[10]

The preoccupation of Federalists with the history of weak regimes brought down by a lack of coercive power and the place of coercion in a republic is reflected in the fact that twenty-nine of the eighty-five *Federalist* papers discuss some issue relating to war, armies, or the militia.[11] Hamilton in particular dismissed those fearful of a national army, arguing in *Federalist* 8 that, in fact, a weak central state that allowed the nation to disband into separate confederacies was a much more real danger. "Standing armies," he wrote, "must inevitably result from a dissolution of the Confederacy." In such a situation, "the military state becomes elevated above the civil," whereas a unified nation would see its army "rarely, if at all, called into activity for interior defense . . . [and] the civil state remains in full vigor."[12] Although Hamilton denied that Americans would feel the force of the new central state, the Constitution did give the national government significant new military powers with which to enforce the laws. At least in theory, an effective national army could now be created, without the national government having to continuously beg states for troops, and it was simpler for the state militias to be called into national service when required.[13]

After the Constitution was ratified, there certainly were moments when the concept of civilian preeminence was threatened. General Andrew Jackson, for instance, repeatedly disobeyed orders and twice invaded Spanish-controlled Florida, helping to push the Monroe administration into annexation after the fact.[14] Once the dogma of civilian control became widely accepted, military involvement in politics, even in less extreme form than Jackson practiced, appeared decidedly illiberal in the liberal American state. As this study has shown, however, officers in the antebellum republic took control of many policies on the ground, implementing national goals in ways that civilian leaders often did not control and could not have predicted. The attenuated nature of civilian control in this era demonstrates the tendency for American military leaders to insert themselves into political affairs and reach into policymaking terrain.

Bringing the Military (Back?) In

Despite important advances that have pushed APD scholars to open new frontiers of research, when analyzed from a broader perspective the bulk of APD work still concentrates in essentially two main areas: social welfare provision and national regulatory efforts. As Elizabeth Sanders has noted, focusing on these two portions of the American state has meant less intellectual effort has been put into examining the third part of the state, its coercive element.[15] The newer studies certainly have advanced our understanding of politics in many ways, especially by focusing our attention on parts of political life that are too often left by the wayside in conventional inquiries, but they generally do not look at the nation's primary coercive actor, the military, as a central actor in American politics or at how the military can impact economic development. Of the few that do discuss the military, most consider it only insofar as it speaks to some other question, rather than examining how the military itself impacts politics and policies.

I argue that the military should be seen by scholars as a crucial actor in its own right, and that it is at the heart of the American state—the key ingredient in the despotic power of the state.[16] Ignoring its central role has led scholars to overemphasize other portions of the state apparatus at its expense.

Especially because of its coercive power, and its concomitant ability to induce action through coercion or the threat of coercion, the military should be seen as a central force in American political development. If one of the basic definitions of the state is, as Max Weber noted, that it is the organization that "successfully upholds a claim to the monopoly of the legitimate use of physical force in the enforcement of its order,"[17] then it seems odd that we have not paid more attention to the state's institution most capable of supporting its legitimacy through the use of force, that is to say, the military.[18]

Surprisingly, scholars of American political development rarely discuss the national military as an important governing entity, despite its fundamental importance to understanding central state power. This is true even though some of APD's foundational works examine various aspects of the American military. Stephen Skowronek in *Building a New American State*, for instance, examines reform of the Army as one of his major case studies of how the state was reconstituted in the Progressive Era. Similarly, Richard Bensel's *Yankee Leviathan* sees the Army during the Civil War period as a crucial extension of the party state that the Republicans built.[19] Neither of these important works, however, consider how the Army per se impacted political development, or how actors within the military apparatus attempted to shape the contours of the American state through their own entrepreneurial actions. Usually, within the APD tradition, a discussion of the military illustrates some other phenomenon that we are trying to study—be it political parties, bureaucratic reform, or executive power—but it is rarely seen as a source of state power in and of itself.[20] I maintain that that using the military as a lens through which we examine other issues misses out on a fruitful avenue of research by not placing the military and actors within the military apparatus at the center of APD. So I propose here to bring us back to Weber's baseline definition of the state, reminding us of something we have already known for a long time, even when we decline to focus on it—coercion matters.

A closer examination of the APD oeuvre reveals that work within the APD tradition has, for the most part, not yet intersected with the rich historical literature on the American military, or for that matter with comparative work within political science that has long directed its spotlight on questions surrounding armies and their impact on state development. So far, these streams of research have remained separate from each other. Instead we have talked about American political development being "shaped by war and trade," in the phraseology of one well-known collection.[21] This concept of war shaping developmental politics is certainly important to any determination regarding how the military has impacted American politics, but it is not the entire story. Indeed, of the essays in Ira Katznelson and Martin Shefter's edited volume, only one, Katznelson's own contribution, analyzes how the military molded the character of the American state, rather than seeing the military merely as a creature of other interests or as a tool through which other, perhaps more important, events occurred.[22] Even Katznelson's chapter sidesteps the issue of whether the military itself was an active participant in the policies he discusses, such as Indian removal, and instead pursues a discussion of how presidents and Congress used the military to act in various ways, thereby influencing the development of the central state. None of this critique is meant to deny the value of examining how elected officials use the military as an institution of government; rather, it serves to highlight underexplored avenues of investigation that can be found by looking at the military and actors within the military acting in their own right.

Much remains to be done to complete the picture of how the military did (and still does) act endogenously to influence political development. A rich historical literature exists on the American military, one that has yet to be fully mined by APD scholars who are interested in the ways that the military has effected institutional change. A full description of this literature would be overwhelming, but as a brief summary, we can divide it into three broad categories. First, there are older works, mostly from the 1950s and 1960s, in which historians dug through official records of the War Department and the Army to sketch out some of the basic activities the military engaged in domestically prior to World Wars I and II. Examples of this genre include works by William Goetzmann and Forest Hill on the Army engineers, Francis Paul Prucha's groundbreaking books on American relations with Indian tribes, and Leonard White's series on administrative history (which included substantial material on the military bureaucracies).[23] The second subset of this literature includes more recent work on similar themes, especially in relation to the military's influence on culture and technology. This portion of the field includes Merritt Roe Smith's well-known monograph on Harper's Ferry Armory, along with updated versions of the older work on Army engineers by Todd Shallat and Paul Paskoff.[24] Finally, the third portion encompasses the area generally known as the "new" military history. This category of work started during the 1970s as a younger generation of scholars began questioning the typical emphasis of military historians upon battles and strategy. Instead, the recent literature adds to the mix an examination of how armies affect the culture and are affected by it, while simultaneously stressing the experience of the common soldier (similar to the social history movement's emphasis on the ordinary person's perspective).[25] Representative examples of this movement include Jill Lepore's *The Name of War* and Fred Anderson's *A People's Army*, both of which consider how wars and battles shaped American identity.[26]

Engaging this literature may open up promising areas of exploration for political scientists interested in questions of coercive power. The new military history and the recent surge of interest in the military are especially ripe for engagement with American political development. As I have shown, the Army contributed to the nationwide emergence of a mature industrial economy, in a way that APD has until now largely missed. Some scholars such as Shallat and Paskoff have focused on one aspect of this story, the Army's socioeconomic role, while other scholars only examine the coercive side of the military.[27] My work brings together both sides of what the Army did and demonstrates that, across the board, the Army was a central player in antebellum economic development. Moreover, some of the new military history tends to marginalize politics in its treatment of the military's activities, choosing instead to foreground questions of society and culture. My work seeks to integrate politics with the military's influence on society by considering how the military's important economic contributions also affected national identity and cohesion.

The Challenge of Expansionism, West and East

Considering the U.S. Army's actions in comparative perspective is also instructive in seeing how important the antebellum military was to the nation's development. In this section I compare U.S. territorial expansion during the nineteenth century to that of Russia. Despite their radically differing forms of government, both nations were faced with similar challenges in the course of expanding their borders: incorporating native peoples, confronting the empires around them that challenged their sovereignty, and enforcing the will of the central state on remote frontiers. Policymakers in both nations used a combination of military strength, political incorporation, and support from private enterprise to achieve their goals. The fortunes of both nations intertwined around the question of Alaska, whose ultimate sale to the United States curtailed Russia's attempt to extend its reach across the globe while heralding the emergence of the American empire. Despite radically differing political systems, American policymakers used techniques of empire building remarkably similar to those of Russia.[28]

The greatest distinction between the two, of course, related to the basic form of governance. The distinction between these two great powers did not escape notice at the time. In a remarkable passage at the end of the first part of *Democracy in America*, Alexis de Tocqueville explicitly compared Russia and the United States while predicting inevitable conflict between these emerging world powers:

> There are at the present time two great nations in the world, which started from different points, but seem to tend towards the same end. I allude to the Russians and the Americans. Both of them have grown up unnoticed; and while the attention of mankind was directed elsewhere, they have suddenly placed themselves in the front rank among the nations, and the world learned their existence and their greatness at almost the same time. All other nations seem to have nearly reached their natural limits, and they have only to maintain their power; but these are still in the act of growth. All the others have stopped, or continue to advance with extreme difficulty; these alone are proceeding with ease and celerity along a path to which no limit can be perceived. The American struggles against the obstacles that nature opposes to him; the adversaries of the Russian are men. The former combats the wilderness and savage life; the latter, civilization with all its arms. The conquests of the American are therefore gained by the plowshare; those of the Russian by the sword. The Anglo-American relies upon personal interest to accomplish his ends and gives free scope to the unguided strength and common sense of the people; the Russian centers all the authority of society in a single arm. The principal instrument of the former is freedom; of the latter, servitude. Their starting-point is different and their courses are not the same; yet each of them seems marked out by the will of Heaven to sway the destinies of half the globe.[29]

In this passage, Tocqueville digresses briefly from his examination of America itself to note its similarities and differences with Russia, another emerging power expanding on the other side of the globe, "still in the act of growth." He asserts that America faces no limits to its expansion beyond nature, while

Russia has to fight against other men; America conquers with economic and agricultural might, Russia with force; American society is based on freedom, Russia's on servitude. In truth, the accuracy of these distinctions, however commonplace they may seem, is questionable. Tocqueville ignores the existence of native peoples in the United States, allowing him to claim that Americans are expanding onto a blank canvas. He also overlooks slavery in the South while seemingly placing serfdom at the center of Russian society. If anything, one could argue that the U.S. version of expansion was more brutal, involving the forced removal and extermination of hundreds of thousands of natives.

Nevertheless, Tocqueville's observations are a useful starting point to begin our comparison of the United States and Russia. Although they had differing forms of government, the process of change in both nations was quite similar. Both were increasing their territorial size, both conquered the native peoples who stood in their way, and the strategies used to pacify the indigenous populations were in many cases the same. When needed, both used violence to achieve their goals. Eventually, the two rising empires would clash over the fate of Russia's American possessions, the Alaska territory. U.S. commercial and naval strength overwhelmed Russia's efforts to maintain its hold on a far-off possession, ultimately culminating in the sale of Alaska to the United States.

The United States and Russia faced similar challenges to their growing territorial acquisitions from the empires around them. Sometimes this took the form of actual violence, but more often came about through other means, such as allying with the native peoples against the colonizing nation, or working together with private enterprises to undermine the ability of that nation to act. Both the United States and Russia responded with their own efforts at creating allies among the native population, working with private enterprises themselves, or simply using armed force.

Like those of the United States, Russia's efforts to deal with the native populations it conquered relied upon a mixture of concessions, outright bribery, and resorting to force when needed. Led from Moscow, the Russian state faced competition for territory and resources from the empires around it. On the western front, Russia entered into conflict with established nations such as Poland, Lithuania, Sweden, the Austro-Hungarian Empire, Britain, France, and the Ottoman Empire. To the east it fought against native groups including the Kazan, Astrakhan, Siberian, Nogai, and Tatar.[30] Expansion toward the east eventually led all the way to Alaska and competition with Britain and the United States over the American continent.

As early as the year 1500, facing attacks on all sides, the Muscovite state became obsessed with security. In addition to threats from Poland-Lithuania and Sweden, conquering indigenous peoples on the eastern front was not a simple process. The native cultures consisted of highly organized societies that in some cases had their own functioning governments. Several were allied with Poland-Lithuania, Russia's primary strategic rival in this early period. They fought back and raided into the Russian heartland as well. In this sense, Russia's problems here mirrored those that the United States faced later, with native tribes allying with the British against the encroaching American presence. The security concerns at this early stage helped to convince Russia's leaders to increase the size and scope of the national military and devote ever-increasing resources to it.[31]

Initially, from the period 1550–1680, Russia's leaders were content to let much of the conquering in the East take place through private hands. The Cossacks, for example, were essentially used as a proxy force that conducted raids into these lands. This marshaling of private coercive power allowed Russia to concentrate its military prowess on threats from the west. The type of force used in defeating the indigenous peoples was more like a cavalry force than a typical army, not unlike the cavalry forces Americans would later use to overcome Indian tribes.[32]

Interestingly, Russia had no interest in eliminating the native populations. Unlike the American case, where outright extermination often came to be the hallmark of Indian removal policy, Russia's leaders preferred to maintain the native populations so that they could become integral parts of the emerging serf-based economic system. They used incentives such as payments to the locals to keep them happy and were more than willing to use force when they felt it needed. As the nation was expanding geographically and experienced a shortage of agricultural laborers, serfdom became the answer, as Peter Kolchin has argued. Cossacks became landowners in the new far-flung empire and part of the new organization. In this respect, oddly enough, the Russian autocratic system was far less destructive of native populations than the American democracy, contra Tocqueville.[33]

In the Great Northern War, fought from 1700 to 1721, Russia allied with the Polish-Lithuanian Empire against Sweden in the culmination of a long struggle for territory and resources. The primary prize was control of the

Baltic Sea region. Over the course of a long series of battles, Russia defeated Sweden and seized the territories of Estonia and Latvia. The war itself was fought largely on Polish territory, and the end result within several decades was increasing Russian encroachment on Polish lands. By 1800 Poland was entirely swallowed up by the empires around it, with Russia receiving a large share of the proceeds. Peter the Great, the czar who led the victorious campaign, proclaimed at the war's conclusion that Russia was now an empire, not merely a czardom, and he crowned himself emperor. Russia now had gained European colonies in addition to its eastern, Asiatic possessions.[34]

Toward the east, Siberia became one of Russia's most prized new acquisitions. Contrary to the popular image of Siberia as a barren wasteland that was home to refugees and political prisoners, many Russians viewed it as a new frontier that would transform their nation and lead to a resurgence of its identity. The fur trade, discussed further below, was the main economic asset offered by Siberia, and the Russian central government worked hard to maintain its control over this expanding trade. Up to the time of Peter the Great, merchants and traders moved ahead of the state to get involved in the fur business. But after that point, as historian C. M. Foust explains, "the state alone was left with the organization, the funds and the impetus for sustained and large-scale expansion and colonization."[35] Merchants and other private actors operated largely under the aegis of state control. The most important *gosti* (merchants) lived in Moscow and served the Muscovite government, in exchange for which they received preferential treatment and tax exemptions. Traders returning west had to pass through a customs house, pay a tax on their pelts, and give a portion of the best ones directly to the state. A special department of the government was organized in 1637 to oversee this trade. The new bureaucracy had autonomy over Siberia, sending *voevody* (governors) to conquer land and maintain peaceful relations with the native peoples. Later, at the end of the eighteenth century, the Russian American corporation was established, a public venture, to continue pressing the state's interests in trade farther east, all the way to Alaska.[36]

To contrast this to the American experience, consider the factory system, set up in 1796 under the Washington administration. The factories, as discussed in Chapter 1, were trading posts located near Army forts that were designed to help manage and regulate private trade with Indian tribes. Run by agents of the Indian Affairs Office, they were conceived as a way of protecting the tribes from predatory trading, as well as a method of overseeing continued westward expansion. The system initially was supported by private interests.

Over time, however, actors such as John Jacob Astor's American Fur Company came to oppose it, believing that it was eating into profits and making it harder to continue pushing farther west and seeking new opportunities. As the factories continued to face Astor's powerful opposition, and continued losing money as well, they were shut down by Congress in 1822.[37] The Russian system was more heavily centralized and seems to have been more successful in keeping state control over trading in a frontier region.

Siberia's importance extended beyond control of the territory to how Russians viewed their expanding nation and how they viewed themselves. Historian Mark Bassin has demonstrated the centrality of Siberia to Russia's self-image. As he explains, Siberia became less important economically due to the decline of the fur trade, and therefore it became portrayed as a barren wasteland, fit only for exiles (hence the popular image). It was largely ignored by policymakers and was an underdeveloped region. Certain opposition figures, who were themselves exiled to Siberia in the 1820s, started to see Siberia as a land that had the potential to become a model for the new society they envisioned. Known as the Decembrists, they focused particularly on the lack of serfdom in the far East. Modeling themselves partially on the American example of a frontier society, they argued that a new, less hierarchical society could be created. Others, who were proponents of nationalism, saw in Siberia the glorious image of Cossacks and heralded the triumph of expansionism.[38] This, too, seems comparable to the American example, as Richard Slotkin and others have argued: the western frontier was seen as a land of myth, involved in the creation of a new self-image of the rugged individual in American culture.[39]

Though not the only causative factor behind the meeting of the two expanding empires, the fur trade was a central reason for why the United States and Russia intersected in the American far Northwest. Economic interests drove private interests in both nations as well as governments to focus attention on this region. Russia was able to overcome British opposition to control the Alaskan territory, but eventually lost it in a struggle of commercial and naval power with the United States.

As mentioned earlier, both nations relied on a combination of private-public cooperation in extending their empires toward the fur-rich region of the northwest American continent. The initial exploration of Alaska by Russia was ordered by Peter the Great in 1725. Vitus Bering led the expedition, and the straits between the Russian mainland and Alaska were named after him when he proved that the two continents were not linked. He saw the coastline, and the published reports of him sighting potential fur opportunities there led to a rush to get them. The first settlement was in 1784 at Kodiak Island, which became the headquarters of the Russian American Fur Corporation, a government-sponsored entity, starting in 1799. Later the headquarters were moved to Sitka, farther south. By 1818 there were twenty-four trading posts on the Alaskan coasts worth over 7 million rubles a year.[40]

Starting from 1805 the Russians began to worry about potential American encroachment on what they considered their exclusive zone of operation. The primary competition came from John Jacob Astor's American Fur Company, a private enterprise that was strongly supported by officials of the U.S. government and chartered by the state of New York. Astor's agents conflicted with Russia's traders as both were interested in the same product, though neither was willing to directly confront each other in any kind of violent way. Russia complained to the U.S. government regarding these activities, but at first the Americans did not make any attempt to stop these incursions. Negotiations continued, and in 1812 the Russian American Corporation and Astor signed an agreement that excluded Americans from Russian areas, but in exchange gave Astor the exclusive right to supply Russian colonies with other needed goods.[41]

The War of 1812 temporarily disrupted American commerce in the far Northwest, but the war's end led to a resurgent American presence and increased Russian apprehension. Americans had now extended their trading all the way to China, infringing on what Russians perceived to be their exclusive area of interest. In 1818 the Russian navy officially took control of the Russian American Corporation, banning Americans from the coastline altogether. The ban was, however, ineffective. Finally, in 1821, Czar Alexander I issued an *ukase* (decree) claiming the entire Northwest for Russia and banning all British and American merchants from entering. He sent three warships to enforce his decree. Both the British and Americans vigorously protested, and in 1824 the czar was compelled to back down, through the eventual realization that the Russians could not stop commerce from proceeding, and that the United States was willing to go to war over the issue. Secretary of State John Quincy Adams went so far as to declare that the Russians had no right to any colonies in the entirety of the American continent.[42]

The 1830s and 1840s saw an increased American presence in the far Northwest. Primarily, as the United States expanded to the west, it became easier for traders to make their way out to Alaska and its environs, and simpler for them to turn a profit through trading. At the same time, the fur trade declined, with fewer pelts available every year. Yankee merchants soon turned instead to whaling expeditions, a development the Russians found troubling as they could not compete with the sheer numbers of Americans who kept coming. Finally, after the United States annexed the Southwest from Mexico after the Mexican-American war, and settled its claim to Oregon, further expansion started to seem inevitable. San Francisco now became the port of call for many merchants and they held increasing weight with American policymakers and diplomats.[43]

American expansionist desires in the 1850s included Cuba, Canada, perhaps more of Mexico, and Alaska as well. Senators such as William Gwin of California and William H. Seward of New York worked together to promote continued territorial expansion, especially to the far northwest region. Both men, despite holding opposite views on slavery, "envisioned a worldwide commercial empire in which the United States would be the center," starting with Russia's American possessions.[44] Seward, for instance, gave a speech in 1853, proclaiming:

> If the Future which you seek consists in this: that these thirty-one States shall continue to exist for a period as long as human foresight is allowed to anticipate after coming events; that they shall be all the while free; that they shall remain distinct and independent in domestic economy, and nevertheless be only one in commerce and foreign affairs; that there shall arise from among them and within their common domain even more than thirty-one other equal States, alike free, independent, and united; that the borders of the Federal Republic so peculiarly constituted shall be extended so that it shall greet the sun when he touches the Tropic, and when he sends his glancing rays towards the Polar circle, and shall include even distant islands in either ocean; that our population now counted by tens of millions shall ultimately be reckoned by hundreds of millions; that our wealth shall increase a thousand fold and our commercial connections shall be multiplied, and our political influence be enhanced in proportion with this wide development, and that mankind shall come to recognize in us a successor of the few great states which have alternately borne commanding sway in the world—if this and only this is desired, then I am free to say that if, as you will readily promise, our public and private virtues shall be preserved, nothing seems to me more certain than the attainment of this Future.[45]

In 1852, when Russia sent ships to patrol the waters of Alaska in an effort to stop further American intrusions, Gwin offered an amendment to the naval appropriations bill to pay for a survey and reconnaissance of Bering's straits and the northern Pacific region. This appropriation of $125,000 eventually led to a series of expeditions from 1853 to 1859 that increased scientific knowledge of the region and assisted commercial enterprises such as whaling.[46] The overall effect was to send the U.S. Navy directly into the heart of Russia's claim and expose just how weak it was. The Navy was central to the expanding commercial empire that the United States was designing, with men like Seward at its heart.[47]

In essence, Russia had in this one instance expanded too far, and the United States was perfectly positioned to push back and compel Russia to surrender this outlying colony. The American Civil War did not stop western merchants from continuing their trade, and Russian policymakers began to realize that the Alaskan colony was becoming a financial disaster for the empire. In addition, Russia saw how aggressive the United States had been in consistently growing and seizing more and more territory, fighting the British, French, Mexicans, and Indian tribes, and Russia feared becoming the next target of America's military might. In the end, with Seward as the secretary of state, the sale of Alaska was concluded in 1867.[48] Russia's imperial project was, at least here, temporarily halted in the face of superior commercial power, fears of military conflict, and geographic advantages enjoyed by the United States.

The drive to territorial enlargement displayed by both Russia and the United States could perhaps be best encapsulated by the views of two different men. Seward was one of the leading Americans behind the impending drive toward an American overseas empire. Speaking in Sitka, Alaska, in 1869, Seward celebrated the land, its people, and the joining of Alaska to the United States. The native tribes of the territory, however, would soon be gone: "they will merely serve the turn until civilized white men come."[49]

Like Seward, Alexander Herzen believed in the necessity of territorial expansion. Herzen, who was exiled in 1852 due to his liberal views, argued that Russia, like the United States, was taming an uncivilized wilderness and bringing it into the fold of a great empire. As Russia purchased Chinese territories around the Amur and Ussuri Rivers in the 1850s and 1860s, Herzen celebrated the fact that the nation could continue to expand, despite losses in the Crimean War and despite the impending sale of Alaska. Herzen was a liberal voice in nineteenth-century Russia who believed in Peter the Great's westernizing ideas. But unlike Seward, he opposed Russian military occupation of Siberia and decried the treatment of its natives.[50]

Tocqueville was therefore wrong in his proclamation that Russia was entirely driven by motives worse than the United States, that Russia was a nation of serfs and autocracy and the United States the land of freedom and democracy. The situation was just not that simple to categorize. He was correct, however, in noticing the expansionary tendencies of both nations, in the growing empires each one had. Both faced similar challenges in their expansions, from dealing with indigenous peoples, maintaining stable relations with them, incorporating them, or using coercion when needed; both dealt with conflicts with the empires that surrounded them; and at the intersection of the two empires they crossed paths over Alaska's future. Policymakers in the United States used similar tactics and thereby built the foundations of the nascent American empire.

"So Many Cords of Affection"

What the military does matters not only for its economic and political impact but also for its effect on the country's sense of national cohesion, as well as how Americans view themselves, other groups within the nation, and their government. In *Federalist* 14, as part of his argument about the desirability of a large republic, James Madison predicted that the new national government would increase ties between the different parts of the union, thus undermining the traditional theory of the small republic:

> Let it be remarked . . . that the intercourse throughout the Union will be facilitated by new improvements. Roads will everywhere be shortened, and kept in better order; accommodations for travelers will be multiplied and meliorated; an interior navigation on our eastern side will be opened throughout, or nearly throughout, the whole extent of the thirteen States. The communication between the Western and Atlantic districts, and between different parts of each, will be rendered more and more easy by those numerous canals with which the beneficence of nature has intersected our country, and which art finds it so little difficult to connect and complete.[51]

Madison argued that the new government would naturally be involved in the business of improving the national infrastructure. Though he did not specify an agency or institution that would handle these needs, I have shown that many of the tasks he described were carried out by the Army—building roads and canals, and easing navigation, as well as protecting frontier communities from foreign threats:

> the States which lie at the greatest distance from the heart of the Union, and which, of course, may partake least of the ordinary circulation of its benefits, will be at the same time immediately contiguous to foreign nations, and will consequently stand, on particular occasions, in greatest need of its strength and resources. . . . Hearken not to the unnatural voice which tells you that the people of America, knit together as they are by so many cords of affection, can no longer live together as members of the same family; can no longer continue the mutual guardians of their mutual happiness; can no longer be fellow citizens of one great, respectable, and flourishing empire.[52]

Madison therefore sees no contradiction between governing a large territory and maintaining republican government. Indeed, according to his theory, the "cords of affection" that bind Americans together will only be strengthened by the actions of a more powerful central state.[53] Similarly, Thomas Jefferson would later argue that internal improvements would mean "new channels of communication will be opened between the States, the lines of separation will disappear, their interests will be identified, and their union cemented by new and indissoluble ties."[54]

The use of force was also seen by many as deeply impacting national identity and culture, partly due to its ability to unite disparate groups within the nation. Following the War of 1812, for example, several prominent figures highlighted its beneficial effects for the country, despite the fact that the war itself ended in a stalemate. John Adams, for instance, told Thomas Jefferson that President James Madison "acquired more glory, and established more Union than all his three Predecessors [*sic*]" by waging war. Former secretary of the treasury Albert Gallatin similarly noted that citizens "are more American; they feel and act more as a nation" in the war's wake.[55]

Despite the fact that the Army failed to create a cohesive national community capable of preventing the sectional tensions that would tear the nation apart, as Richard Bensel notes,[56] at the very least the economy the Army helped to build became a cornerstone of the Union's ultimate victory. One of the primary reasons for the North's triumph was its robust industrial base, which largely owed its existence to the Army's socioeconomic activities. The Army's promotion of new manufacturing methods, its technological innovation, and its building of a superior railroad infrastructure all made the North stronger and more capable of winning the war. Although the Army could not, in the end, prevent war from coming, it helped to underwrite the emerging economic juggernaut that ultimately triumphed.

NOTES

Introduction

1. On the importance of a robust public sector for economic development, see Robert H. Bates, *Prosperity and Violence: The Political Economy of Development* (New York: W. W. Norton, 2009); Mark Dincecco, *State Capacity and Economic Development: Present and Past* (New York: Cambridge University Press, 2017); Peter Evans and James E. Rauch, "Bureaucracy and Growth: A Cross-National Analysis of the Effects of 'Weberian' State Structures on Economic Growth," *American Sociological Review* 64:5 (October 1999): 748–65.

2. Stephen Skowronek, *Building a New American State: The Expansion of National Administrative Capacities, 1877–1920* (New York: Cambridge University Press, 1982), 24.

3. Elizabeth Sanders, "The Three American States," *Clio* 15:1 (2004–5): 1, 46–47. On the creation of the modern national security state, see Michael Hogan, *A Cross of Iron: Harry S. Truman and the Origins of the National Security State, 1945–1954* (New York: Cambridge University Press, 2000). On the impact of World War II, see James T. Sparrow, *Warfare State: World War II Americans and the Age of Big Government* (New York: Oxford University Press, 2011).

4. I thank Richard Bensel for suggesting the "socioeconomic" terminology.

5. For the purposes of this study, I define the "early American political economy" as the fluid combination of economic developments and political contributions to economic change from the period 1787–1860.

6. The core-periphery terminology (though not the precise conceptualization I use) is borrowed from work in comparative political sociology and especially Immanuel Wallerstein's world-systems theory. See Wallerstein, "The Rise and Future Demise of the World Capitalist System: Concepts for Comparative Analysis," *Comparative Studies in Society and History* 16:4 (September 1974): 387–415.

7. Adam Smith, *An Inquiry into the Nature and Causes of the Wealth of Nations* (Chicago: University of Chicago Press, 1976 [1776]), book 4, 477.

8. Joseph A. Schumpeter, *Capitalism, Socialism and Democracy* (New York: Harper and Brothers, 1942).

9. Alexis de Tocqueville, *Democracy in America: Historical-Critical Edition of De la démocratie en Amérique*, ed. Eduardo Nolla, trans. James T. Schleifer, bilingual French-English edition (Indianapolis: Liberty Fund, 2010), volume 1, accessed February 24, 2020, https://oll.libertyfund.org/titles/2285#Tocqueville_1532-01_EN_1203.

10. Albert Fishlow, *American Railroads and the Transformation of the Ante-bellum Economy* (Cambridge, MA: Harvard University Press, 1965); Fishlow, "Internal Transportation in the Nineteenth and Early Twentieth Centuries," in Stanley L. Engerman and Robert E. Gallman,

eds., *The Cambridge Economic History of the United States* (volume 2: *The Long Nineteenth Century*) (New York: Cambridge University Press, 2000): 543–642; Robert William Fogel, *Railroads and American Economic Growth: Essays in Econometric History* (Baltimore: Johns Hopkins University Press, 1964); George Rogers Taylor, *The Transportation Revolution, 1815–1860* (New York: Rinehart, 1951).

11. Gavin Wright, "The Role of Nationhood in the Economic Development of the USA," in Alice Teichova and Herbert Matis, eds., *Nation, State, and the Economy in History* (New York: Cambridge University Press, 2003), 387–403, quote at 395; Max M. Edling, *A Revolution in Favor of Government: Origins of the U.S. Constitution and the Making of the American State* (New York: Oxford University Press, 2003); Edling, *A Hercules in the Cradle: War, Money, and the American State, 1783–1867* (Chicago: University of Chicago Press, 2014).

12. Oscar Handlin and Mary Flug Handlin, *Commonwealth: A Study of the Role of Government in the American Economy: Massachusetts, 1774–1861* (New York: New York University Press, 1947); Louis Hartz, *Economic Policy and Democratic Thought: Pennsylvania, 1776–1860* (Cambridge, MA: Harvard University Press, 1948); William J. Novak, *The People's Welfare: Law and Regulation in Nineteenth-Century America* (Chapel Hill: University of North Carolina Press, 1996).

13. Naomi R. Lamoreaux and John Joseph Wallis, "Fixing the Machine That Would Not Go of Itself: State Constitutional Change and the Creation of an Open-Access Social Order in the Mid-Nineteenth Century United States," working paper (2018), available at https://economics.yale.edu/sites/default/files/files/Faculty/Lamoreaux/Lamoreaux%20Wallis%2C%20Fixing%20the%20Machine%2C%202018-09-16.pdf. See also John Joseph Wallis, "The Other Foundings: Federalism and the Constitutional Structure of American Government," in Douglas A. Irwin and Richard Sylla, eds., *Founding Choices: American Economic Policy in the 1790s* (Chicago: University of Chicago Press, 2011), 177–216.

14. Forest G. Hill, *Roads, Rails, and Waterways: The Army Engineers and Early Transportation* (Norman: University of Oklahoma Press, 1957); Hill, "Formative Relations of American Enterprise, Government, and Science," *Political Science Quarterly* 75:3 (September 1960): 400–419; Carter Goodrich, *Government Promotion of American Canals and Railroads, 1800–1890* (New York: Columbia University Press, 1960).

15. Laurence J. Malone, *Opening the West: Federal Internal Improvements Before 1860* (Westport, CT: Greenwood Press, 1998). More broadly, see Jeremy Atack and Peter Passell, *A New Economic View of American History* (2nd ed.) (New York: W. W. Norton, 1994), esp. chapters 6–9 and 16.

16. Francis Paul Prucha, *Broadax and Bayonet: The Role of the United States Army in the Development of the Northwest, 1815–1860* (Lincoln: University of Nebraska Press, 1973 [1953,]); William H. Goetzmann, *Army Exploration in the American West, 1803–1863* (Lincoln: University of Nebraska Press, 1959).

17. Colleen A. Dunlavy, *Politics and Industrialization: Early Railroads in the United States and Prussia* (Princeton, NJ: Princeton University Press, 1994); Zachary Callen, *Railroads and American Political Development: Infrastructure, Federalism, and State Building* (Lawrence: University Press of Kansas, 2016).

18. On Smith, see Warren J. Samuels, "The Political Economy of Adam Smith," *Ethics* 87:3 (April 1977): 189–207; Max Weber, *The Protestant Ethic and the "Spirit" of Capitalism and Other Writings* (New York: Penguin Books, 2002).

19. For example, see Joel Mokyr, "Technological Inertia in Economic History," *Journal of Economic History* 52:2 (June 1992): 325–38; David S. Landes, *The Wealth and Poverty of Nations: Why Some Are So Rich and Some Are So Poor* (New York: W.W. Norton, 1999); Gregory Clark, *A Farewell to Alms: A Brief Economic History of the World* (Princeton: Princeton University Press, 2008).

20. Charles Wolf, *Markets or Governments: Choosing Between Imperfect Alternatives* (Cambridge, MA: MIT Press, 1990).

21. Karl Polanyi, *The Great Transformation* (New York: Farrar and Rinehart, 1944).

22. Oliver E. Williamson, *The Economic Institutions of Capitalism: Firms, Markets, Relational Contracting* (New York: Free Press, 1985).

23. Douglass C. North, *Structure and Change in Economic History* (New York: Norton, 1981), 20; North, *Institutions, Institutional Change, and Economic Performance* (New York: Cambridge University Press, 1990). See also Ha-Joon Chang, *Kicking Away the Ladder: Policies and Institutions for Economic Development in Historical Perspective* (London: Anthem Press, 2002), and Kenneth W. Dam, *The Law-Growth Nexus: The Rule of Law and Economic Development* (Washington, DC: Brookings Institution Press, 2006). On how to think about the rule of law as a concept, see Matthew D. McCubbins, Daniel B. Rodriguez, and Barry R. Weingast, "The Rule of Law Unplugged," University of Texas School of Law, Public Law and Legal Theory Research Paper Series Number 158.

24. Douglass C. North and Barry R. Weingast, "Constitutions and Commitment: The Evolution of Institutional Governing Public Choice in Seventeenth-Century England," *Journal of Economic History* 49:4 (December 1989): 803–32. See also Weingast, "The Economic Role of Political Institutions: Market-Preserving Federalism and Economic Development," *Journal of Law, Economics, and Organization* 11:1 (April 1995): 1–31; Douglass C. North, "Institutions and Credible Commitment," *Journal of Institutional and Theoretical Economics* 149:1 (March 1993): 11–23.

25. Douglass C. North, John Joseph Wallis, and Barry C. Weingast, *Violence and Social Orders: A Conceptual Framework for Interpreting Recorded Human History* (New York: Cambridge University Press, 2012). See also Naomi R. Lamoreaux and John Joseph Wallis, eds., *Organizations, Civil Society, and the Roots of Development* (Chicago: University of Chicago Press, 2017); Stephan Haggard, Andrew MacIntyre, and Lydia Tiede, "The Rule of Law and Economic Development," *Annual Review of Political Science* 11 (2008): 205–34; Barry R. Weingast, "The Political Foundations of Democracy and the Rule of the Law," *American Political Science Review* 91:2 (June 1997): 245–63.

26. Margaret Levi, "The State of the Study of the State," in Ira Katznelson and Helen V. Milner, eds., *Political Science: The State of the Discipline* (New York: W. W. Norton, 2002), 33–55.

27. Dani Rodrik, Arvind Subramanian, and Francesco Trebbi, "Institutions Rule: The Primacy of Institutions over Geography and Integration in Economic Development," *Journal of Economic Growth* 9:2 (June 2004): 131–65.

28. Daron Acemoglu and James A. Robinson, *Why Nations Fail: The Origins of Power, Prosperity, and Poverty* (New York: Crown, 2012). For more on this question, see Stanley L. Engerman and Kenneth L. Sokoloff, "Debating the Role of Institutions in Political and Economic Development: Theory, History, and Findings," *Annual Review of Political Science* 11 (2008): 119–35; Peter Gourevitch, "The Role of Politics in Economic Development," *Annual Review of Political Science* 11 (2008): 137–59; Daron Acemoglu, Francisco A. Gallego, and James A.

Robinson, "Institutions, Human Capital, and Development," *Annual Review of Economics* 6 (2014): 875–912.

29. Peter A. Hall and David Soskice, eds., *Varieties of Capitalism: The Institutional Foundations of Comparative Advantage* (New York: Oxford University Press, 2001); Peter A. Hall and Kathleen Thelen, "Institutional Change in Varieties of Capitalism," *Socio-economic Review* 7:1 (January 2009): 7–34; Rafael LaPorta, Florencio Lopez-de-Silanes, and Andrei Shleifer, "The Economic Consequences of Legal Origins," *Journal of Economic Literature* 46:2 (June 2008): 285–332; Kathleen Thelen, "Varieties of Capitalism: Trajectories of Liberalization and the New Politics of Social Solidarity," *Annual Review of Political Science* 15 (2012): 137–59.

30. Paul Pierson, *Politics in Time: History, Institutions, and Social Analysis* (Princeton: Princeton University Press, 2004); B. Guy Peters, Jon Pierre, and Desmond S. King, "The Politics of Path Dependency: Political Conflict in Historical Institutionalism," *Journal of Politics* 67:4 (November 2005): 1275–1300.

31. Portions of this section of the chapter were previously published as William D. Adler and Andrew J. Polsky, "Building the New American Nation: Economic Development, Public Goods, and the Early U.S. Army," *Political Science Quarterly* 125:1 (Spring 2010): 87–110. I thank the Academy of Political Science for permission to reproduce that material here.

32. Robert E. Gallman, "Economic Growth and Structural Change in the Long Nineteenth Century," in Engerman and Gallman, *The Cambridge Economic History of the United States*, 1–55.

33. Thomas C. Cochran, *Frontiers of Change: Early Industrialism in America* (New York: Oxford University Press, 1981), chapters 2 and 3; Douglass C. North, *Growth and Welfare in the American Past: A New Economic History* (Englewood Cliffs, NJ: Prentice-Hall, 1966), 17–23; Jeremy Atack, Fred Bateman, and William N. Parker, "Northern Agriculture and the Westward Movement," in Engerman and Gallman, *The Cambridge Economic History of the United States*: 285–328. I do not enter here into the recent scholarly debate over the impact of slavery on the American economy and the so-called new history of capitalism. For more on that, see Alan L. Olmstead and Paul W. Rhode, "Cotton, Slavery, and the New History of Capitalism," *Explorations in Economic History* 67 (2018): 1–17; Eric Hilt, "Economic History, Historical Analysis, and the 'New History of Capitalism,'" *Journal of Economic History* 77:2 (June 2017): 511–36.

34. Peter H. Lindert and Jeffrey G. Williamson, *Unequal Gains: American Growth and Inequality since 1700* (Princeton, NJ: Princeton University Press, 2016), 10. See also 84–85.

35. Stanley Elkins and Eric McKitrick, *The Age of Federalism: The Early American Republic, 1788–1800* (New York: Oxford University Press, 1993), chapters 2 and 5; Gordon S. Wood, *Empire of Liberty: A History of the Early Republic, 1789–1815* (New York: Oxford University Press, 2009), chapters 3 and 10.

36. Edling, *A Revolution in Favor of Government*; Edling, *A Hercules in the Cradle*.

37. Patrick Griffin, *American Leviathan: Empire, Nation, and Revolutionary Frontier* (New York: Hill and Wang, 2008); Francis Paul Prucha, *The Sword of the Republic: The United States Army on the Frontier, 1783–1846* (Lincoln: University of Nebraska Press, 1969), especially chapters 1 and 3.

38. Stanley L. Engerman and Kenneth L. Sokoloff, *Economic Development in the Americas Since 1500: Endowments and Institutions* (New York: Cambridge University Press, 2012), chapter 7; Engerman and Sokoloff, "Once Upon a Time in the Americas: Land and Immigration Policies in the New World," in Dora L. Costa and Naomi R. Lamoreaux, eds., *Understanding Long-Run Economic Growth: Geography, Institutions, and the Knowledge Economy*

(Chicago: University of Chicago Press, 2011), 13–48; Farley Grubb, "U.S. Land Policy: Founding Choices and Outcomes, 1781–1802," in Irwin and Sylla, eds., *Founding Choices*, 259–89.

39. On the importance of railroad transportation to the growth of American agricultural production, see Jeremy Atack, "The Impact of Access to Rail Transportation on Agricultural Improvement: The American Midwest as a Test Case, 1850–1860," *Journal of Transport and Land Use* 4:2 (Summer 2011): 5–18; Dave Donaldson and Richard Hornbeck, "Railroads and American Economic Growth: A 'Market Access' Approach," *Quarterly Journal of Economics* 131:2 (May 2016): 799–858.

40. On the lack of engineers in the early nation, see Robert G. Angevine, *The Railroad and the State: War, Politics, and Technology in Nineteenth-Century America* (Stanford, CA: Stanford University Press, 2004), 22; Todd Shallat, *Structures in the Stream: Water, Science, and the Rise of the U.S. Army Corps of Engineers* (Austin: University of Texas Press, 1994), 94.

41. See Guillaume Vandenbroucke, "The American Frontier: Technology Versus Immigration," *Review of Economic Dynamics* 11:2 (April 2008): 283–301, which finds that productivity growth and lower cost of transportation were more important than increased immigration to U.S. economic growth in the nineteenth century; and Vandenbroucke, "The U.S. Westward Expansion," *International Economic Review* 49:1 (February 2008): 81–110, which sees lower transportation costs as central to westward migration. See also Berthold Herrendorf, James A. Schmitz, Jr., and Arilton Teixera, "The Role of Transportation in U.S. Economic Development: 1840–1860," *International Economic Review* 53:3 (August 2012): 693–716.

42. On the importance of sound governance and public goods provisioning to economic development, see Joachim Ahrens, *Governance and Economic Development: A Comparative Institutional Approach* (Northampton, MA: Edward Elgar, 2002).

43. Lindert and Williamson, *Unequal Gains*, 10.

44. Gallman, "Economic Growth and Structural Change," 5.

45. Lindert and Williamson, *Unequal Gains*, 103. Gallman estimates that "between 1774 and 1909 the American real gross national product increased about 175-fold, or at an average rate of 3.9 percent per year." See Gallman, "Economic Growth and Structural Change," 2.

46. For examples, see Robert W. Coakley, *The Role of Federal Military Forces in Domestic Disorders, 1789–1878* (Washington, DC: Center of Military History, 1988).

47. Mancur Olson, *The Logic of Collective Action: Public Goods and the Theory of Groups* (Cambridge, MA: Harvard University Press, 1965). I do not enter here into the debate over whether governments provide these goods more efficiently than markets. For more, see Paul Samuelson, "The Pure Theory of Public Expenditure," *Review of Economics and Statistics* 36:4 (November 1954): 387–89; William A. Niskanen, "Bureaucrats and Politicians," *Journal of Law and Economics* 18:3 (December 1975): 617–43; James Buchanan, *The Demand and Supply of Public Goods* (New York: McNally, 1968).

48. *Annals of Congress*, 10th Congress, 1st Session, at 1019–56 and 2196; Leonard D. White, *The Jeffersonians: A Study in Administrative History, 1801–1829* (New York: Macmillan, 1961), 532–34; Lindsay Schakenbach Regele, *Manufacturing Advantage: War, the State, and the Origins of American Industry, 1776–1848* (Baltimore: Johns Hopkins University Press, 2019), chapter 3.

49. Mark Pitcavage, "An Equitable Burden: The Decline of the State Militias, 1783–1858," Ph.D. dissertation, Ohio State University, 1995.

50. Prucha, *Broadax and Bayonet*; Prucha, *The Sword of the Republic*; Ira Katznelson, "Flexible Capacity: The Military and Early American Statebuilding," in Katznelson and Martin

Shefter, eds., *Shaped by War and Trade: International Influences on American Political Development* (Princeton, NJ: Princeton University Press, 2002), 82–110.

51. Prucha, *The Sword of the Republic*; Scott A. Silverstone, *Divided Union: The Politics of War in the Early American Republic* (Ithaca, NY: Cornell University Press, 2004).

52. Prucha, *Broadax and Bayonet*; Goetzmann, *Army Exploration in the American West*, especially chapter 10; Robert M. Utley, *Frontiersmen in Blue: The United States Army and the Indian, 1848–1865* (Lincoln: University of Nebraska Press, 1967).

53. Michael Mann, "The Autonomous Power of the State: Its Origins, Mechanisms and Results," *European Journal of Sociology* 25:2 (1984): 185–213; Mann, *The Sources of Social Power*, volume 1: *A History of Power from the Beginning to A.D. 1760* (Cambridge: Cambridge University Press, 1986), especially chapter 1; Mann, *The Sources of Social Power*, volume 2: *The Rise of Classes and Nation-States, 1760–1914* (Cambridge: Cambridge University Press, 1993), especially chapter 3.

54. Hillel Soifer and Matthias vom Hau, "Unpacking the *Strength* of the State: The Utility of State Infrastructural Power," *Studies in Comparative International Development* 43:3–4 (2008): 219–30, quote at 222.

55. Hillel Soifer, "State Infrastructural Power: Approaches to Conceptualization and Measurement," *Studies in Comparative International Development* 43:3–4 (2008): 231–51. In Soifer's terms, the way I use Mann's work here is a "national capabilities approach that sees state infrastructural power as a characteristic of the central state and highlights the extent of the resources at its disposal for exercising this power via its institutions of control" (235–36).

56. Jessica Fortin-Rittberger, "Exploring the Relationship Between Infrastructural and Coercive State Capacity," *Democratization* 21:7 (2014): 1244–64.

57. Harold D. Lasswell, *Who Gets What, When, How* (New York: Whittlesey House, 1936). For more on distributive politics, see Eric Kramon and Daniel N. Posner, "Who Benefits from Distributive Politics? How the Outcome One Studies Affects the Answer One Gets," *Perspectives on Politics* 11:2 (June 2013): 461–74; Miriam Golden and Brian Min, "Distributive Politics Around the World," *Annual Review of Political Science* 16 (2013): 73–99.

58. William B. Skelton, "The Commanding Generals and the Question of Civil Control in the Antebellum U.S. Army," *American Nineteenth Century History* 7:2 (June 2006): 153–72; Skelton, *An American Profession of Arms: The Army Officer Corps, 1784–1861* (Lawrence: University Press of Kansas, 1992).

59. John P. Burke, "The Institutional Presidency," in Michael Nelson, ed., *The Presidency and the Political System* (8th ed.) (Washington, DC: CQ Press, 2006), 383–409, especially 383–85.

60. Richard Pious, "The Presidency and the Nominating Process: Politics and Power," in Michael Nelson, ed., *The Presidency and the Political System* (8th ed.) (Washington, DC: CQ Press, 2006), 195–218.

61. Nelson W. Polsby, "The Institutionalization of the U.S. House of Representatives," *American Political Science Review* 62:1 (March 1968):144–68.

62. On entrepreneurship and political development, see Adam D. Sheingate, "Political Entrepreneurship, Institutional Change, and American Political Development," *Studies in American Political Development* 17:2 (Fall 2003): 185–203; Sheingate, "The Terrain of the Political Entrepreneur," in Stephen Skowronek and Matthew Glassman, eds., *Formative Acts: American Politics in the Making* (Philadelphia: University of Pennsylvania Press, 2007), 13–31. More generally, see John Kingdon, *Agendas, Alternatives, and Public Policies* (New York: Harper Collins, 1995).

63. Shirley Anne Warshaw, "The Formation and Use of the Cabinet," in Phillip G. Henderson, ed., *The Presidency Then and Now* (Lanham, MD: Rowman and Littlefield, 2000), 115–37; Lindsay M. Chervinsky, "George Washington and the First Presidential Cabinet," *Presidential Studies Quarterly* 48:1 (March 2018): 139–52.

64. On bureaucrats initiating policy reforms, see Jan Schnellenbach, "Public Entrepreneurship and the Economics of Reform," *Journal of Institutional Economics* 3:2 (2007): 183–202; Paul Teske and Mark Schneider, "The Bureaucratic Entrepreneur: The Case of City Managers," *Public Administration Review* 54:4 (July–August 1994): 331–40; Schneider and Teske, "Toward a Theory of the Political Entrepreneur: Evidence from Local Government," *American Political Science Review* 86:3 (September 1992): 737–47.

65. In particular, compare to Daniel P. Carpenter, *The Forging of Bureaucratic Autonomy: Reputations, Networks, and Policy Innovation in Executive Agencies, 1862–1928* (Princeton, NJ: Princeton University Press, 2001); Carpenter, *Reputation and Power: Organizational Image and Pharmaceutical Regulation at the FDA* (Princeton, NJ: Princeton University Press, 2010). I define bureaucratic autonomy in a similar manner to Carpenter: "when bureaucrats take actions consistent with their own wishes, actions to which politicians and organized interests defer even though they would prefer that other actions (or no action at all) be taken" (Carpenter, *The Forging of Bureaucratic Autonomy,* 4) and "bureaucratic autonomy prevails when a politically differentiated agency takes self-consistent action that neither politicians nor organized interests prefer but that they either cannot or will not overturn or constrain in the future" (Carpenter, *The Forging of Bureaucratic Autonomy,* 16). I specify my points of departure from Carpenter's theory in further detail in Chapter 4.

66. Soifer, "State Infrastructural Power"; Soifer and vom Hau, "Unpacking the *Strength* of the State"; Luciana Cingolani, Kaj Thomsson, and Denis de Crombrugghe, "Minding Weber More Than Ever? The Impacts of State Capacity and Bureaucratic Autonomy on Development Goals," *World Development* 72 (August 2015): 191–207.

67. Francis Fukuyama, "What Is Governance?" *Governance* 26:3 (July 2013): 347–68; Mark Dincecco and Gabriel Katz, "State Capacity and Long-Run Economic Performance," *Economic Journal* 126:590 (February 2016): 189–218.

68. Although he is concerned with a later era, see Richard Franklin Bensel, *Sectionalism and American Political Development: 1880–1980* (Madison: University of Wisconsin Press, 1984), on the topic of sectionalism.

69. This issue is discussed extensively in Angevine, *The Railroad and the State.*

70. J. C. A. Stagg, *Mr. Madison's War: Politics, Diplomacy, and Warfare in the Early American Republic, 1783–1830* (Princeton, NJ: Princeton University Press, 1983).

71. Matthew Karp, *This Vast Southern Empire: Slaveholders at the Helm of American Foreign Policy* (Cambridge, MA: Harvard University Press, 2016), chapters 4 and 5.

72. Silverstone, *Divided Union.*

73. Notable exceptions to this general pattern of overlooking the military's role include Bensel, *Yankee Leviathan: The Origins of Central State Authority in America, 1859–1877* (New York: Cambridge University Press, 1990); Robert P. Saldin, *War, the American State, and Politics Since 1898* (New York: Cambridge University Press, 2011); Marc Allen Eisner, *From Warfare State to Welfare State: World War I, Compensatory State Building, and the Limits of the Modern Order* (University Park: Pennsylvania State University Press, 2000); Aaron L. Friedberg, *In the Shadow of the Garrison State: America's Anti-statism and Its Cold War Grand Strategy* (Princeton, NJ: Princeton University Press, 2000); Bartholomew Sparrow, *From the*

Outside In: World War II and the American State (Princeton, NJ: Princeton University Press, 1996). The last three, however, look only at the modern period. Brian Balogh, *A Government out of Sight: The Mystery of National Authority in Nineteenth-Century America* (New York: Cambridge University Press, 2009), includes some material on the early military but focuses primarily on other institutions of the national government, while Sheldon D. Pollack, *War, Revenue, and State Building: Financing the Development of the American State* (Ithaca, NY: Cornell University Press, 2009), engages with the fiscal end of the equation rather than the military side.

74. Katznelson and Shefter, *Shaped by War and Trade.*

75. Skowronek, *Building a New American State*, especially chapter 2.

76. Bensel, *Yankee Leviathan.*

77. Theda Skocpol, *Protecting Soldiers and Mothers: The Political Origins of Social Policy in the United States* (Cambridge, MA: Harvard University Press, 1992).

78. Carpenter, *The Forging of Bureaucratic Autonomy.*

79. Some work prior to Skowronek had, in fact, already made the point that the early national government was not completely uninvolved in economic regulation; see for example John G. Burke, "Bursting Boilers and the Federal Power," *Technology and Culture* 7:1 (Winter 1966): 1–23.

80. Balogh, *Government out of Sight.* A somewhat similar argument about the modern era and government programs that are hidden from mainstream view is made by Suzanne Mettler, *The Submerged State: How Invisible Government Policies Undermine American Democracy* (Chicago: University of Chicago Press, 2011).

81. Colin Moore, *American Imperialism and the State, 1893–1921* (New York: Cambridge University Press, 2017); Moore, "State Building Through Partnership: Delegation, Public-Private Partnerships, and the Political Development of American Imperialism, 1898–1916," *Studies in American Political Development* 25:1 (April 2011): 27–55. On associational state building, see also Carol Nackenoff, "The Private Roots of American Political Development: The Immigrants' Protective League's 'Friendly and Sympathetic Touch,' 1908–1924," *Studies in American Political Development* 28:2 (October 2014): 129–60; Adam Sheingate, "Why Can't Americans See the State?" *The Forum* 7:4 (2010) https://doi.org/10.2202/1540-8884.1336; Chloe N. Thurston, *At the Boundaries of Homeownership: Credit, Discrimination, and the American State* (New York: Cambridge University Press, 2018).

82. Edling, *A Revolution in Favor of Government.* See also Gregory Ablavsky, "The Savage Constitution," *Duke Law Journal* 63:5 (February 2014): 999–1089.

83. Laura Jensen, *Patriots, Settlers, and the Origins of American Social Policy* (New York: Cambridge University Press, 2003); Michelle Landis Dauber, *The Sympathetic State: Disaster Relief and the Origins of the American Welfare State* (Chicago: University of Chicago Press, 2013.

84. Stefan Heumann, "State, Nation, and Empire: The Formation of the US," *Journal of Political Power* 4:3 (2011): 375–93; Heumann, "The Tutelary Empire: State- and Nation-Building in the 19th Century United States," Ph.D. dissertation, University of Pennsylvania, 2009.

85. David F. Ericson, "The Federal Government and Slavery: Following the Money Trail," *Studies in American Political Development* 19:1 (Spring 2005): 105–16; Ericson, *Slavery in the American Republic: Developing the Federal Government, 1791–1861* (Lawrence: University Press of Kansas, 2011); Ericson, "The United States Military, State Development, and Slavery in the Early Republic," *Studies in American Political Development* 31:1 (April 2017): 130–48.

86. Karp, *This Vast Southern Empire.*

87. Stephen J. Rockwell, *Indian Affairs and the Administrative State in the Nineteenth Century* (New York: Cambridge University Press, 2013); William H. Bergmann, *The American National State and the Early West* (New York: Cambridge University Press, 2012).

88. Andrew S. Kelly, "The Political Development of Scientific Capacity in the United States," *Studies in American Political Development* 28:1 (April 2014): 1–25.

89. Jerry L. Mashaw, "Recovering American Administrative Law: Federalist Foundations, 1787–1801," *Yale Law Journal* 115:6 (April 2006): 1256–344; Mashaw, "Reluctant Nationalists: Federal Administration and Administrative Law in the Republican Era, 1801–1829," *Yale Law Journal* 116:8 (June 2007): 1636–740; Mashaw, "Administration and 'The Democracy'": Administrative Law from Jackson to Lincoln, 1829–1861," *Yale Law Journal* 117:8 (June 2008): 1568–693; Mashaw, *Creating the Administrative Constitution: The Lost One Hundred Years of American Administrative Law* (New Haven, CT: Yale University Press, 2012).

90. Paul Frymer, *Building an American Empire: The Era of Territorial and Political Expansion* (Princeton, NJ: Princeton University Press, 2017); Frymer, "Building an American Empire: Territorial Expansion in the Antebellum Era," *UC Irvine Law Review* 1:3 (September 2011): 913–54; Frymer, "'A Rush and a Push and the Land Is Ours': Territorial Expansion, Land Policy, and U.S. State Formation," *Perspectives on Politics* 12:1 (March 2014): 119–44.

91. Regele, *Manufacturing Advantage.*

92. Richard R. John, *Spreading the News: The American Postal System from Franklin to Morse* (Cambridge, MA: Harvard University Press, 1995). The importance of the Post Office to technological innovation has also been empirically confirmed by Daron Acemoglu, Jacob Moscona, and James A. Robinson, "State Capacity and American Technology: Evidence from the Nineteenth Century," *American Economic Review* 106:5 (May 2016): 61–67. On the connections between postal offices, state capacity, and economic development, see Jeffrey L. Jensen and Adam J. Ramey, "Going Postal: State Capacity and Violent Dispute Resolution," *Journal of Comparative Economics* 48:4 (December 2020): 779–96.

93. Richard R. John, "Governmental Institutions as Agents of Change: Rethinking American Political Development in the Early Republic, 1787–1835," *Studies in American Political Development* 11:2 (Fall 1997): 347–80; John, "Ruling Passions: Political Economy in Nineteenth-Century America," *Journal of Policy History* 18:1 (2006): 1–18.

94. Desmond King and Robert C. Lieberman, "Ironies of State Building: A Comparative Perspective on the American State," *World Politics* 61:3 (July 2009): 547–88.

95. William J. Novak, "The Myth of the 'Weak' American State," *American Historical Review* 113:3 (June 2008): 752–72; Gautham Rao, "The New Historiography of the Early Federal Government: Institutions, Contexts, and the Imperial State," *William and Mary Quarterly* 77:1 (January 2020): 97–128. See also Rao, *National Duties: Custom Houses and the Making of the American State* (Chicago: University of Chicago Press, 2016); Rao, "Administering Entitlement: Governance, Public Health Care, and the Early American State," *Law and Social Inquiry* 37:3 (Summer 2012): 627–56.

96. The extensive literature on the relationship between war and state building includes Richard Bean, "War and the Birth of the Nation State," *Journal of Economic History* 33:1 (March 1973): 203–21; Brian M. Downing, *The Military Revolution and Political Change: Origins of Democracy and Autocracy in Early Modern Europe* (Princeton, NJ: Princeton University Press, 1992); Thomas Ertman, *Birth of the Leviathan: Building States and Regimes in Medieval and Early Modern Europe* (New York: Cambridge University Press, 1997); Karen A.

Rasler and William R. Thompson, "War Making and State Making: Government Expenditures, Tax Revenues, and Global Wars," *American Political Science Review* 79:2 (June 1985): 491–507; Hendrik Spruyt, *The Sovereign State and Its Competitors: An Analysis of Systems Change* (Princeton, NJ: Princeton University Press, 1994); Charles Tilly, ed., *The Formation of National States in Western Europe* (Princeton, NJ: Princeton University Press, 1975); Tilly, "War Making and State Making as Organized Crime," in Peter Evans, Dietrich Rueschemeyer, and Theda Skocpol, eds., *Bringing the State Back In* (New York: Cambridge University Press, 1985), 169–91; Tilly, *Coercion, Capital, and European States,* A.D. *990–1992* (Malden, MA: Blackwell, 1990); Sidney Tarrow, *War, States, and Contention: A Comparative Historical Study* (Ithaca, NY: Cornell University Press, 2015). One book that raises this issue in comparison to American developments is Bruce D. Porter, *War and the Rise of the State: The Military Foundations of Modern Politics* (New York: Free Press, 1994).

97. Sanders, "The Three American States."

98. Friedberg, *In the Shadow of the Garrison State*; Hogan, *A Cross of Iron*; Sparrow, *From the Outside In*; Amy B. Zegart, *Flawed by Design: The Evolution of the CIA, JCS, and NSC* (Stanford, CA: Stanford University Press, 1999).

99. Katznelson, "Flexible Capacity."

100. Katznelson, "Flexible Capacity," 89.

101. Merritt Roe Smith, *Harpers Ferry Armory and the New Technology: The Challenge of Change* (Ithaca, NY: Cornell University Press, 1977); Smith, "Army Ordnance and the 'American System' of Manufacturing, 1815–1861," in Smith, ed., *Military Enterprise and Technological Change: Perspectives on the American Experience* (Cambridge, MA: MIT Press, 1985), 39–86.

102. Regele, *Manufacturing Advantage.*

103. Mark R. Wilson, *The Business of Civil War: Military Mobilization and the State, 1861–1865* (Baltimore: Johns Hopkins University Press, 2006); Wilson, "The Politics of Procurement: Military Origins of Bureaucratic Autonomy," *Journal of Policy History* 18:1 (2006): 44–73.

104. Todd Shallat, "Building Waterways, 1802–1861: Science and the United States Army in Early Public Works," *Technology and Culture* 31:1 (January 1990): 18–50; Shallat, *Structures in the Stream.*

105. Angevine, *The Railroad and the State.*

106. Christopher McGrory Klyza, "The United States Army, Natural Resources, and Political Development in the Nineteenth Century," *Polity* 35:1 (Fall 2002): 1–28.

107. Katznelson, "Flexible Capacity"; Ericson, "The Federal Government and Slavery"; Klyza, "The United States Army, Natural Resources, and Political Development"; Angevine, *The Railroad and the State.*

108. Bensel, *Yankee Leviathan*; Theodore J. Crackel, *Mr. Jefferson's Army: Political and Social Reform of the Military Establishment, 1801–1809* (New York: New York University Press, 1987); Crackel, "The Military Academy in the Context of Jeffersonian Reform," in Robert M. S. McDonald, ed., *Thomas Jefferson's Military Academy: Founding West Point* (Charlottesville: University of Virginia Press, 2004), 99–117; Richard H. Kohn, *Eagle and Sword: The Beginnings of the Military Establishment in America* (New York: Free Press, 1975).

109. Angevine, *The Railroad and the State*; John Lauritz Larson, *Internal Improvement: National Public Works and the Promise of Popular Government in the Early United States* (Chapel Hill: University of North Carolina Press, 2001); Stephen Minicucci, "Internal Improvements and the Union, 1790–1860," *Studies in American Political Development* 18:2 (Fall 2004): 160–85.

110. Shallat, "Building Waterways"; Shallat, *Structures in the Stream*; Smith, "Army Ordnance and the 'American System'"; Wilson, "The Politics of Procurement."

111. Andrew J. Polsky, "'Mr. Lincoln's Army' Revisited: Partisanship, Institutional Position, and Union Army Command, 1861–1865," *Studies in American Political Development* 16:2 (Fall 2002): 176–207; William B. Skelton, "Professionalization in the U.S. Army Officer Corps During the Age of Jackson," *Armed Forces and Society* 1:4 (August 1975): 443–71; Skelton, *An American Profession of Arms*.

112. Ian Lustick, "History, Historiography, and Political Science: Multiple Historical Records and the Problem of Selection Bias," *American Political Science Review* 90:3 (September 1996): 605–18.

Chapter 1

1. On the importance of the rule of law to economic development, see Douglass C. North, *Institutions, Institutional Change, and Economic Performance* (New York: Cambridge University Press, 1990); on the state's need to preserve authority and manage violence, see Douglass C. North, John Joseph Wallis, and Barry C. Weingast, *Violence and Social Orders: A Conceptual Framework for Interpreting Recorded Human History* (New York: Cambridge University Press, 2012). A critique of studies that linearly link law to economic performance can be found in Harry N. Scheiber, "Regulation, Property Rights, and Definition of 'The Market': Law and the American Economy," *Journal of Economic History* 41:1 (March 1981): 103–9.

2. Bruce D. Porter, *War and the Rise of the State: The Military Foundations of Modern Politics* (New York: Free Press, 1994), 3.

3. Christopher McGrory Klyza, "The United States Army, Natural Resources, and Political Development in the Nineteenth Century," *Polity* 35:1 (Fall 2002): 1–28. See also Mancur Olson, *The Logic of Collective Action: Public Goods and the Theory of Groups* (Cambridge, MA: Harvard University Press, 1965).

4. *Annals of Congress*, 10th Congress, 1st Session, at 1019–56 and 2196; Leonard D. White, *The Jeffersonians: A Study in Administrative History, 1801–1829* (New York: Macmillan, 1961), 532–34.

5. David C. Hendrickson, *Peace Pact: The Lost World of the American Founding* (Lawrence: University Press of Kansas, 2003); Richard H. Kohn, *Eagle and Sword: The Beginnings of the Military Establishment in America* (New York: Free Press, 1975), 99.

6. Kevin M. Gannon, "Escaping 'Mr. Jefferson's Plan of Destruction': New England Federalists and the Idea of a Northern Confederacy, 1803–1804," *Journal of the Early Republic* 21:3 (Autumn 2001): 413–43, quote on 414–15.

7. James Madison, Alexander Hamilton, and John Jay, *The Federalist Papers*, ed. Isaac Kramnick (New York: Penguin, 1987).

8. Madison, Hamilton, and Jay, *The Federalist Papers*, 115.

9. Madison, Hamilton, and Jay, *The Federalist Papers*, 116–17.

10. On opposition to standing armies, see Lawrence Delbert Cress, *Citizens in Arms: The Army and Militia in American Society to the War of 1812* (Chapel Hill: University of North Carolina Press, 1982); Cress, "Radical Whiggery on the Role of the Military: Ideological Roots of the American Revolutionary Militia," *Journal of the History of Ideas* 40:1 (January–March 1979): 43–60; Marcus Cunliffe, *Soldiers and Civilians: The Martial Spirit in America, 1775–1865* (New York: Little, Brown, 1968); Kohn, *Eagle and Sword*, chapter 1.

11. Kohn, *Eagle and Sword*, 70.

12. Max M. Edling, *A Revolution in Favor of Government: Origins of the U.S. Constitution and the Making of the American State* (New York: Oxford University Press, 2003), chapter 5.

13. Harry M. Ward, *The Department of War, 1781–1795* (Pittsburgh: University of Pittsburgh Press, 1962), 42.

14. Ward, *The Department of War*, 75–78; Keith L. Dougherty, *Collective Action Under the Articles of Confederation* (New York: Cambridge University Press, 2001), chapter 6.

15. Hendrickson, *Peace Pact*; Kohn, *Eagle and Sword*, 74–75, 83–85; Porter, *War and the Rise of the State*, 252–53.

16. Kohn, *Eagle and Sword*, 74. See also Edling, *A Revolution in Favor of Government*, chapter 5.

17. U.S. Constitution, Article I, Section 8; Kohn, *Eagle and Sword*, 75–81.

18. Robert W. Coakley, *The Role of Federal Military Forces in Domestic Disorders, 1789–1878* (Washington, DC: Center of Military History, 1988), 3–15.

19. Ward, *The Department of War*, 100–102.

20. Coakley, *The Role of Federal Military Forces*, 19–23; the law was made permanent in 1795 (67).

21. John R. Howe, Jr., "Republican Thought and the Political Violence of the 1790s," *American Quarterly* 19:2 (Summer 1967): 147–65; Stanley Elkins and Eric McKitrick, *The Age of Federalism: The Early American Republic, 1788–1800* (New York: Oxford University Press, 1993), chapter 15.

22. Theodore J. Crackel, *Mr. Jefferson's Army: Political and Social Reform of the Military Establishment, 1801–1809* (New York: New York University Press, 1987), 42–44; on the demobilization of the New Army, see Elkins and McKitrick, *The Age of Federalism*, 730–32; Kohn, *Eagle and Sword*, chapter 13.

23. Crackel, *Mr. Jefferson's Army*, 38–45.

24. Henry Dearborn to Brigadier General James Wilkinson, May 12, 1801, and Dearborn to the Commanding Officer of West Point, April 15, 1801, in National Archives, Records of the Office of the Secretary of War (RG 107), Letters Sent by the Secretary of War Relating to Military Affairs, 1800–1889; Crackel, *Mr. Jefferson's Army*, 58–65. For a somewhat strained interpretation of Jefferson's constitutional position in relation to West Point, see David N. Mayer, "'Necessary and Proper': West Point and Jefferson's Constitutionalism," in Robert M. S. McDonald, ed., *Thomas Jefferson's Military Academy: Founding West Point* (Charlottesville: University of Virginia Press, 2004), 54–76.

25. Miscellaneous Letters, in National Archives, Records of the Office of the Secretary of War (RG 107), Letters Sent to the President by the Secretary of War, 1800–1863.

26. Crackel, *Mr. Jefferson's Army*, 38–45, 60–61. Crackel, "The Military Academy in the Context of Jeffersonian Reform," in McDonald, *Thomas Jefferson's Military Academy*, 99–117, further argues that Jefferson's reforms of the Army fit neatly into his broader policies regarding national power.

27. Kohn, *Eagle and Sword*, 303. Porter, *War and the Rise of the State*, 255, disagrees, arguing that Jefferson hobbled military capabilities until the Civil War; this interpretation seems dubious, given the evidence for a highly capable antebellum Army.

28. Scott A. Silverstone, *Divided Union: The Politics of War in the Early American Republic* (Ithaca, NY: Cornell University Press, 2004), 74–80.

29. White, *The Jeffersonians*, 423–29.

30. Coakley, *The Role of Federal Military Forces*, 88. Data on the expanded size of the Army is from Susan B. Carter, Scott Sigmund Gartner, Michael R. Haines, Alan L. Olmstead, Richard Sutch, and Gavin Wright, eds., *Historical Statistics of the United States: Earliest Times to the Present* (Millennial Edition), volume 5 (New York: Cambridge University Press, 2006), 353. The officer corps was also expanded from two hundred to five hundred and filled with loyal Republicans, according to Crackel, *Mr. Jefferson's Army*, 170.

31. Crackel, *Mr. Jefferson's Army*, 169–78.

32. White, *The Jeffersonians*, 431–32.

33. White, *The Jeffersonians*, 460–64; Coakley, *The Role of Federal Military Forces*, 88–90.

34. Silverstone, *Divided Union*, 81–84; Coakley, *The Role of Federal Military Forces*, 89–90; White, *The Jeffersonians*, 468–73. On the embargo's effectiveness and its impact on Britain, see Jeffrey A. Frankel, "The 1807–1809 Embargo Against Great Britain," *Journal of Economic History* 42:2 (June 1982): 291–308.

35. White, *The Jeffersonians*, 468–73.

36. Brian Schoen, "Calculating the Price of Union: Republican Economic Nationalism and the Origins of Southern Sectionalism, 1790–1828," *Journal of the Early Republic* 23:2 (Summer 2003): 173–206.

37. William W. Freehling, *Prelude to Civil War: The Nullification Controversy in South Carolina, 1816–1836* (New York: Harper and Row, 1966).

38. David F. Ericson, "The Nullification Crisis, American Republicanism, and the Force Bill Debate," *Journal of Southern History* 61:2 (May 1995): 249–70; Schoen, "Calculating the Price of Union"; Keith E. Whittington, "The Political Constitution of Federalism in Antebellum America: The Nullification Debate as an Illustration of Informal Mechanisms of Constitutional Change," *Publius* 26:2 (Spring 1996): 1–24.

39. Coakley, *The Role of Federal Military Forces*, 94–98.

40. Richard B. Latner, "The Nullification Crisis and Republican Subversion," *Journal of Southern History* 43:1 (February 1977): 19–38, quote on 31.

41. Latner, "The Nullification Crisis."

42. Lewis Cass to Winfield Scott, November 18, 1832; Cass to Scott, December 3, 1832; Cass to Scott, January 26, 1833, in National Archives, Records of the Office of the Secretary of War (RG 107), Confidential and Unofficial Letters Sent by the Secretary of War, 1814–1847.

43. Lewis Cass to Col. Twiggs or Officer Commanding at the Arsenal, Augusta, December 14, 1832; Cass to Wilson Sumpkin, Governor of Georgia, December 14, 1832, in National Archives, Records of the Office of the Secretary of War (RG 107), Confidential and Unofficial Letters Sent by the Secretary of War, 1814–1847.

44. Coakley, *The Role of Federal Military Forces*, 94–101.

45. Coakley, *The Role of Federal Military Forces*, 101–3; Ericson, "The Nullification Crisis"; Freehling, *Prelude to Civil War.*

46. Richard B. Morris, "Andrew Jackson, Strikebreaker," *American Historical Review* 55:1 (October 1949): 54–68; Coakley, *The Role of Federal Military Forces*, 105–6.

47. Samuel Watson, "United States Army Officers Fight the 'Patriot War': Responses to Filibustering on the Canadian Border, 1837–1839," *Journal of the Early Republic* 18:3 (Autumn 1998): 485–519; Coakley, *The Role of Federal Military Forces*, 110–16.

48. Coakley, *The Role of Federal Military Forces*, 115.

49. Joel R. Poinsett to Winfield Scott, October 26, 1839, in National Archives, Records of the Office of the Secretary of War (RG 107), Confidential and Unofficial Letters Sent by the Secretary of War, 1814–1847.

50. Watson, "United States Army Officers."

51. Report of the Major General of the Army, Alexander Macomb, November 29, 1838, 25th Congress, 3rd Session, H. Doc. 2 (U.S. Serial Set) (all Reports from the Secretary of War or officers contained in the U.S. Serial Set); Coakley, *The Role of Federal Military Forces*, 112–17.

52. Report of the Major General of the Army, November 29, 1838; Coakley, *The Role of Federal Military Forces*, 118–9.

53. Report of the Major General Commanding the Army, Alexander Macomb, November 27, 1839, 26th Congress, 1st Session, S. Doc. 1; Report of the Secretary of War, J. R. Poinsett, December 5, 1840, 26th Congress, 2nd Session, S. Doc. 1; Annual Message from the President of the United States to the Two Houses of Congress, December 2, 1839, 26th Congress, 1st Session, S. Doc. 1.

54. Annual Message from the President of the United States to the Two Houses of Congress, December 9, 1840, 26th Congress, 2nd Session, S. Doc. 1.

55. Coakley, *The Role of Federal Military Forces*, 119–25; William W. Wiecek, "'A Peculiar Conservatism' and the Dorr Rebellion: Constitutional Clash in Jacksonian America," *American Journal of Legal History* 22:3 (July 1978): 237–53.

56. Coakley, *The Role of Federal Military Forces*, 119–25; Wiecek, "'A Peculiar Conservatism.'"

57. Coakley, *The Role of Federal Military Forces*, 127.

58. Seth Rockman, "The Unfree Origins of American Capitalism," in Cathy Matson, ed., *The Economy of Early America: Historical Perspectives and New Directions* (University Park: Pennsylvania State University Press, 2006), 335–61.

59. Tommy R. Young II, "The United States Army and the Institution of Slavery in Louisiana, 1803–1835," *Louisiana Studies* 13 (Fall 1974): 201–22, quote on 202.

60. David F. Ericson, *Slavery in the American Republic: Developing the Federal Government, 1791–1861* (Lawrence: University Press of Kansas, 2011); Matthew Karp, *This Vast Southern Empire: Slaveholders at the Helm of American Foreign Policy* (Cambridge, MA: Harvard University Press, 2016).

61. Matthew Mason, *Slavery and Politics in the Early American Republic* (Chapel Hill: University of North Carolina Press, 2006), 107.

62. Report of the Major General of the Army, Alexander Macomb, November 1831, 22nd Congress, 1st Session, H. Doc. 2.

63. Young, "The United States Army and the Institution of Slavery."

64. Coakley, *The Role of Federal Military Forces*, 128–37. For more on the federal government's involvement in enforcing the fugitive slave law, see David F. Ericson, "The Federal Government and Slavery: Following the Money Trail," *Studies in American Political Development* 19:1 (Spring 2005): 105–16; Don Fehrenbacher, *The Slaveholding Republic: An Account of the United States Government's Relations to Slavery* (New York: Oxford University Press, 2001), especially chapters 7 and 8. See also James Oakes, "The Political Significance of Slave Resistance," *History Workshop Journal* 22:1 (1986): 89–107.

65. Karp, *This Vast Southern Empire*, 220.

66. Elkins and McKitrick, *The Age of Federalism*, 462.

67. Max M. Edling and Mark D. Kaplanoff, "Alexander Hamilton's Fiscal Reform: Transforming the Structure of Taxation in the Early Republic," *William and Mary Quarterly* 61:4 (October 2004): 713–44.

68. Coakley, *The Role of Federal Military Forces*, 28–65.

69. Elkins and McKitrick, *The Age of Federalism*, 461–85; Kohn, *Eagle and Sword*, 158–70.

70. For more on the Jay Treaty, see Elkins and McKitrick, *The Age of Federalism*, 406–36.

71. Elkins and McKitrick, *The Age of Federalism*, 643–62.

72. See Elkins and McKitrick, *The Age of Federalism*, 549–79, for more on the XYZ Affair.

73. Elkins and McKitrick, *The Age of Federalism*, 595; Kohn, *Eagle and Sword*, 221–29.

74. On the Alien and Sedition Acts, see Geoffrey R. Stone, *Perilous Times: Free Speech in Wartime from the Sedition Act of 1798 to the War on Terrorism* (New York: Norton, 2004), chapter 1; Elkins and McKitrick, *The Age of Federalism*, 590–93; Kohn, *Eagle and Sword*, chapter 10.

75. Elkins and McKitrick, *The Age of Federalism*, 696–700; Coakley, *The Role of Federal Military Forces*, 69–77; Dwight F. Henderson, "Treason, Sedition, and Fries' Rebellion," *American Journal of Legal History* 14:4 (October 1970): 308–18.

76. Coakley, *The Role of Federal Military Forces*, 77–82.

77. Coakley, *The Role of Federal Military Forces*, 82–83, quote on 83.

78. John H. Aldrich, *Why Parties? The Origin and Transformation of Political Parties in America* (Chicago: University of Chicago Press, 1995), chapter 5.

79. Fehrenbacher, *The Slaveholding Republic*; Karp, *This Vast Southern Empire*, chapters 3 and 4.

80. Annual Message of the President of the United States to the Two Houses of Congress, December 2, 1851, 32nd Congress, 1st Session, S. Exec. Doc. 1; Durwood Ball, *Army Regulars on the Western Frontier, 1848–1861* (Norman: University of Oklahoma Press, 2001), 89–90.

81. Ball, *Army Regulars*, 127–38; Robert E. May, "Young American Males and Filibustering in the Age of Manifest Destiny: The United States Army as a Cultural Mirror," *Journal of American History* 78:3 (December 1991): 857–86.

82. Ball, *Army Regulars*, 93–97; Silverstone, *Divided Union*, chapter 6

83. Karp, *This Vast Southern Empire*, 199–215.

84. For several examples of officers and enlisted Army regulars assisting filibustering attempts, see May, "Young American Males"; see also Ball, *Army Regulars*, chapter 7.

85. Ball, *Army Regulars*, 93–103; May, "Young American Males."

86. Jefferson Davis to John E. Wool, January 12, 1854, in National Archives, Records of the Office of the Secretary of War (RG 107), Letters Sent by the Secretary of War Relating to Military Affairs, 1800–1889.

87. Ball, *Army Regulars*, 97–103; May, "Young American Males."

88. Ball, *Army Regulars*, 103–6; Coakley, *The Role of Federal Military Forces*, 137–44.

89. Report of the Secretary of War, Jefferson Davis, December 1, 1856, 34th Congress, 3rd Session, S. Exec. Doc. 5. On southern fears of expanded national power, see Mason, *Slavery and Politics in the Early American Republic*, especially 235–37.

90. Report of the Secretary of War, Jefferson Davis, December 1, 1856, 34th Congress, 3rd Session, S. Exec. Doc. 5; Coakley, *The Role of Federal Military Forces*, 145–58.

91. Coakley, *The Role of Federal Military Forces*, 173–87; Ball, *Army Regulars*, 181–87.

92. Ball, *Army Regulars*, 153–63; Coakley, *The Role of Federal Military Forces*, 194–209; William H. Goetzmann, *Army Exploration in the American West, 1803–1863* (Lincoln: University of Nebraska Press, 1959), chapter 10.

93. Ball, *Army Regulars*, 161–71; Coakley, *The Role of Federal Military Forces*, 209–26.

94. Fred Anderson and Andrew Cayton, *The Dominion of War: Empire and Liberty in North America, 1500–2000* (New York: Penguin, 2005), chapter 4; R. Douglas Hurt, *The Indian Frontier, 1763–1846* (Albuquerque: University of New Mexico Press, 2002); Francis Paul Prucha, *The Sword of the Republic: The United States Army on the Frontier, 1783–1846* (Lincoln: University of Nebraska Press, 1969), 1–6; Robert M. Utley, *Frontiersmen in Blue: The United States Army and the Indian, 1848–1865* (Lincoln: University of Nebraska Press, 1967), chapter 1.

95. Francois Furstenberg, "The Significance of the Trans-Appalachian Frontier in Atlantic History," *American Historical Review* 113:3 (June 2008): 647–77, quote at 665.

96. On international cooperation and competition with native tribes, see Richard White, *The Middle Ground: Indians, Empires, and Republics in the Great Lakes Region, 1650–1815* (New York: Cambridge University Press, 1991).

97. Kohn, *Eagle and Sword*, 41–43.

98. Alan S. Brown, "The Role of the Army in Western Settlement: Josiah Harmar's Command, 1785–1790," *Pennsylvania Magazine of History and Biography* 93 (April 1969): 161–78; Kohn, *Eagle and Sword*, 65–68; Prucha, *Sword of the Republic*, 7–8.

99. Ward, *The Department of War*, 68.

100. Anderson and Cayton, *Dominion of War*, 191–95. See also Colin G. Calloway, *The Shawnees and the War for America* (New York: Viking, 2007).

101. Kohn, *Eagle and Sword*, 92–104; Prucha, *Sword of the Republic*, chapter 3; Henry Knox to the Governor of Georgia, July 11, 1792, and August 31, 1792, in National Archives, Records of the Office of the Secretary of War (RG 107), Correspondence of the War Department Relating to Indian Affairs, Military Pensions, and Fortifications, 1791–1797.

102. Andrew R. L. Cayton, "'Separate Interests' and the Nation-State: The Washington Administration and the Origins of Regionalism in the Trans-Appalachian West," *Journal of American History* 79:1 (June 1992): 39–67, quote on 47.

103. Cayton, "'Separate Interests.'"

104. Anderson and Cayton, *Dominion of War*, 191–95; Cayton, "'Separate Interests,'" 51–53; Hurt, *The Indian Frontier*, 108–15; Kohn, *Eagle and Sword*, 104–26, 139–57; Prucha, *Sword of the Republic*, chapter 2.

105. William H. Bergmann, *The American National State and the Early West* (New York: Cambridge University Press, 2012), chapter 2.

106. Henry Dearborn to His Excellency George Clinton, Esq., October 23, 1801, in National Archives, Records of the Office of the Secretary of War (RG 107), Miscellaneous Letters Sent by the Secretary of War, 1800–1809.

107. John J. Carter, *Covert Operations as a Tool of Presidential Foreign Policy in American History from 1800 to 1920: Foreign Policy in the Shadows* (Lewiston, NY: Edwin Mellen Press, 2000), 21–22.

108. Hurt, *The Indian Frontier*, 116–19.

109. Bergmann, *The American National State and the Early West*, 250–51; Prucha, *Sword of the Republic*, 104–18. For a more negative view of the Army's importance, see Roger L. Nichols, "The Army and the Indians 1800–1830—a Reappraisal: The Missouri Valley Example," *Pacific Historical Review* 41 (1972): 151–68.

110. David S. Heidler and Jeanne T. Heidler, *Old Hickory's War: Andrew Jackson and the Quest for Empire* (Baton Rouge: Louisiana State University Press, 2003), 7–27; Anderson and

Cayton, *Dominion of War*, 231–34; Hurt, *The Indian Frontier*, 124–33; Prucha, *Sword of the Republic*, 112–18.

111. John C. Calhoun to Major General Andrew Jackson, Nashville, TN, December 26, 1817, in National Archives, Records of the Office of the Secretary of War (RG 107), Letters Sent by the Secretary of War Relating to Military Affairs, 1800–1889.

112. Heidler and Heidler, *Old Hickory's War*.

113. John C. Calhoun to General Andrew Jackson, December 24, 1819, in National Archives, Records of the Office of the Secretary of War (RG 107), Confidential and Unofficial Letters Sent by the Secretary of War, 1814–1847.

114. John Missall and Mary Lou Missall, *The Seminole Wars: America's Longest Indian Conflict* (Gainesville: University Press of Florida, 2004), 52–72.

115. A. J. Langguth, *Driven West: Andrew Jackson and the Trail of Tears to the Civil War* (New York: Simon & Schuster, 2010), 43–88.

116. Annual Message from the President of the United States to the Two Houses of Congress, December 7, 1830, 21st Congress, 2nd Session, S. Doc. 1; Annual Message from the President of the United States to the Two Houses of Congress, December 6, 1831, 22nd Congress, 1st Session, H. Doc. 2.

117. Quote from Report of the Secretary of War, December 1830, 21st Congress, 2nd Session, S. Doc. 1; see also Report of the Bureau of Indian Affairs, November 17, 1829, 21st Congress, 1st Session, S. Doc. 1; Hurt, *The Indian Frontier*, 138–44; Prucha, *Sword of the Republic*, 254–57.

118. Hurt, *The Indian Frontier*, 144–51; Prucha, *Sword of the Republic*, 258–61.

119. Hurt, *The Indian Frontier*, 154–63; Prucha, *Sword of the Republic*, 262–68; John Eaton to President Jackson, February 21, 1831, in National Archives, Records of the Office of the Secretary of War (RG 107), Letters Sent to the President by the Secretary of War, 1800–1863.

120. Report of the Major General of the Army, Alexander Macomb, November 1831, 22nd Congress, 1st Session, H. Doc. 2; Hurt, *The Indian Frontier*, 164–88; Prucha, *Sword of the Republic*, 212–31. On the removal of the Potawatomies, see Joel Poinsett to General Macomb, June 19, 1837, and Poinsett to Major General Edmund P. Gaines, July 28, 1837, in National Archives, Records of the Office of the Secretary of War (RG 107), Letters Sent by the Secretary of War Relating to Military Affairs, 1800–1889.

121. Annual Message from the President of the United States to the Two Houses of Congress, December 6, 1836, 24th Congress, 2nd Session, H. Doc. 2; Annual Message from the President of the United States to the Two Houses of Congress, December 5, 1837, 25th Congress, 2nd Session, S. Doc. 1; Annual Message from the President of the United States to the Two Houses of Congress, December 4, 1838, 25th Congress, 3rd Session, H. Doc. 2; Report of the Secretary of War, Lewis Cass, November 30, 1835, 24th Congress, 1st Session, H. Doc. 2; Report of the Secretary of War Ad Interim, B. F. Butler, December 3, 1836, 24th Congress, 2nd Session, H. Doc. 2; Report of the Secretary of War, Joel R. Poinsett, December 2, 1837, 25th Congress, 2nd Session, S. Doc. 1; Report of the Secretary of War, Joel R. Poinsett, November 28, 1838, 25th Congress, 3rd Session, H. Doc. 2; Missall and Missall, *The Seminole Wars*, chapters 5–10; Prucha, *Sword of the Republic*, chapter 14.

122. Report of the Secretary of War, John H. Eaton, November 30, 1829, 21st Congress, 1st Session, S. Doc. 1.

123. Report of the Secretary of War, Lewis Cass, November 27, 1834, 23rd Congress, 2nd Session, S. Doc. 1.

124. Annual Message from the President of the United States to the Two Houses of Congress, December 2, 1845, 29th Congress, 1st Session, S. Doc. 1; Hurt, *The Indian Frontier*, chapter 8; Prucha, *Sword of the Republic*, chapter 18.

125. Report of the Secretary of War, William L. Marcy, November 29, 1845, 29th Congress, 1st Session, S. Doc. 1.

126. Report of the Secretary of War, Charles M. Conrad, December 4, 1852, 32nd Congress, 2nd Session, S. Exec. Doc. 1. See also Report of the Secretary of War, Charles M. Conrad, November 29, 1851, 32nd Congress, 1st Session, S. Exec. Doc. 1; Report of the Secretary of War, Jefferson Davis, December 1, 1853, 33rd Congress, 1st Session, S. Exec. Doc. 1; see also Utley, *Frontiersmen in Blue*, 80–90.

127. Ball, *Army Regulars*, chapter 3; Utley, *Frontiersmen in Blue*, 115–20.

128. Crackel, *Mr. Jefferson's Army*, 100–108; Prucha, *Sword of the Republic*, chapter 4.

129. J. C. A. Stagg, *Mr. Madison's War: Politics, Diplomacy, and Warfare in the Early American Republic, 1783–1830* (Princeton, NJ: Princeton University Press, 1983).

130. James Monroe to Governor Tompkins of New York, February 4, 1815, in National Archives, Records of the Office of the Secretary of War (RG 107), Confidential and Unofficial Letters Sent by the Secretary of War, 1814–1847.

131. Prucha, *Sword of the Republic*, 104–19; Silverstone, *Divided Union*, 84–103.

132. Anderson and Cayton, *Dominion of War*, 227.

133. Arthur Scherr, "Thomas Jefferson's Nationalist Vision of New England and the War of 1812," *The Historian* 69:1 (Spring 2007): 1–35.

134. Anderson and Cayton, *Dominion of War*, 236–40; Carter, *Covert Operations*, 34–40; Heidler and Heidler, *Old Hickory's War*.

135. Anderson and Cayton, *Dominion of War*, 267–70; John S. D. Eisenhower, *So Far from God: The U.S. War with Mexico, 1846–1848* (New York: Anchor Books, 1990), chapter 3; Karp, *This Vast Southern Empire*, chapter 5.

136. Annual Message of the President of the United States to the Two Houses of Congress, December 2, 1845, 29th Congress, 1st Session, S. Doc. 1; Report of Marcy, November 29, 1845,; Anderson and Cayton, *Dominion of War*, 276–79; Eisenhower, *So Far from God*, 50–68; John H. Schroeder, *Mr. Polk's War: American Opposition and Dissent, 1846–1848* (Madison: University of Wisconsin Press, 1973), 8–19.

137. Anderson and Cayton, *Dominion of War*, 279–84; Eisenhower, *So Far from God*; Paul Frymer, "'A Rush and a Push and the Land Is Ours: Territorial Expansion, Land Policy, and U.S. State Formation." *Perspectives on Politics* 12:1 (March 2014): 119–44.

138. Annual Message of the President of the United States to the Two Houses of Congress, December 5, 1848, 30th Congress, 2nd Session, H. Exec. Doc. 1.

139. Michael J. Gerhardt, "Constitutional Construction and Departmentalism: A Case Study of the Demise of the Whig Presidency," *University of Pennsylvania Journal of Constitutional Law* 12:2 (January 2010): 425–59.

140. This point was first highlighted in Frederick Jackson Turner's famous essay "The Significance of the Frontier in American History," presented at the July 12, 1893, meeting of the American Historical Association in Chicago.

141. Brown, "The Role of the Army in Western Settlement"; Kohn, *Eagle and Sword*, chapter 4.

142. Prucha, *Sword of the Republic*, 22–25.

143. Bergmann, *The American National State and the Early West*, chapter 2; Prucha, *Sword of the Republic*, 29–38.

144. Francis Paul Prucha, *Broadax and Bayonet: The Role of the United States Army in the Development of the Northwest, 1815–1860* (Lincoln: University of Nebraska Press, 1973 [1953]), 11–13; Stephen J. Rockwell, *Indian Affairs and the Administrative State in the Nineteenth Century* (New York: Cambridge University Press, 2013), 61–62, 71–75, 124–29.

145. Prucha, *Broadax and Bayonet*, 3–9, 149–71; Prucha, *Sword of the Republic*, 124–28.

146. Report of the Adjutant General, R. Jones, November 28, 1849, 31st Congress, 1st Session, S. Exec. Doc. 1.

147. Prucha, *Broadax and Bayonet*, 10.

148. Bergmann, *The American National State and the Early West*, chapter 5; Prucha, *Broadax and Bayonet*, 11–13; Prucha, *Sword of the Republic*, 135–37, 205–7.

149. Prucha, *Sword of the Republic*, 149–51.

150. Report of the Commissioner of Indian Affairs, T. Hartley Crawford, November 25, 1843, 28th Congress, 1st Session, S. Doc. 1; see also attached letters from A. Brunson to General Walter Cunningham, September 27, 1843, and from T. Hartley Crawford to Secretary of War J. M. Porter on October 20, 1843.

151. Report of the Secretary of War, George W. Crawford, November 30, 1849, 31st Congress, 1st Session, S. Exec. Doc. 1, and attached letter from Crawford to Brigadier General Bennet Riley.

152. Robert W. Frazer, *Forts and Supplies: The Role of the Army in the Economy of the Southwest, 1846–1861* (Albuquerque: University of New Mexico Press, 1983), 120, 152, and quote on 189.

153. Prucha, *Broadax and Bayonet*, 69.

154. Richard R. John, *Spreading the News: The American Postal System from Franklin to Morse* (Cambridge, MA: Harvard University Press, 1995).

155. Statement of Henry Dearborn, July 10, 1803, in National Archives, Records of the Office of the Secretary of War (RG 107), Miscellaneous Letters Sent by the Secretary of War, 1800–1809.

156. Prucha, *Broadax and Bayonet*, 185–86; Michael L. Tate, *The Frontier Army in the Settlement of the West* (Norman: University of Oklahoma Press, 1999), 62–67.

157. Tate, *The Frontier Army*, 62–64; see also Frazer, *Forts and Supplies*, 140–41.

158. On the importance of the Santa Fe Trail and the Army's recognition of the need to protect migrants and traders, see Utley, *Frontiersmen in Blue*, chapter 4.

159. Report of the Secretary of War, John C. Spencer, December 1, 1841, 27th Congress, 2nd Session, H. Doc. 2; Prucha, *Sword of the Republic*, 360–61; Tate, *The Frontier Army*; Richard White, *"It's Your Misfortune and None of My Own": A History of the American West* (Norman: University of Oklahoma Press, 1991), chapter 8.

160. Frazer, *Forts and Supplies*.

161. Report of the Secretary of War, Jefferson Davis, December 1, 1856.

Chapter 2

1. For more on collective goods and the early American state, see Christopher McGrory Klyza, "The United States Army, Natural Resources, and Political Development in the Nineteenth Century," *Polity* 35:1 (Fall 2002): 1–28. More generally, see Mancur Olson, *The Logic of*

Collective Action: Public Goods and the Theory of Groups (Cambridge, MA: Harvard University Press, 1965).

2. Robert G. Angevine, *The Railroad and the State: War, Politics, and Technology in Nineteenth-Century America* (Stanford, CA: Stanford University Press, 2004), 22; Todd Shallat, *Structures in the Stream: Water, Science, and the Rise of the U.S. Army Corps of Engineers* (Austin: University of Texas Press, 1994), 94.

3. Angevine, *The Railroad and the State*, 22–24; Shallat, *Structures in the Stream*, 80.

4. Henry Dearborn to Brigadier General James Wilkinson, May 12, 1801, and Dearborn to the Commanding Officer of West Point, April 15, 1801, in National Archives, Records of the Office of the Secretary of War (RG 107), Letters Sent by the Secretary of War Relating to Military Affairs, 1800–1889; Theodore J. Crackel, *Mr. Jefferson's Army: Political and Social Reform of the Military Establishment, 1801–1809* (New York: New York University Press, 1987), 58–65.

5. Angevine, *The Railroad and the State*, 24–25; Shallat, *Structures in the Stream*, 81.

6. Shallat, *Structures in the Stream*, 100; Wayne Wei-Siang Hsieh, *West Pointers and the Civil War: The Old Army in War and Peace* (Chapel Hill: University of North Carolina Press, 2009), 18–25.

7. Shallat, *Structures in the Stream*, 91–97.

8. William Crawford to Brigadier General Joseph Swift, June 11, 1816, in National Archives, Records of the Office of the Secretary of War (RG 107), Letters Sent by the Secretary of War Relating to Military Affairs, 1800–1889.

9. Report of Captain G. W. Hughes of the Topographical Engineers relative to the working of copper ore, April 10, 1844, in Annual Report of the Secretary of War, 28th Congress, 1st Session, S. Doc. 291.

10. Shallat, *Structures in the Stream*, 84.

11. William H. Crawford to General Simon Bernard, May 6, 1816, in National Archives, Records of the Office of the Secretary of War (RG 107), Letters Sent by the Secretary of War Relating to Military Affairs, 1800–1889; Forest G. Hill, *Roads, Rails, and Waterways: The Army Engineers and Early Transportation* (Norman: University of Oklahoma Press, 1957), 6–9, 33, 49–55, 75–77; Shallat, *Structures in the Stream*, 128–39.

12. Forest G. Hill, "Formative Relations of American Enterprise, Government, and Science," *Political Science Quarterly* 75:3 (September 1960): 400–419, at 405–6.

13. Shallat, *Structures in the Stream*, 9.

14. Robert Kagan, *Dangerous Nation* (New York: Alfred A. Knopf, 2006), expresses a similar skepticism regarding claims that the United States was isolationist in its early years. For a somewhat different perspective on how international pressures shaped American state power, see Aristide R. Zolberg, "International Engagement and American Democracy: A Comparative Perspective," in Ira Katznelson and Martin Shefter, eds., *Shaped by War and Trade: International Influences on American Political Development* (Princeton, NJ: Princeton University Press, 2002), 24–54.

15. Hill, *Roads, Rails, and Waterways*, 5.

16. Frank N. Schubert, *The Nation Builders: A Sesquicentennial History of the Corps of Topographical Engineers, 1838–1863* (Fort Belvoir, VA: Office of History, U.S. Army Corps of Engineers, 1988), 5–8.

17. Schubert, *The Nation Builders*, 8.

18. Report of the Secretary of War, November 21, 1831, 22nd Congress, 1st Session, H. Doc. 2; William H. Goetzmann, *Army Exploration in the American West, 1803–1863* (Lincoln: Uni-

versity of Nebraska Press, 1959), chapter 1; Schubert, *The Nation Builders*, chapter 2; Shallat, *Structures in the Stream*, chapter 2.

19. Shallat, *Structures in the Stream*, 118; Shallat, "Engineering Policy: The U.S. Army Corps of Engineers and the Historical Foundation of Power," *Public Historian* 11:3 (Summer 1989): 6–27; Paul F. Paskoff, *Troubled Waters: Steamboat Disasters, River Improvements, and American Public Policy, 1821–1860* (Baton Rouge: Louisiana State University Press, 2007).

20. Tables 2, 4, and 5 were produced using the same methodology. Data was collected from the secretary of war's annual reports for the years 1829 to 1860 (prior to 1829 no unified report was issued, making any earlier accounting more challenging). The nation was divided into four sections: Northeast, South, Old Northwest, and West. Every state or territory mentioned was categorized into one of those sections, and then each individual project was counted and classified. Certain projects were unclassifiable either because they crossed the boundary between sections (such as improvements to the Mississippi River and mineralogical and geological surveys), or because the precise location could not be determined with the available information (such as surveys of the Gallean and Black Rivers). Projects not listed in these official reports were not included. The following is a breakdown of how states and territories were categorized: Northeast: New York, New Jersey, Maine, Rhode Island, Massachusetts, Connecticut, Delaware, New Hampshire, Pennsylvania, Maryland, Vermont; South: North Carolina, Florida, Louisiana, Alabama, Georgia, Virginia, South Carolina, Washington, DC, Arkansas, Tennessee, Kentucky, Mississippi; Old Northwest: Indiana, Illinois, Wisconsin, Michigan, Ohio; West: Iowa, Texas, Missouri, California, Oregon Territory, Louisiana Territory, New Mexico Territory. Some projects that crossed into two sections were placed into one of them by author's choice. Contact the author for further details.

21. Paskoff, *Troubled Waters*, 6.

22. Annual Report of the Chief of the Corps of Topographical Engineers, November 6, 1845, 29th Congress, 1st Session, S. Doc. 1.

23. Annual Report of the Chief of the Corps, November 6, 1845; Report of the Chief Topographical Engineer, November 1, 1843, 28th Congress, 1st Session, S. Doc. 1.

24. Laurence J. Malone, *Opening the West: Federal Internal Improvements Before 1860* (Westport, CT: Greenwood Press, 1998), 86–87.

25. Goetzmann, *Army Exploration in the American West*, chapter 1; Schubert, *The Nation Builders*, 44–46; Richard White, *"It's Your Misfortune and None of My Own": A History of the American West* (Norman: University of Oklahoma Press, 1991), chapter 5.

26. Carter Goodrich, *Government Promotion of American Canals and Railroads, 1800–1890* (New York: Columbia University Press, 1960). See also John Lauritz Larson, *Internal Improvement: National Public Works and the Promise of Popular Government in the Early United States* (Chapel Hill: University of North Carolina Press, 2001), who accepts Goodrich's basic thesis.

27. Malone, *Opening the West*.

28. William Crawford to Major James Kearney, May 31, 1816, in National Archives, Records of the Office of the Secretary of War (RG 107), Letters Sent by the Secretary of War Relating to Military Affairs, 1800–1889.

29. Larson, *Internal Improvement*, 137.

30. Karen M. O'Neill, *Rivers by Design: State Power and the Origin of U.S. Flood Control* (Durham, NC: Duke University Press, 2006), 19–22.

31. Quoted in Angevine, *The Railroad and the State*, 18.

32. Hill, *Roads, Rails, and Waterways*, 57–76.

33. Goetzmann, *Army Exploration in the American West*, 8–9. For more on the General Survey Act, see Angevine, *The Railroad and the State*, 16–17; Klyza, "The United States Army, Natural Resources, and Political Development," 7–8.

34. Hill, *Roads, Rails, and Waterways*, 61–81.

35. Paul Lucier, "Commercial Interests and Scientific Disinterestedness: Consulting Geologists in Antebellum America," *Isis* 86:2 (June 1995): 245–67.

36. Angevine, *The Railroad and the State*, 18–21, 48; Hill, *Roads, Rails, and Waterways*, 96–105.

37. Angevine, *The Railroad and the State*, 35–40, 95–101; Colleen A. Dunlavy, *Politics and Industrialization: Early Railroads in the United States and Prussia* (Princeton, NJ: Princeton University Press, 1994), 56–61; Hill, *Roads, Rails, and Waterways*, 114–30; Report of the Secretary of War, J. R. Poinsett, November 28, 1838, 25th Congress, 3rd Session, H. Doc. 2.

38. Richard Bensel, *Yankee Leviathan: The Origins of Central State Authority in America, 1859–1877* (New York: Cambridge University Press, 1990), 85.

39. Angevine, *The Railroad and the State*, 65. On the origins of the War Department, see Harry M. Ward, *The Department of War, 1781–1795* (Pittsburgh: University of Pittsburgh Press, 1962). For more on the Army's advanced bureaucratic structure, see Mark R. Wilson, *The Business of Civil War: Military Mobilization and the State, 1861–1865* (Baltimore: Johns Hopkins University Press, 2006), especially chapter 2.

40. For a slightly different perspective on bureaucracy in the antebellum era, but one that still disagrees with the "courts and parties" paradigm, see Richard R. John, "Affairs of Office: The Executive Departments, the Election of 1828, and the Making of the Democratic Party," in Meg Jacobs, William J. Novak, and Julian E. Zelizer, eds., *The Democratic Experiment: New Directions in American Political History* (Princeton, NJ: Princeton University Press, 2003), 50–84.

41. Charles F. O'Connell, Jr., "The Corps of Engineers and the Rise of Modern Management, 1827–1856," in Merritt Roe Smith, ed., *Military Enterprise and Technological Change: Perspectives on the American Experience* (Cambridge, MA: MIT Press, 1985), 87–116; Angevine, *The Railroad and the State*, 66–70.

42. Alfred D. Chandler, Jr., *The Visible Hand: The Managerial Revolution in American Business* (Cambridge, MA: Belknap Press of Harvard University Press, 1977).

43. Merritt Roe Smith, *Harper's Ferry Armory and the New Technology: The Challenge of Change* (Ithaca, NY: Cornell University Press, 1977), 28–106.

44. Henry Dearborn to Eli Whitney, June 16, 1801, in National Archives, Records of the Office of the Secretary of War (RG 107), Miscellaneous Letters Sent by the Secretary of War, 1800–1889; Smith, *Harper's Ferry Armory*, chapter 3; Lindsay Schakenbach Regele, *Manufacturing Advantage: War, the State, and the Origins of American Industry, 1776–1848* (Baltimore: Johns Hopkins University Press, 2019), 61–62.

45. Regele, *Manufacturing Advantage*, 74–81.

46. Merritt Roe Smith, "Army Ordnance and the 'American System' of Manufacturing, 1815–1861," in Smith, *Military Enterprise and Technological Change*, 39–86; Smith, "Military Entrepreneurship," in Otto Mayr and Robert C. Post, eds., *Yankee Enterprise: The Rise of the American System of Manufactures* (Washington, DC: Smithsonian Institution Press, 1981), 63–102; Smith, *Harper's Ferry Armory*; James J. Farley, *Making Arms in the Machine Age: Philadelphia's*

Frankford Arsenal, 1816–1870 (University Park: Pennsylvania State University Press, 1994); Regele, *Manufacturing Advantage*, 149–54.

47. Regele, *Manufacturing Advantage*, 100–101.

48. Alex Roland, "Science and War," *Osiris*, 2nd ser., 1 (1985): 247–72, esp. 253–54.

49. Smith, "Army Ordnance and the 'American System'," 78.

50. David Hounshell, *From the American System to Mass Production, 1800–1932: The Development of Manufacturing Technology in the United States* (Baltimore: Johns Hopkins University Press, 1985); Vernon W. Ruttan, *Is War Necessary for Economic Growth? Military Procurement and Technology Development* (New York: Oxford University Press, 2006), chapter 2. For more on the relationship between military spending and economic development, see Alex Roland, "Science, Technology, and War," *Technology and Culture* 36:2 (April 1995): S83–S100.

51. Michael L. Tate, *The Frontier Army in the Settlement of the West* (Norman: University of Oklahoma Press, 1999), 62–67; Paskoff, *Troubled Waters*, 22–23.

52. Francis Paul Prucha, *Broadax and Bayonet: The Role of the United States Army in the Development of the Northwest, 1815–1860* (Lincoln: University of Nebraska Press, 1973 [1953]).

53. Paul Frymer, *Building an American Empire: The Era of Territorial and Political Expansion* (Princeton, NJ: Princeton University Press, 2017).

54. White, *"It's Your Misfortune and None of My Own,"* 155–56. On the importance of the Northwest Ordinance to the country's economic development, see Gavin Wright, "The Role of Nationhood in the Economic Development of the USA," in Alice Teichova and Herbert Matis, eds., *Nation, State, and the Economy in History* (New York: Cambridge University Press, 2003), 387–403, especially 390–95.

55. Crackel, *Mr. Jefferson's Army*, 109; Francis Paul Prucha, *The Sword of the Republic: The United States Army on the Frontier, 1783–1846* (Lincoln: University of Nebraska Press, 1969), chapter 4.

56. Report of the Secretary of War, George W. Crawford, November 30, 1849, 31st Congress, 1st Session, S. Ex. Doc. 1; John S. D. Eisenhower, *So Far From God: The U.S. War with Mexico, 1846–1848* (New York: Anchor Books, 1990), 205–10; White, *"It's Your Misfortune and None of My Own,"* 157.

57. Henry Dearborn to General James Wilkinson, July 17, 1801, and Dearborn to Butler, April 16, 1802, in National Archives, Records of the Office of the Secretary of War (RG 107), Letters Sent by the Secretary of War Relating to Military Affairs, 1800–1889; Prucha, *Sword of the Republic*, 183.

58. William Crawford to Major General Alexander Macomb, May 29, 1816, in National Archives, Records of the Office of the Secretary of War (RG 107), Letters Sent by the Secretary of War Relating to Military Affairs, 1800–1889.

59. William H. Bergmann, *The American National State and the Early West* (New York: Cambridge University Press, 2012), especially chapter 4.

60. Prucha, *Sword of the Republic*, 182–89; Prucha, *Broadax and Bayonet*, chapter 3.

61. Goetzmann, *Army Exploration in the American West*; Prucha, *Sword of the Republic*, chapter 8.

62. Prucha, *Sword of the Republic*, 81–83; White, *"It's Your Misfortune and None of My Own,"* 119–21.

63. Alan Taylor, "The Science of Distant Empire, 1768–1811," in Douglas Seefeldt, Jeffrey L. Hantman, and Peter S. Onuf, eds., *Across the Continent: Jefferson, Lewis and Clark, and the*

Making of America (Charlottesville: University of Virginia Press, 2005), 16–44; William H. Goetzmann, *When the Eagle Screamed: The Romantic Horizon in American Diplomacy, 1800–1860* (New York: John Wiley and Sons, 1966), chapter 1; Goetzmann, *Exploration and Empire: The Explorer and Scientist in the Winning of the American West* (New York: Norton, 1978 [1966]), chapter 1.

64. Prucha, *Sword of the Republic*, 88–93.

65. Goetzmann, *Exploration and Empire*, chapter 5.

66. Goetzmann, *Exploration and Empire*, 46–53; Shallat, *Structures in the Stream*, 70–71; White, *"It's Your Misfortune and None of My Own,"* 121.

67. Goetzmann, *Exploration and Empire*, 60–62; Prucha, *Sword of the Republic*, 144–46.

68. Goetzmann, *Army Exploration in the American West*, chapter 3. See also the excellent biography of Frémont by Tom Chaffin, *Pathfinder: John Charles Frémont and the Course of American Empire* (New York: Hill and Wang, 2002).

69. Howard Stansbury, *An Expedition to the Valley of the Great Salt Lake of Utah* (Philadelphia: Lippincott, Grambo, 1855); John Williams Gunnison, *The Mormons or Latter Day Saints in the Valley of the Great Salt Lake, a History of Their Rise and Progress, Peculiar Doctrines, Present Conditions and Projects* (Philadelphia: Lippincott, Grambo, 1852); Norman F. Furniss, *The Mormon Conflict, 1850–1859* (New Haven, CT: Yale University Press, 1960), 32–33.

70. Goetzmann, *Exploration and Empire*, 240–50.

71. Angevine, *The Railroad and the State*, 114–15.

72. George W. Crawford to Colonel J. J. Abert, July 11, 1849, in Report of the Secretary of War, November 30, 1849, 31st Congress, 1st Session, S. Ex. Doc. 1.

73. Jefferson Davis to Brevet Brigadier General Joseph G. Totten, Chief Engineer, April 5, 1853; Davis to Governor Isaac J. Stevens, Washington Territory, April 8, 1853; and Davis to Lt. R. S. Williamson, May 6, 1853, all in National Archives, Records of the Office of the Secretary of War (RG 107), Letters Sent by the Secretary of War Relating to Military Affairs, 1800–1889; Goetzmann, *Army Exploration in the American West*, chapter 7.

74. Angevine, *The Railroad and the State*, 117.

75. Goetzmann, *Army Exploration in the American West*, chapter 8; Goetzmann, *Exploration and Empire*, chapter 8.

76. Angevine, *The Railroad and the State*, 115–17; Goetzmann, *Army Exploration in the American West*, 295–303.

77. Schubert, *The Nation Builders*, 23–24.

78. Goetzmann, *Army Exploration in the American West*, 109–51; Goetzmann, *Exploration and Empire*, 253–57.

79. Goetzmann, *Army Exploration in the American West*, 375–78, 406–18.

80. Lucille E. Horgan, *Forged in War: The Continental Congress and the Origins of Military Supply and Acquisition Policy* (Westport, CT: Greenwood Press, 2002); Paul A. C. Koistinen, *Beating Plowshares into Swords: The Political Economy of American Warfare, 1606–1865* (Lawrence: University Press of Kansas, 1996), 52–58; Erna Risch, *Quartermaster Support of the Army, 1775–1939* (Washington, DC: Center of Military History, 1989), chapters 1–5.

81. Koistinen, *Beating Plowshares into Swords*, 92–98; Risch, *Quartermaster Support of the Army*, chapter 6.

82. Wilson, *The Business of Civil War*, 46–49.

83. Mark R. Wilson, "The Politics of Procurement: Military Origins of Bureaucratic Autonomy," *Journal of Policy History* 18:1 (2006): 44–73, quote on 58.

84. Wilson, "The Politics of Procurement," 62. On the organizational synthesis, see Brian Balogh, "Reorganizing the Organizational Synthesis: Federal-Professional Relations in Modern America," *Studies in American Political Development* 5:2 (Summer 1991): 119–72; Louis Galambos, "The Emerging Organizational Synthesis in Modern American History," *Business History Review* 44:3 (Autumn 1970): 279–90; Galambos, "Technology, Political Economy, and Professionalism: Central Themes in the Organizational Synthesis," *Business History Review* 57:4 (Winter 1983): 471–93.

Chapter 3

1. Richard H. Kohn, *Eagle and Sword: The Beginnings of the Military Establishment in America* (New York: Free Press, 1975); Theodore J. Crackel, *Mr. Jefferson's Army: Political and Social Reform of the Military Establishment, 1801–1809* (New York: New York University Press, 1987).

2. Michael Lipsky, *Street-Level Bureaucracy: Dilemmas of the Individual in Public Services* (New York: Russell Sage Foundation, 1983).

3. Timothy Lindberg, "Legislating for American Empire: Territorial Policy and the House Committee on Territories," *Congress and the Presidency* 47:2 (2020): 153–74.

4. Andrew J. Polsky, "The Presidency at War," in Michael Nelson, ed., *The Presidency and the Political System* (8th ed.) (Washington, DC: CQ Press, 2006), 557–75; Mariah Zeisberg, *War Powers: The Politics of Constitutional Authority* (Princeton, NJ: Princeton University Press, 2013).

5. Shirley Anne Warshaw, "The Formation and Use of the Cabinet," in Phillip G. Henderson, ed., *The Presidency Then and Now* (Lanham, MD: Rowman and Littlefield, 2000), 115–37.

6. William B. Skelton, *An American Profession of Arms: The Army Officer Corps, 1784–1861* (Lawrence: University Press of Kansas, 1992), 131.

7. William B. Skelton, "The Commanding Generals and the Question of Civil Control in the Antebellum U.S. Army," *American Nineteenth Century History* 7:2 (June 2006): 153–72. On questions of territorial governance, see also Lindberg, "Legislating for American Empire."

8. Skelton, *An American Profession of Arms*; Samuel J. Watson, "Professionalism, Social Attitudes, and Civil-Military Accountability in the United States Army Officer Corps, 1815–1846," Ph.D. dissertation, Rice University, 1996.

9. Stephen Skowronek, *Building a New American State: The Expansion of National Administrative Capacities, 1877–1920* (New York: Cambridge University Press, 1982).

10. Samuel Huntington, *The Soldier and the State: The Theory and Politics of Civil-Military Relations* (Cambridge, MA: Harvard University Press, 1957).

11. Peter D. Feaver, *Armed Servants: Agency, Oversight, and Civil-Military Relations* (Cambridge, MA: Harvard University Press, 2005). Other work that criticizes Huntington includes Morris Janowitz, *The Professional Soldier: A Social and Political Portrait* (Glencoe, IL: Free Press, 1960); Eliot A. Cohen, *Supreme Command: Soldiers, Statesmen, and Leadership in Wartime* (New York: Anchor, 2003); Cohen, "The Unequal Dialogue: The Theory and Reality of Civil-Military Relations and the Use of Force," in Peter D. Feaver and Richard H. Kohn, eds., *Soldiers and Civilians: The Civil-Military Gap and American National Security* (Cambridge, MA: MIT Press, 2001); Thomas S. Langston, *Uneasy Balance: Civil-Military Relations in Peacetime Since 1783* (Baltimore: Johns Hopkins University Press, 2003); Charles A. Stevenson, *Warrior and Politicians: US Civil-Military Relations Under Stress* (New York: Routledge, 2006). A unique

perspective that is more sympathetic with Huntington can be found in Richard D. Hooker, Jr., "Soldiers of the State: Reconsidering American Civil-Military Relations," *Parameters* 33:4 (Winter 2003–4): 4–18.

12. Russell Weigley, "The American Civil-Military Cultural Gap: A Historical Perspective, Colonial Times to the Present," in Feaver and Kohn, eds., *Soldiers and Civilians.*

13. See also Susan M. Browne, "War-Making and U.S. State Formation: Mobilization, Demobilization, and the Inherent Ambiguities of Federalism," in Diane E. Davis and Anthony W. Pereira, eds., *Irregular Armed Forces and Their Role in Politics and State Formation* (New York: Cambridge University Press, 2003), 232–52.

14. Skelton, *An American Profession of Arms.*

15. One example of the embargo's lack of popularity can be found in a petition to Congress by New York merchants, printed in the *Annals of Congress*, 10th Congress, 2nd Session, February 6, 1809, at 1777–80.

16. Scott A. Silverstone, *Divided Union: The Politics of War in the Early American Republic* (Ithaca, NY: Cornell University Press, 2004), 74–80.

17. For one prominent example, see Ralph Ketcham, *Presidents Above Party: The First American Presidency, 1789–1829* (Chapel Hill: University of North Carolina Press, 1984).

18. *Annals of Congress*, 10th Congress, 1st Session, December 18, 1807, at 50.

19. Annals of Congress, 10th Congress, 2nd Session, December 26, 1808, at 910; Leonard White, *The Jeffersonians: A Study in Administrative History, 1801–1829* (New York: Macmillan, 1961), 32–35; Crackel, *Mr. Jefferson's Army*, 170–78.

20. Brian Schoen, "Calculating the Price of Union: Republican Economic Nationalism and the Origins of Southern Sectionalism, 1790–1828," *Journal of the Early Republic* 23:2 (Summer 2003): 173–206.

21. Crackel, *Mr. Jefferson's Army*, 169–70.

22. White, *The Jeffersonians*, 423–26.

23. Robert W. Coakley, *The Role of Federal Military Forces in Domestic Disorders, 1789–1878* (Washington, DC: Center of Military History, 1988), 90.

24. Stephen Skowronek, *The Politics Presidents Make* (Cambridge, MA: Harvard University Press, 1997); Leroy G. Dorsey, ed., *The Presidency and Rhetorical Leadership* (College Station: Texas A&M University Press, 2002), 28–30.

25. Coakley, *The Role of Federal Military Forces*, 94–101.

26. Lewis Cass to Winfield Scott, November 18, 1832, in National Archives, Records of the Office of the Secretary of War (RG 107), Confidential and Unofficial Letters Sent by the Secretary of War, 1814–1847.

27. Lewis Cass to Winfield Scott, January 26, 1833, in National Archives, Records of the Office of the Secretary of War (RG 107), Confidential and Unofficial Letters Sent by the Secretary of War, 1814–1847.

28. David F. Ericson, "The Nullification Crisis, American Republicanism, and the Force Bill Debate," *The Journal of Southern History* 61:2 (May 1995), 249–70, esp. 254.

29. Richard B. Latner, "The Nullification Crisis and Republican Subversion," *Journal of Southern History* 43:1 (February 1977), 19–38.

30. Coakley, *The Role of Federal Military Forces*, 101–3.

31. On the widespread popular support behind the Patriot movement, see Andrew Bonthius, "The Patriot War of 1837–1838: Locofocoism with a Gun?" *Labour/Le Travail* 52 (Fall 2003): 9–43.

32. Annual Message from the President of the United States to the Two Houses of Congress, December 4, 1838, 25th Congress, 3rd Session, H. Doc. 2.

33. Annual Message from the President of the United States to the Two Houses of Congress, December 2, 1839, 26th Congress, 1st Session, S. Doc. 1.

34. Annual Message from the President of the United States to the Two Houses of Congress, December 9, 1840, 26th Congress, 2nd Session, S. Doc. 1.

35. Skowronek, *The Politics Presidents Make.*

36. J. R. Poinsett to Major General Winfield Scott, October 26, 1839, in National Archives, Records of the Office of the Secretary of War (RG 107), Confidential and Unofficial Letters Sent by the Secretary of War, 1814–1847.

37. Samuel Watson, "United States Army Officers Fight the 'Patriot War': Responses to Filibustering on the Canadian Border, 1837–1839," *Journal of the Early Republic* 18:3 (Autumn 1998): 485–519, quote on 486.

38. Skowronek, *The Politics Presidents Make.*

39. Coakley, *The Role of Federal Military Forces*, 119–27; Paul M. Thompson, "Is There Anything 'Legal' About Extralegal Action? The Debate over Dorr's Rebellion," *New England Law Review* 36 (Winter 2002): 385–432.

40. Coakley, *The Role of Federal Military Forces*, 119–25.

41. John B. Rae, "Democrats and the Dorr Rebellion," *New England Quarterly* 9:3 (September 1936): 476–83; Michael A. Conron, "Law, Politics, and Chief Justice Taney: A Reconsideration of the *Luther v. Borden* Decision," *American Journal of Legal History* 11:4 (October 1967): 377–88; Thompson, "Is There Anything 'Legal' About Extralegal Action?"

42. Coakley, *The Role of Federal Military Forces*, 28–35; Kohn, *Eagle and Sword*, 158–61; Max M. Edling, *A Revolution in Favor of Government: Origins of the U.S. Constitution and the Making of the American State* (New York: Oxford University Press, 2003), 135–37.

43. Coakley, *The Role of Federal Military Forces*, 43–65; Kohn, *Eagle and Sword*, 161–70.

44. Coakley, *The Role of Federal Military Forces*, 69–77; Peter Levine, "The Fries Rebellion: Social Violence and the Politics of the New Nation," *Pennsylvania History* 40:3 (July 1973): 241–58.

45. Coakley, *The Role of Federal Military Forces*, 77–83; John M. Murrin, "The Jeffersonian Triumph and American Exceptionalism," *Journal of the Early Republic* 20:1 (Spring 2000): 1–25.

46. John H. Aldrich, *Why Parties? The Origin and Transformation of Political Parties in America* (Chicago: University of Chicago Press, 1995), chapter 5; Michael F. Holt, *The Rise and Fall of the American Whig Party: Jacksonian Politics and the Onset of the Civil War* (New York: Oxford University Press, 2003), chapters 21, 22, and 23.

47. Don Fehrenbacher, *The Slaveholding Republic: An Account of the United States Government's Relations to Slavery* (New York: Oxford University Press, 2001).

48. Annual Message of the President of the United States to the Two Houses of Congress, December 2, 1851, 32nd Congress, 1st Session, S. Exec. Doc. 1; Durwood Ball, *Army Regulars on the Western Frontier, 1848–1861* (Norman: University of Oklahoma Press, 2001), 89–90. See also Amy S. Greenberg, "Pirates, Patriots, and Public Meetings: Antebellum Expansionism and Urban Culture," *Journal of Urban History* 31:5 (July 2005): 634–50.

49. Ball, *Army Regulars on the Western Frontier*, 97–106; Robert E. May, "Young American Males and Filibustering in the Age of Manifest Destiny: The United States Army as a Cultural Mirror," *Journal of American History* 78:3 (December 1991): 857–86.

50. Jefferson Davis to B. J. Hallett, Esq., July 9, 1853, in National Archives, Records of the Office of the Secretary of War (RG 107), Letters Sent by the Secretary of War Relating to Military Affairs, 1800–1889. See also Report of the Secretary of War, Jefferson Davis, December 1, 1856, 34th Congress, 3rd Session, S. Exec. Doc. 5.

51. May, "Young American Males."

52. Ball, *Army Regulars on the Western Frontier*, 172–78; Coakley, *The Role of Federal Military Forces*, 145–65.

53. Ball, *Army Regulars on the Western Frontier*, 181–87; Coakley, *The Role of Federal Military Forces*, 173–93.

54. Ball, *Army Regulars on the Western Frontier*, 153–71; Coakley, *The Role of Federal Military Forces*, 194–226.

55. Polsky, "The Presidency at War"; William G. Howell and Jon Pevehouse, *While Dangers Gather: Congressional Checks on Presidential War Powers* (Princeton, NJ: Princeton University Press, 2007).

56. James Monroe to Governor Tompkins of New York, February 4, 1815, and Monroe to Governor of Vermont, February 10, 1815, in National Archives, Records of the Office of the Secretary of War (RG 107), Confidential and Unofficial Letters Sent by the Secretary of War, 1814–1847.

57. Fred Anderson and Andrew Cayton, *The Dominion of War: Empire and Liberty in North America, 1500–2000* (New York: Penguin, 2005), 225–29; J. C. A. Stagg, *Mr. Madison's War: Politics, Diplomacy, and Warfare in the Early American Republic, 1783–1830* (Princeton, NJ: Princeton University Press, 1983); Charles A. Stevenson, *Congress at War: The Politics of Conflict Since 1789* (Washington, DC: Potomac Books, 2007), chapter 3.

58. Daniel Walker Howe, *What Hath God Wrought: The Transformation of America, 1815–1848* (New York: Oxford University Press, 2007), 63–72; Silverstone, *Divided Union*, 84–103.

59. Watson, "Professionalism, Social Attitudes, and Civil-Military Accountability," 163.

60. William B. Skelton, "Professionalization in the U.S. Army Officer Corps During the Age of Jackson," *Armed Forces and Society* 1:4 (August 1975): 443–71, at 448–49; Skelton, "High Army Leadership in the Era of the War of 1812: The Making and Remaking of the Officer Corps," *William and Mary Quarterly*, 3rd ser., 51:2 (April 1994): 253–74.

61. Anderson and Cayton, *Dominion of War*, chapter 5; Howe, *What Hath God Wrought*, 63–72; Skelton, *An American Profession of Arms*, 84–86.

62. David S. Heidler and Jeanne T. Heidler, *Old Hickory's War: Andrew Jackson and the Quest for Empire* (Baton Rouge: Louisiana State University Press, 2003), 42–46.

63. William H. Crawford to Major General Andrew Jackson, July 9, 1816, in National Archives, Records of the Office of the Secretary of War (RG 107), Confidential and Unofficial Letters Sent by the Secretary of War, 1814–1847.

64. Heidler and Heidler, *Old Hickory's War*, 70.

65. John C. Calhoun to Major General Andrew Jackson, December 29, 1817, in National Archives, Records of the Office of the Secretary of War (RG 107), Letters Sent by the Secretary of War Relating to Military Affairs, 1800–1889; Heidler and Heidler, *Old Hickory's War*, 90–92.

66. John C. Calhoun to General Andrew Jackson, December 28, 1818, in National Archives, Records of the Office of the Secretary of War (RG 107), Confidential and Unofficial Letters Sent by the Secretary of War, 1814–1847.

67. Skelton, *An American Profession of Arms*, 332–35.

68. Annual Message from the President of the United States to the Two Houses of Congress, December 7, 1847, 30th Congress, 1st Session, S. Exec. Doc. 1.

69. Annual Message from the President of the United States to the Two Houses of Congress, December 2, 1845, 29th Congress, 1st Session, S. Doc. 1; Report of the Secretary of War, W. L. Marcy, November 29, 1845, 29th Congress, 1st Session, S. Doc. 1; Anderson and Cayton, *Dominion of War*, 276–79; Robert W. Merry, *A Country of Vast Designs: James K. Polk, the Mexican War, and the Conquest of the American Continent* (New York: Simon and Schuster, 2009).

70. John H. Schroeder, *Mr. Polk's War: American Opposition and Dissent, 1846–1848* (Madison: University of Wisconsin Press, 1973).

71. John S. D. Eisenhower, *So Far from God: The U.S. War with Mexico, 1846–1848* (New York: Anchor Books, 1990), 50.

72. Eisenhower, *So Far from God*, 89–97.

73. Eisenhower, *So Far from God*, 210–19; Skelton, *An American Profession of Arms*, 334–45; Report of the Secretary of War, W. L. Marcy, December 2, 1847, 30th Congress, 1st Session, S. Exec. Doc. 1.

74. Eisenhower, *So Far from God*, 358–68.

75. Henry Knox to Brigadier General And. Pickens, April 21, 1792, and Knox to Pickens, August 15, 1792, in National Archives, Records of the Office of the Secretary of War (RG 107), Correspondence of the War Department Relating to Indian Affairs, Military Pensions, and Fortifications, 1791–1797.

76. Kohn, *Eagle and Sword*, 92–96; Mark Puls, *Henry Knox: Visionary General of the American Revolution* (New York: Palgrave Macmillan, 2008), chapter 10; Harry M. Ward, *The Department of War, 1781–1795* (Pittsburgh: University of Pittsburgh Press, 1962), 106.

77. Kohn, *Eagle and Sword*, 97–98.

78. John Grenier, *The First Way of War: American War Making on the Frontier* (New York: Cambridge University Press, 2005), 193–203; Kohn, *Eagle and Sword*, 101–26, 139–57; Puls, *Henry Knox*, chapter 10; Ward, *The Department of War*, 106–28.

79. R. Douglas Hurt, *The Indian Frontier, 1763–1846* (Albuquerque: University of New Mexico Press, 2002), 116–19, 133–36.

80. Heidler and Heidler, *Old Hickory's War*, 7–27; Hurt, *The Indian Frontier*, 124–33.

81. Hurt, *The Indian Frontier*, 168–88; Francis Paul Prucha, *The Sword of the Republic: The United States Army on the Frontier, 1783–1846* (Lincoln: University of Nebraska Press, 1969), 212–31; Report of the Major General of the Army, Alexander Macomb, November 1831, 22nd Congress, 1st Session, H. Doc. 2.

82. Report of the Secretary of War, Lewis Cass, November 30, 1835, 24th Congress, 1st Session, H. Doc. 2; Report of the Secretary of War Ad Interim, Benjamin F. Butler, December 3, 1836, 24th Congress, 2nd Session, H. Doc. 2; John Missall and Mary Lou Missall, *The Seminole Wars: America's Longest Indian Conflict* (Gainesville: University Press of Florida, 2004), 93–111; Prucha, *Sword of the Republic*, 269–73.

83. Annual Message from the President of the United States to the Two Houses of Congress, December 6, 1836, 24th Congress, 2nd Session, H. Doc. 2.

84. Benjamin F. Butler, Secretary of War Ad Interim, to Major General Thomas S. Jesup, January 4, 1837, in National Archives, Records of the Office of the Secretary of War (RG 107), Letters Sent by the Secretary of War Relating to Military Affairs, 1800–1889.

85. Report of the Major General of the Army, Alexander Macomb, November 20, 1837, 25th Congress, 2nd Session, S. Doc. 1.

86. Joel Poinsett to Major General Thomas S. Jesup, July 25, 1837, in National Archives, Records of the Office of the Secretary of War (RG 107), Letters Sent by the Secretary of War Relating to Military Affairs, 1800–1889. See also Missall and Missall, *Seminole Wars*, 144–50.

87. Joel Poinsett to General Edmund Gaines, August 9, 1837, and Poinsett to Gaines, August 14, 1837, in National Archives, Records of the Office of the Secretary of War (RG 107), Letters Sent by the Secretary of War Relating to Military Affairs, 1800–1889.

88. Annual Message from the President of the United States to the Two Houses of Congress, December 5, 1837, 25th Congress, 2nd Session, S. Doc. 1.

89. Ball, *Army Regulars on the Western Frontier*, chapter 3; Robert W. Frazer, *Forts and Supplies: The Role of the Army in the Economy of the Southwest, 1846–1861* (Albuquerque: University of New Mexico Press, 1983), chapters 4 and 6; Report of the Secretary of War, Charles M. Conrad, November 29, 1851, 32nd Congress, 1st Session, S. Ex. Doc. 1; Report of the Secretary of War, Charles M. Conrad, December 4, 1852, 32nd Congress, 2nd Session, S. Ex. Doc. 1.

90. Skelton, "The Commanding Generals," 165–67.

91. Ball, *Army Regulars on the Western Frontier*, 70–71, 139–49.

92. W. Neil Franklin, "Pennsylvania-Virginia Rivalry for the Indian Trade of the Ohio Valley," *Mississippi Valley Historical Review* 20:4 (March 1934): 463–80; Jack M. Sosin, "The British Indian Department and Dunmore's War," *Virginia Magazine of History and Biography* 74:1, part 1 (January 1966): 34–50; Kohn, *Eagle and Sword*, 60–65.

93. Alan S. Brown, "The Role of the Army in Western Settlement: Josiah Harmar's Command, 1785–1790," *Pennsylvania Magazine of History and Biography* 93 (April 1969): 161–78.

94. William H. Bergmann, *The American National State and the Early West* (New York: Cambridge University Press, 2012), chapter 3.

95. Henry Dearborn to Daniel Bissell, July 6, 1802, in National Archives, Records of the Office of the Secretary of War (RG 107), Letters Sent by the Secretary of War Relating to Military Affairs, 1800–1889.

96. Henry Dearborn to John Hamtramck, April 2, 1803, in National Archives, Records of the Office of the Secretary of War (RG 107), Letters Sent by the Secretary of War Relating to Military Affairs, 1800–1889; Dearborn to Vice President Aaron Burr, March 16, 1801, Dearborn to Lt. Col. Tousand, March 18, 1801, Dearborn to Lt. Peter Dransy, Dearborn to Mr. Edward Wright, March 20, 1801, Dearborn to David Henley, March 20, 1801, Dearborn to Major General William Heath, March 26, 1801, in National Archives, Records of the Office of the Secretary of War (RG 107), Miscellaneous Letters Sent by the Secretary of War, 1800–1809.

97. Francis Paul Prucha, *Broadax and Bayonet: The Role of the United States Army in the Development of the Northwest, 1815–1860* (Lincoln: University of Nebraska Press, 1973 [1953]), 9.

98. Prucha, *Broadax and Bayonet*, 18–23; Report of the Major General, Alexander Macomb, November 21, 1831, 22nd Congress, 1st Session, H. Doc. 2; Ron Field, *Forts of the American Frontier, 1820–91: Central and Northern Plains* (Westminster, MD: Osprey, 2005), 13–15.

99. Michael L. Tate, *The Frontier Army in the Settlement of the West* (Norman: University of Oklahoma Press, 1999), 29–30; Prucha, *Broadax and Bayonet*, 25–26; see also Report of the Secretary of War, John C. Spencer, December 1, 1841, 27th Congress, 2nd Session, H. Doc. 2.

100. This point is similar to the argument regarding bureaucrats made in Daniel P. Carpenter, *The Forging of Bureaucratic Autonomy: Reputations, Networks, and Policy Innovation in Executive Agencies, 1862–1928* (Princeton, NJ: Princeton University Press, 2001).

101. Annual Message from the President of the United States to the Two Houses of Congress, December 7, 1841, 27th Congress, 2nd Session, H. Doc. 2.

102. Report of the Secretary of War, John C. Spencer, December 1, 1841, 27th Congress, 2nd Session, H. Doc. 2; Prucha, *Broadax and Bayonet*, 29.

103. Report of the Adjutant General, R. Jones, November 28, 1849, 31st Congress, 1st Session, S. Ex. Doc. 1; Prucha, *Broadax and Bayonet*, 27–28.

104. Prucha, *Broadax and Bayonet*, xi.

105. Richard Bruce Winders, *Mr. Polk's Army: The American Military Experience in the Mexican War* (College Station: Texas A&M University Press, 1997), 8; Robert H. Thonhoff, "Taylor's Trail in Texas," *Southwestern Historical Quarterly* 70:1 (July 1966): 7–22.

106. Report of the Secretary of War, John C. Spencer, December 1, 1841, 27th Congress, 2nd Session, H. Doc. 2.

107. Field, *Forts of the American Frontier 1820–91: Central and Northern Plains*, 13–15; Report of the Secretary of War, John C. Spencer, December 1, 1841, 27th Congress, 2nd Session, H. Doc. 2; Coakley, *The Role of Federal Military Forces*, esp. chapter 8.

108. Robert M. Utley, *Fort Scott National Historic Site* (Oro Valley, AZ: Western National Parks Association, 1991).

109. Annual Message from the President of the United States to the Two Houses of Congress, December 5, 1848, 30th Congress, 2nd Session, H. Exec. Doc. 1; Tate, *The Frontier Army in the Settlement of the West*, 30–31.

110. Report of the Secretary of War, Charles M. Conrad, November 30, 1850, 31st Congress, 2nd Session, H. Exec. Doc. 1.

111. Tate, *The Frontier Army in the Settlement of the West*, 114–15.

112. Frazer, *Forts and Supplies*, 61–65; Field, *Forts of the American Frontier, 1820–91: The Southern Plains and Southwest*, 43–44.

113. Frazer, *Forts and Supplies*, 118–41, 147–60.

114. Report of the Chief, Topographical Engineers, J. J. Abert, November 17, 1848, 30th Congress, 2nd Session, H. Exec. Doc. 1.

115. Report of the Secretary of War, Jefferson Davis, December 1, 1856, 34th Congress, 3rd Session, S. Exec. Doc. 5.

116. Fort data for years prior to 1820 and post-1850 does not seem to be easily available. However, this more limited period does include many of the major changes in fort locations and population movement during the antebellum era.

117. Population data downloaded from http://www.nhgis.org, Minnesota Population Center, National Historical Geographic Information System: Version 2.0, Minneapolis: University of Minnesota, 2011.

118. Prucha, *Broadax and Bayonet*, 18.

119. Louis Hartz, *The Liberal Tradition in America* (New York: Harvest Books, 1955). See also Aziz Rana, *The Two Faces of American Freedom* (Cambridge, MA: Harvard University Press, 2014).

Chapter 4

1. Shirley Anne Warshaw, "The Formation and Use of the Cabinet," in Phillip G. Henderson, ed., *The Presidency Then and Now* (Lanham, MD: Rowman and Littlefield, 2000), 115–37.

2. Stephen Skowronek, *Building a New American State: The Expansion of National Administrative Capacities, 1877–1920* (New York: Cambridge University Press, 1982).

3. Skowronek, *Building a New American State*, 20, 23.

4. Richard Franklin Bensel, *Yankee Leviathan: The Origins of Central State Authority in America, 1859–1877* (New York: Cambridge University Press, 1990), 85, 91.

5. Daniel Carpenter, *The Forging of Bureaucratic Autonomy: Reputations, Networks, and Policy Innovation in Executive Agencies, 1862–1928* (Princeton, NJ: Princeton University Press, 2001), chapter 2, quote at 50.

6. Mark R. Wilson, "The Politics of Procurement: Military Origins of Bureaucratic Autonomy," *Journal of Policy History* 18:1 (2006): 44–73; Wilson, *The Business of Civil War: Military Mobilization and the State, 1861–1865* (Baltimore: Johns Hopkins University Press, 2006).

7. Wilson, *The Business of Civil War*, 40.

8. Stephen J. Rockwell, *Indian Affairs and the Administrative State in the Nineteenth Century* (New York: Cambridge University Press, 2013), especially 31–34 and 306–18.

9. On Jesup, see Erna Risch, *Quartermaster Support of the Army, 1775–1939* (Washington, DC: Center of Military History, 1989); on Abert, see Frank N. Schubert, *The Nation Builders: A Sesquicentennial History of the Corps of Topographical Engineers, 1838–1863* (Fort Belvoir, VA: Office of History, U.S. Army Corps of Engineers, 1988).

10. Carpenter, *The Forging of Bureaucratic Autonomy*, 19–20.

11. Samuel P. Huntington, *The Soldier and the State: The Theory and Politics of Civil-Military Relations* (Cambridge, MA: Harvard University Press, 1957). On professionalization in the antebellum period, see William B. Skelton, *An American Profession of Arms: The Army Officer Corps, 1784–1861* (Lawrence: University Press of Kansas, 1992); Samuel J. Watson, "How the Army Became Accepted: West Point Socialization, Military Accountability, and the Nation-State During the Jacksonian Era," *American Nineteenth Century History* 7:2 (June 2006): 219–51.

12. Matthew D. McCubbins, Roger G. Noll, and Barry R. Weingast, "Administrative Procedures as Instruments of Political Control," *Journal of Law, Economics, and Organization* 3:2 (Autumn 1987): 243–77; Terry Moe, "An Assessment of the Positive Theory of 'Congressional Dominance,'" *Legislative Studies Quarterly* 12:4 (November 1987): 475–520.

13. See, for example, John Ferejohn and Charles Shipan, "Congressional Influence on Bureaucracy," *Journal of Law, Economics, and Organization* 6:1 (April 1990): 1–20; Jonathan R. Macey, "Organizational Design and Political Control of Administrative Agencies," *Journal of Law, Economics, and Organization* 8:1 (March 1992): 93–110; Thomas H. Hammond and Jack H. Knott, "Who Controls the Bureaucracy? Presidential Power, Congressional Dominance, Legal Constraints, and Bureaucratic Autonomy in a Model of Multi-institutional Policy-Making," *Journal of Law, Economics, and Organization* 12:1 (March 1996): 119–66; David Epstein and Sharyn O'Halloran, "Asymmetric Information, Delegation, and the Structure of Policy-Making," *Journal of Theoretical Politics* 11:1 (1999): 37–56; Charles R. Shipan, "Congress and the Bureaucracy," in Paul J. Quirk and Sarah A. Binder, eds., *The Legislative Branch* (New York: Oxford University Press, 2005): 432–58; Barry R. Weingast, "Caught in the Middle: The President, Congress, and the Political-Bureaucratic System," in Joel D. Aberbach and Mark A. Peterson, eds., *The Executive Branch* (New York: Oxford University Press, 2005): 312–43; Michael M. Ting, "A Strategic Theory of Bureaucratic Redundancy," *American Journal of Political Science* 47:2 (April 2003): 274–92.

14. Keith E. Whittington and Daniel P. Carpenter, "Executive Power in American Institutional Development," *Perspectives on Politics* 1:3 (September 2003): 495–513.

15. Amy B. Zegart, *Flawed by Design: The Evolution of the CIA, JCS, and NSC* (Stanford, CA: Stanford University Press, 1999).

16. Paul Pierson, *Politics in Time: History, Institutions, and Social Analysis* (Princeton: Princeton University Press, 2004); Karen Orren and Stephen Skowronek, *The Search for American Political Development* (New York: Cambridge University Press, 2004).

17. See William R. Lowry, "Can Bureaucracies Change Policy?" *Journal of Policy History* 20:2 (2008): 287–306, for a review of this literature, as well as case studies that attempt to demonstrate the difficulty of bureaucratically led policymaking.

18. See Ruth Anne French-Hodson, "New Economics of Organization and Nineteenth-Century Bureaucracies: A Study of the Bureau of Indian Affairs," M.Phil. thesis, Merton College, University of Oxford, 2007, especially the introduction.

19. Of course, the national security state Zegart analyzes is created in the twentieth century, and is not entirely comparable to the earlier developments discussed here. However, her model is still useful as a point of reference when discussing the War Department's bureaucracy, as we can sift through her claims and pinpoint which ones are relevant to an earlier period.

20. On presidential resources in the premodern era, see John P. Burke, "The Institutional Presidency," in Michael Nelson, ed., *The Presidency and the Political System* (8th ed.) (Washington, DC: CQ Press, 2006): 383–409.

21. Henry Dearborn to Aaron Burr, March 16, 1801, and October 21, 1801, in National Archives, Records of the Office of the Secretary of War (RG 107), Miscellaneous Letters Sent by the Secretary of War, 1800–1809.

22. On the annual message as a tool of public communication, see Michael J. Korzi, *A Seat of Popular Leadership: The Presidency, Political Parties, and Democratic Government* (Amherst: University of Massachusetts Press, 2004).

23. Annual Message from the President of the United States to the Two Houses of Congress, December 7, 1830, 21st Congress, 2nd Session, S. Doc. 1; Annual Message from the President of the United States to the Two Houses of Congress, December 2, 1834, 23rd Congress, 2nd Session, S. Doc. 1.

24. Nelson W. Polsby, "The Institutionalization of the U.S. House of Representatives," *American Political Science Review* 62:1 (March 1968): 144–68.

25. Todd Shallat, *Structures in the Stream: Water, Science, and the Rise of the U.S. Army Corps of Engineers* (Austin: University of Texas Press, 1994), 154. On the importance of implementation for the success of policy, see Jeffrey L. Pressman and Aaron B. Wildavsky, *Implementation: How Great Expectations in Washington Are Dashed in Oakland* (Berkeley: University of California Press, 1974).

26. Paul A. C. Koistinen, *Beating Plowshares into Swords: The Political Economy of American Warfare, 1606–1865* (Lawrence: University Press of Kansas, 1996), 56–57.

27. On congressional deference to executive actors (albeit in a very different context), see Lawrence A. Becker, *Doing the Right Thing: Collective Action and Procedural Choice in the New Legislative Process* (Columbus: Ohio State University Press, 2005).

28. On distributive politics, see the classic essay by Theodore J. Lowi, "American Business, Public Policy, Case-Studies, and Political Theory," *World Politics* 16:4 (July 1964): 677–715. This raises an important question: if members of Congress received no distributional benefits from peripheral Army activities, why did they continue to fund them? One possible explanation is that much of what the Army did was not funded directly by Congress. The General Survey Act, for instance, did not require any additional appropriations, with engineers simply sent by the War Department's Board of Engineers for Internal Improvements while their salaries

continued to be paid as usual by normal appropriations. Other activities in the periphery, such as the initial building of the Natchez Trace, occurred without prior authorization, and the labor was performed by soldiers in the course of their regular duties. Finally, to the extent such projects were funded, some members of Congress had an ideological stake in promoting expansionist policies (although most projects did not require this funding to proceed).

29. Stephen Minicucci, "Internal Improvements and the Union, 1790–1860," *Studies in American Political Development* 18:2 (Fall 2004): 160–85.

30. Billy Joe Peyton, "'To Make the Crooked Ways Straight and the Rough Ways Smooth': The Federal Government's Role in Laying Out and Building the Cumberland Road," Ph.D. dissertation, West Virginia University, 1999.

31. Robert G. Angevine, *The Railroad and the State: War, Politics, and Technology in Nineteenth-Century America* (Stanford, CA: Stanford University Press, 2004), for instance, highlights the horse-trading character of some railroad funding in this era. On logrolling generally, see William H. Riker and Steven J. Brams, "The Paradox of Vote Trading," *American Political Science Review* 67:4 (December 1973): 1235–47.

32. Warshaw, "The Formation and Use of the Cabinet."

33. For a recent prominent work viewing civil-military relations in this manner, see Peter D. Feaver, *Armed Servants: Agency, Oversight, and Civil-Military Relations* (Cambridge, MA: Harvard University Press, 2005). The classic statement on the subject is Huntington, *The Soldier and the State.*

34. John Lauritz Larson, *Internal Improvement: National Public Works and the Promise of Popular Government in the Early United States* (Chapel Hill: University of North Carolina Press, 2001).

35. Mitchel A. Sollenberger, "Presidential Vetoes 1789–Present: A Summary Overview." Congressional Research Service, Report 98–148, April 2004. On the increasing use of the veto from Jackson forward, see Nolan McCarty, "Presidential Vetoes in the Early Republic: Changing Constitutional Norms or Electoral Reform?" *Journal of Politics* 71:2 (April 2009): 369–84.

36. Daniel Carpenter and Gisela Sin, "Policy Tragedy and the Emergence of Regulation: The Food, Drug, and Cosmetic Act of 1938," *Studies in American Political Development* 21:2 (Fall 2007): 149–80.

37. Carpenter and Sin, "Policy Tragedy," 179. See also Daniel P. Carpenter and Colin D. Moore, "Robust Action and the Strategic Use of Ambiguity in a Bureaucratic Cohort: FDA Officers and the Evolution of New Drug Regulations, 1950–70," in Stephen Skowronek and Matthew Glassman, eds., *Formative Acts: American Politics in the Making* (Philadelphia: University of Pennsylvania Press, 2007): 340–62.

38. George Bomford to Lewis Cass, October 28, 1831, printed in Annual Report of the Secretary of War, Lewis Cass, November 21, 1831, 22nd Congress, 1st Session, H. Doc. 2; Annual Report of the Secretary of War, J. R. Poinsett, November 28, 1838, 25th Congress, 3rd Session, H. Doc. 2; Annual Report of the Secretary of War, J. R. Poinsett, November 30, 1839, 26th Congress, 1st Session, S. Doc. 1; Report from the Ordnance Department, November 29, 1839, 26th Congress, 1st Session, S. Doc. 1; Annual Report of the Secretary of War, J. R. Poinsett, December 5, 1840, 26th Congress, 2nd Session, S. Doc. 1; Report from the Ordnance Department, November 30, 1840, 26th Congress, 2nd Session, S. Doc. 1; Annual Report of the Secretary of War, John Spencer, December 1, 1841, 27th Congress, 2nd Session, H. Doc. 2; Report of the Chief of the Ordnance Department, November 22, 1841, 27th Congress, 2nd Session,

H. Doc. 2; Annual Report of the Secretary of War, John Spencer, November 26, 1842, 27th Congress, 3rd Session, H. Exec. Doc. 2; Annual Report of the Secretary of War, J. M. Porter, November 30, 1843, 28th Congress, 1st Session, S. Doc. 1; Annual Report of the Secretary of War, William Wilkins, November 30, 1844, 28th Congress, 2nd Session, S. Doc. 1; Report of the Chief of the Ordnance Department, November 1, 1844, 28th Congress, 2nd Session, S. Doc. 1; Annual Report of the Secretary of War, W. L. Marcy, November 29, 1845, 29th Congress, 1st Session, S. Doc. 1; Report of the Ordnance Department, October 31, 1845, 29th Congress, 1st Session, S. Doc. 1.

39. Annual Message from the President of the United States to the Two Houses of Congress, December 5, 1837, 25th Congress, 2nd Session, S. Doc. 1.

40. Colleen A. Dunlavy, *Politics and Industrialization: Early Railroads in the United States and Prussia* (Princeton, NJ: Princeton University Press, 1994), 126.

41. Christopher McGrory Klyza, "The United States Army, Natural Resources, and Political Development in the Nineteenth Century," *Polity* 35:1 (Fall 2002): 1–28.

42. Report of the Secretary of War Ad Interim, B. F. Butler, December 3, 1836, 24th Congress, 2nd Session, H. Doc. 2; Report from the Ordnance Department, November 12, 1836, 24th Congress, 2nd Session, H. Doc. 2; Report from the Ordnance Department, November 20, 1837, 25th Congress, 2nd Session, S. Doc. 1; Report of the Chief of the Ordnance Department, November 28, 1838, 25th Congress, 3rd Session, H. Doc. 2; Annual Report of the Secretary of War, J. R. Poinsett, November 30, 1839, 26th Congress, 1st Session, S. Doc. 1; Annual Report of the Secretary of War, John Spencer, November 26, 1842, 27th Congress, 3rd Session, H. Exec. Doc. 2; Annual Report of the Secretary of War, J. M. Porter, November 30, 1843, 28th Congress, 1st Session, S. Doc. 1; Annual Report of the Secretary of War, W. L. Marcy, November 29, 1845, 29th Congress, 1st Session, S. Doc. 1.

43. Annual Message of the President to the Two Houses of Congress, December 2, 1845, 29th Congress, 1st Session, S. Doc. 1; Report from the Ordnance Department, November 20, 1847, 30th Congress, 1st Session, S. Ex. Doc. 1; Klyza, "The United States Army, Natural Resources, and Political Development."

44. On political entrepreneurship, see Adam D. Sheingate, "Political Entrepreneurship, Institutional Change, and American Political Development," *Studies in American Political Development* 17:2 (Fall 2003): 185–203; Jan Schnellenbach, "Public Entrepreneurship and the Economics of Reform," *Journal of Institutional Economics* 3:2 (2007): 183–202.

45. Merritt Roe Smith, *Harper's Ferry Armory and the New Technology: The Challenge of Change* (Ithaca, NY: Cornell University Press, 1977), 28–30; Harry M. Ward, *The Department of War, 1781–1795* (Pittsburgh: University of Pittsburgh Press, 1962): 83–138.

46. Henry Dearborn to Lt. Col. Toussard, April 14, 1801, and June 1, 1801; and Dearborn to Major Cushing, June 1, 1801, National Archives, Records of the Office of the Secretary of War (RG 107), Letters Sent by the Secretary of War Relating to Military Affairs, 1800–1889.

47. Henry Dearborn to Decius Wadsworth, April 7, 1802, in National Archives, Records of the Office of the Secretary of War (RG 107), Letters Sent by the Secretary of War Relating to Military Affairs, 1800–1889; Dearborn to Eli Whitney, June 16, 1801, in National Archives, Records of the Office of the Secretary of War (RG 107), Miscellaneous Letters Sent by the Secretary of War, 1800–1809.

48. Henry Dearborn to Bissell, July 6, 1802, in National Archives, Records of the Office of the Secretary of War (RG 107), Letters Sent by the Secretary of War Relating to Military Affairs, 1800–1889.

49. Henry Dearborn to Major Daniel Jackson, April 30, 1801, in National Archives, Records of the Office of the Secretary of War (RG 107), Letters Sent by the Secretary of War Relating to Military Affairs, 1800–1889.

50. Angevine, *The Railroad and the State*, 9–11.

51. Larson, *Internal Improvement*, 110, 127–28, 137, 141.

52. American State Papers, Military Affairs, volume 2, House of Representatives, 15th Congress, 2nd Session, at 533–37; Angevine, *The Railroad and the State*, 16–18; Larson, *Internal Improvement*, 141–47.

53. David R. Mayhew, "Wars and American Politics," *Perspectives on Politics* 3:3 (September 2005): 473–93, quote on 476.

54. Angevine, *The Railroad and the State*, 18–21, 48.

55. Angevine, *The Railroad and the State*, 87–101; Charles F. O'Connell, Jr., "The Corps of Engineers and the Rise of Modern Management, 1827–1856," in Merritt Roe Smith, ed., *Military Enterprise and Technological Change: Perspectives on the American Experience* (Cambridge, MA: MIT Press, 1985): 87–116.

56. Angevine, *The Railroad and the State*, 61–63; Forest G. Hill, *Roads, Rails, and Waterways: The Army Engineers and Early Transportation* (Norman: University of Oklahoma Press, 1957), 90–94; Frank N. Schubert, *The Nation Builders: A Sesquicentennial History of the Corps of Topographical Engineers, 1838–1863* (Fort Belvoir, VA: Office of History, U.S. Army Corps of Engineers, 1988), 23–26.

57. Carpenter, *The Forging of Bureaucratic Autonomy*, 43.

58. Wilson, "The Politics of Procurement"; Wilson, *The Business of Civil War.*

59. Wilson, *The Business of Civil War*, 40.

60. Carpenter, *The Forging of Bureaucratic Autonomy*, 19–20.

61. Daniel Wirls and Stephen Wirls, *The Invention of the United States Senate* (Baltimore: Johns Hopkins University Press, 2004); James Sterling Young, *The Washington Community, 1800–1828* (New York: Columbia University Press, 1966). See, however, Allan G. Bogue and Mark Paul Marlaire, "Of Mess and Men: The Boardinghouse and Congressional Voting, 1821–1842," *American Journal of Political Science* 19:2 (May 1975): 207–30, who criticize Young's theory of early American political culture.

62. Shallat, *Structures in the Stream*, 128.

63. Larson, *Internal Improvement.*

64. Merritt Roe Smith, "Army Ordnance and the 'American System' of Manufacturing, 1815–1861," in Smith, *Military Enterprise and Technological Change*, 39–86, esp. 43–50.

65. Smith, "Army Ordnance and the 'American System'."

66. Lindsay Schakenbach Regele, *Manufacturing Advantage: War, the State, and the Origins of American Industry, 1776–1848* (Baltimore: Johns Hopkins University Press, 2019), chapters 3 and 6.

67. Smith, "Army Ordnance and the 'American System'," 70–74.

68. Smith, *Harper's Ferry Armory*, 266–69.

69. Tom Chaffin, *Pathfinder: John Charles Frémont and the Course of American Empire* (New York: Hill and Wang, 2002), 60.

70. In this respect I have been influenced by the argument put forward in Ira Katznelson and John S. Lapinski, "At the Crossroads: Congress and American Political Development," *Perspectives on Politics* 4 (2006): 243–60.

71. Shallat, *Structures in the Stream*, 43; Schubert, *The Nation Builders*, 4.

72. Schubert, *The Nation Builders*, chapter 1; Shallat, *Structures in the Stream*, 43–62.

73. Garry David Ryan, "War Department Topographical Bureau, 1831–1863: An Administrative History," Ph.D. dissertation, American University, 1968, 20–22.

74. Ryan, "War Department Topographical Bureau," 47–48.

75. *Journal of the House of Representatives of the United States*, volume 14, January 19, 1821.

76. *Journal of the House*, volume 14, January 19, 1821; *Annals of Congress*, House of Representatives, 16th Congress, 2nd Session, January 19, 1821.

77. *Annals of Congress*, House of Representatives, 16th Congress, 2nd Session, January 20, 1821.

78. *Annals of Congress*, House of Representatives, 16th Congress, 2nd Session, January 20, 1821, at 913.

79. *Annals of Congress*, House of Representatives, 16th Congress, 2nd Session, January 20, 1821, at 924–25.

80. *Annals of Congress*, House of Representatives, 16th Congress, 2nd Session, January 22, 1821, at 933–34, and appendix, at 1798–99.

81. *American State Papers*, Military Affairs, volume 3, Senate, 18th Congress, 2nd Session, January 24, 1825.

82. *Register of Debates*, 18th Congress, 2nd Session, February 11, 1825, at 556.

83. *Register of Debates*, 18th Congress, 2nd Session, February 11, 1825 (quote at 554).

84. *Register of Debates*, 18th Congress, 2nd Session, February 11, 1825.

85. On Jackson's support for improvements, especially for western states and territories, see Laurence J. Malone, *Opening the West: Federal Internal Improvements Before 1860* (Westport, CT: Greenwood Press, 1998).

86. *American State Papers*, Military Affairs, volume 3, 19th Congress, 1st Session, December 1, 1825.

87. *American State Papers*, Military Affairs, volume 3, 19th Congress, 2nd Session, November 18, 1826.

88. *American State Papers*, Military Affairs, volume 3, House of Representatives, 19th Congress, 1st Session, January 16, 1826, p. 185.

89. *American State Papers*, Military Affairs, volume 3, House of Representatives, 19th Congress, 1st Session, January 10, 1826.

90. Richard B. Latner, "The Nullification Crisis and Republican Subversion," *Journal of Southern History* 43:1 (February 1977): 19–38.

91. H.R. 51, 19th Congress, 1st Session, January 16, 1826.

92. Shallat, *Structures in the Stream*, 152–53, for instance, only discusses Abert's actions from 1831 through 1838. Schubert, *The Nation Builders*, chapter 2, starts his examination of their campaign for independence beginning in 1829.

93. *American State Papers*, Military Affairs, volume 3, House of Representatives, 19th Congress, 2nd Session, January 2, 1827, 492–93.

94. *American State Papers*, Military Affairs, volume 3, January 2, 1827, 492–93.

95. *American State Papers*, Military Affairs, volume 3, House of Representatives, 19th Congress, 2nd Session, January 2, 1827, 493–95.

96. H.R. 345, 19th Congress, 2nd Session, January 5, 1827.

97. *Niles' Weekly Register*, November 5, 1825, 157.

98. *Niles' Weekly Register*, October 22, 1825, 121; emphasis in the original.

99. *Literary Casket*, November 11, 1826, 155; *North American; or, Weekly Journal of Politics, Science, and Literature*, November 10, 1827, 202.

100. Schubert, *The Nation Builders*, 17.

101. Quoted in Ryan, "War Department Topographical Bureau," 75.

102. H.R. 57, 21st Congress, 1st Session, January 4, 1830; H.R. 96, 22nd Congress, 1st Session, December 23, 1831; *Register of Debates*, House of Representatives, 21st Congress, 1st Session, March 31, 1830; *American State Papers*, Military Affairs Volume 4, 21st Congress, 2nd Session, January 14, 1831.

103. Annual Report of the Secretary of War, Lewis Cass, November 21, 1831, 22nd Congress, 1st Session, H. Doc. 2; Schubert, *The Nation Builders*, 19–20.

104. Annual Report of the Secretary of War, Lewis Cass, November 21, 1831, 22nd Congress, 1st Session, H. Doc. 2; Shallat, *Structures in the Stream*, 139–40.

105. *Register of Debates*, Senate, 22nd Congress, 1st Session, June 1, 1832, 995. The bill is S. 137, 22nd Congress, 1st Session, March 5, 1832, also noted in *Journal of the Senate of the United States of America*, Volume 21, March 5, 1832, when it passed to a second reading.

106. *Register of Debates*, Senate, 22nd Congress, 1st Session, June 1, 1832.

107. Report from the Topographical Bureau, November 7, 1831, 22nd Congress, 1st Session, H. Doc. 2; Report from the Topographical Bureau, October 30, 1834, 23rd Congress, 2nd Session, S. Doc. 1.

108. *American States Papers*, Military Affairs, volume 3, December 16, 1834, 797 .

109. H.R. 567, 23rd Congress, 2nd Session, December 16, 1834; *Register of Debates*, 23rd Congress, 2nd Session, appendix, December 16, 1834.

110. William H. Goetzmann, *Army Exploration in the American West, 1803–1863* (Lincoln: University of Nebraska Press, 1959), 9–11.

111. Ryan, "War Department Topographical Bureau," 114.

112. Malone, *Opening the West*, chapter 4.

113. *Congressional Globe*, 24th Congress, 2nd Session, February 16, 1837, 190; *Register of Debates*, Senate, 24th Congress, 1st Session, June 10, 1836.

114. S. 52, 24th Congress, 1st Session, January 13, 1836; H.R. 104, 24th Congress, 1st Session, January 12, 1836.

115. *American State Papers*, Military Affairs, volume 6, House of Representatives, 24th Congress, 1st Session, January 12, 1836.

116. *American State Papers*, Military Affairs, volume 6, House of Representatives, 24th Congress, 1st Session, June 23, 1836.

117. *Congressional Globe*, House of Representatives, 25th Congress, 2nd Session, July 2, 1838.

118. Report from the Topographical Bureau, November 2, 1835, 24th Congress, 1st Session, H. Doc. 2; Report from the Topographical Bureau, November 15, 1836, 24th Congress, 2nd Session, H. Doc. 2; Report from the Topographical Bureau, November 7, 1837, 25th Congress, 2nd Session, S. Doc. 1; Annual Report of the Secretary of War, J. R. Poinsett, November 28, 1838, 25th Congress, 3rd Session, H. Doc. 2; Schubert, *The Nation Builders*, 21–24; Shallat, *Structures in the Stream*, 152–53.

119. Report from the Topographical Bureau, November 7, 1837, 25th Congress, 2nd Session, S. Doc. 1.

120. Annual Report of the Secretary of War, J. R. Poinsett, November 28, 1838, 25th Congress, 3rd Session, H. Doc. 2.

121. *Baltimore Sun*, December 20, 1837, 2.

122. *Baltimore Sun*, July 17, 1838, 4.

123. *Army and Navy Chronicle*, February 27, 1840, 136. On the role of service journals in the continuing professionalization of the antebellum military, see Skelton, *An American Profession of Arms*, 204–5.

124. Shallat, *Structures in the Stream*, 170–72; Annual Message of the President of the United States to the Two Houses of Congress, December 5, 1848, 30th Congress, 2nd Session, H. Exec. Doc. 1.

125. Chaffin, *Pathfinder*, 95–97, 242–43; Goetzmann, *Army Exploration in the American West*, 65–108; Vernon L. Volpe, "The Origins of the Fremont Expeditions: John J. Abert and the Scientific Exploration of the Trans-Mississippi West," *The Historian* 62:2 (December 2000): 245–63.

126. Shallat, *Structures in the Stream*, 84.

127. Schubert, *The Nation Builders*, 27.

128. Shallat, *Structures in the Stream*, 106; Ryan, "War Department Topographical Bureau," 143–44, 155–59; Schubert, *The Nation Builders*, 28–29.

129. *Journal of the Senate of the United States of America*, volume 44, February 18, 1853; *Congressional Globe*, 32nd Congress, 2nd Session, February 18, 1853, and February 19, 1853; Goetzmann, *Army Exploration in the American West*, 262–65.

130. Hill, *Roads, Rails, and Waterways*, 135–38.

131. *Baltimore Sun*, October 19, 1849, 1; *New York Daily Times*, May 27, 1853, 3; *New York Daily Times*, June 13, 1853, 3; *New York Daily Times*, July 19, 1853, 8; *New York Daily Times*, April 11, 1854, 1; *American Railway Times*, July 7, 1853, 2; *American Railway Times*, June 1, 1854, 2; *American Railway Times*, March 5, 1857, 1.

132. Goetzmann, *Army Exploration in the American West*, 209–10.

133. Goetzmann, *Army Exploration in the American West*, chapter 7; Angevine, *The Railroad and the State*, 114–19.

134. Matthew Karp, *This Vast Southern Empire: Slaveholders at the Helm of American Foreign Policy* (Cambridge, MA: Harvard University Press, 2016), 201.

135. Goetzmann, *Army Exploration in the American West*, 341–42; Annual Report of the Secretary of War, Jefferson Davis, December 4, 1854, 33rd Congress, 2nd Session, S. Ex. Doc. 1.

136. Shallat, *Structures in the Stream*, 178; Ryan, "War Department Topographical Bureau," 185–92.

137. Schubert, *The Nation Builders*, 74–79; Goetzmann, *Army Exploration in the American West*, 429–33. Goetzmann argues that the Civil War caused the destruction of the topographical corps, but his own evidence clearly indicates the loss of cross-partisan and cross-sectional support for the corps prior to the war's outbreak.

138. Risch, *Quartermaster Support of the Army*, chapters 6–8; Wilson, *The Business of Civil War*.

139. Wilson, "The Politics of Procurement."

140. Wilson, *The Business of Civil War*, 57–58, 74–78.

141. Pamela L. Baker, "The Washington National Road Bill and the Struggle to Adopt a Federal System of Internal Improvement," *Journal of the Early Republic* 22:3 (Autumn 2000):

437–64; Daniel M. Mulcare, "Restricted Authority: Slavery Politics, Internal Improvements, and the Limitation of National Administrative Capacity," *Political Research Quarterly* 61:4 (December 2008): 671–85.

142. Skowronek, *Building a New American State.*

143. Bensel, *Yankee Leviathan.*

144. William D. Adler and Andrew J. Polsky, "Building the New American Nation: Economic Development, Public Goods, and the Early U.S. Army," *Political Science Quarterly* 125:1 (Spring 2010): 87–110.

145. *Congressional Globe*, Senate, 24th Congress, 1st Session, June 2, 1836; emphasis in the original.

Conclusion

1. Two relatively recent important pieces that recognize the unsustainable nature of the weak state argument are Desmond King and Robert C. Lieberman, "Ironies of State Building: A Comparative Perspective on the American State," *World Politics* 61:3 (July 2009): 547–88, and William J. Novak, "The Myth of the 'Weak' American State," *American Historical Review* 113:3 (June 2008): 752–72.

2. On the military and economic development generally, see Vernon W. Ruttan, *Is War Necessary for Economic Growth? Military Procurement and Technology Development* (New York: Oxford University Press, 2006).

3. Federalist #14, in James Madison, Alexander Hamilton, and John Jay, *The Federalist Papers*, edited by Isaac Kramnick (New York: Penguin, 1987).

4. Matthew Karp, *This Vast Southern Empire: Slaveholders at the Helm of American Foreign Policy* (Cambridge, MA: Harvard University Press, 2016).

5. Samuel P. Huntington, *The Soldier and the State: The Theory and Politics of Civil-Military Relations* (Cambridge, MA: Harvard University Press, 1957); Peter D. Feaver, *Armed Servants: Agency, Oversight, and Civil-Military Relations* (Cambridge, MA: Harvard University Press, 2003); Eliot A. Cohen, *Supreme Command: Soldiers, Statesmen, and Leadership in Wartime* (New York: Anchor, 2002).

6. David C. Hendrickson, *Peace Pact: The Lost World of the American Founding* (Lawrence: University Press of Kansas, 2003), 211–19.

7. On Anti-Federalist thought, see Saul Cornell, *The Other Founders: Anti-Federalism and the Dissenting Tradition in America, 1788–1828* (Chapel Hill: University of North Carolina Press, 1999).

8. Don Higginbotham, "The Federalized Militia Debate: A Neglected Aspect of Second Amendment Scholarship," *William and Mary Quarterly*, 3rd ser., 55:1 (January 1998): 39–58. See also Clayton E. Cramer, *Armed America* (New York: Nelson Current, 2006).

9. "Essay by A Farmer and Planter," in Herbert J. Storing, ed., *The Complete Anti-Federalist*, (Chicago: University of Chicago Press, 1981), volume 5, 2.3.

10. Philip B. Kurland and Ralph Lerner, eds., *The Founders' Constitution* (Chicago: University of Chicago Press, 1987), volume 1, chapter 5, document 1. (Thanks to Michael Fisher for pointing me to this letter.) On supply problems during the Revolution, see Lucille E. Horgan, *Forged in War: The Continental Congress and the Origin of Military Supply and Acquisition Policy* (Westport, CT: Greenwood Press, 2002); Erna Risch, *Quartermaster Support of the Army, 1775–1939* (Washington, DC: Center of Military History, 1989), chapters 1–5.

11. Madison, Hamilton, and Jay, *The Federalist Papers*. Calculations by author.

12. Madison, Hamilton, and Jay, *The Federalist Papers*, 116–17.

13. Max M. Edling, *A Revolution in Favor of Government: Origins of the U.S. Constitution and the Making of the American State* (New York: Oxford University Press, 2003), chapter 5. See also Richard H. Kohn, *Eagle and Sword: The Beginnings of the Military Establishment in America* (New York: Free Press, 1975).

14. David S. Heidler and Jeanne T. Heidler, *Old Hickory's War: Andrew Jackson and the Quest for Empire* (Baton Rouge: Louisiana State University Press, 2003); William H. Crawford to Major General Andrew Jackson, July 9, 1816, in National Archives, Records of the Office of the Secretary of War (RG 107), Confidential and Unofficial Letters Sent by the Secretary of War, 1814–1847; John C. Calhoun to Major General Andrew Jackson, December 29, 1817, in National Archives, Records of the Office of the Secretary of War (RG 107), Letters Sent by the Secretary of War Relating to Military Affairs, 1800–1889; John C. Calhoun to General Andrew Jackson, December 28, 1818, in National Archives, Records of the Office of the Secretary of War (RG 107), Confidential and Unofficial Letters Sent by the Secretary of War, 1814–1847.

15. Elizabeth Sanders, "The Three American States," *Clio* 15:1 (Fall–Winter 2004–5): 1, 46–47.

16. Michael Mann, "The Autonomous Power of the State: Its Origins, Mechanisms and Results," *European Journal of Sociology* 25:2 (1984): 185–213.

17. Max Weber, *The Theory of Social and Economic Organization* (New York: Free Press, 1997), 154.

18. Marie Gottschalk's work on the uniqueness of America's prison system echoes some of these same themes, although in a very different context. See Gottschalk, "Hiding in Plain Sight: American Politics and the Carceral State," *Annual Review of Political Science* 11 (2008): 235–60.

19. Richard Franklin Bensel, *Yankee Leviathan: The Origins of Central State Authority in America, 1859–1877* (New York: Cambridge University Press, 1990).

20. See, for instance, Robert P. Saldin, *War, the American State, and Politics Since 1898* (New York: Cambridge University Press, 2011).

21. Ira Katznelson and Martin Shefter, eds., *Shaped by War and Trade: International Influences on American Political Development* (Princeton, NJ: Princeton University Press, 2002).

22. Ira Katznelson, "Flexible Capacity: The Military and Early American Statebuilding," in Katznelson and Shefter, *Shaped by War and Trade*, 82–110.

23. William H. Goetzmann, *Army Exploration in the American West, 1803–1863* (Lincoln: University of Nebraska Press, 1959); Forest G. Hill, *Roads, Rails, and Waterways: The Army Engineers and Early Transportation* (Norman: University of Oklahoma Press, 1957); Hill, "Formative Relations of American Enterprise, Government, and Science," *Political Science Quarterly* 75:3 (September 1960): 400–419; see also Carter Goodrich, *Government Promotion of American Canals and Railroads, 1800–1890* (New York: Columbia University Press, 1960); Francis Paul Prucha, *The Sword of the Republic: The United States Army on the Frontier, 1783–1846* (Lincoln: University of Nebraska Press, 1969); Prucha, *The Great Father: The United States Government and the American Indians* (Lincoln: University of Nebraska Press, 1984); Leonard White, *The Federalists: A Study in Administrative History* (New York: Collier-Macmillan, 1965); White, *The Jeffersonians: A Study in Administrative History, 1801–1829* (New York: Macmillan, 1961); White, *The Jacksonians: A Study in Administrative History, 1829–1861* (New York: Macmillan, 1954); White, *The Republican Era: A Study in Administrative History, 1869–1901* (New York: Macmillan, 1958). On White's contributions to the study of administrative

history as well as their limits, see Richard R. John, "Leonard D. White and the Invention of American Administrative History," *Reviews in American History* 24:2 (1996): 344–60.

24. Merritt Roe Smith, *Harpers Ferry Armory and the New Technology: The Challenge of Change* (Ithaca, NY: Cornell University Press, 1977); Todd Shallat, *Structures in the Stream: Water, Science, and the Rise of the U.S. Army Corps of Engineers* (Austin: University of Texas Press, 1994); Paul F. Paskoff, *Troubled Waters: Steamboat Disasters, River Improvements, and American Public Policy, 1821–1860* (Baton Rouge: Louisiana State University Press, 2007).

25. Peter Paret, "The New Military History," *Parameters* 31 (Autumn 1991): 10–18.

26. Jill Lepore, *The Name of War: King Philip's War and the Origins of American Identity* (New York: Vintage, 1999); Fred Anderson, *A People's Army: Massachusetts Soldiers and Society in the Seven Years' War* (Chapel Hill: University of North Carolina Press, 1996). See also Anderson and Andrew Cayton, *The Dominion of War: Empire and Liberty in North America, 1500–2000* (New York: Penguin, 2005).

27. For examples of recent works that focus on the Army's coercive role, see Durwood Ball, *Army Regulars on the Western Frontier, 1848–1861* (Norman: University of Oklahoma Press, 2001); Anderson and Cayton, *The Dominion of War*; William H. Bergmann, *The American National State and the Early West* (New York: Cambridge University Press, 2012); John Missall and Mary Lou Missall, *The Seminole Wars: America's Longest Indian Conflict* (Gainesville: University Press of Florida, 2004).

28. The notion of comparing Russia and the United States in this manner is not an entirely novel one. Besides the observations cited from Alexis de Tocqueville below, other historians have perceived the potential similarities between these two nations, leading to a small but interesting historiography. In 1952, for instance, Donald Treadgold, "Russian Expansion in the Light of Turner's Study of the American Frontier," *Agricultural History* 26:4 (October 1952): 147–52, pointed out the potential explanatory benefits of examining Russia's expansion through the lens of Frederick Jackson Turner's concept of the frontier mentality, something Turner himself briefly noted as well. One noteworthy work that produced a fruitful comparative account is Peter Kolchin's *Unfree Labor: American Slavery and Russian Serfdom* (Cambridge, MA: Belknap Press of the Harvard University Press, 1987). Besides Kolchin's work, however, there have only been scattered attempts to address these potential comparisons. In a recent book, *Empires Apart: A History of American and Russian Imperialism* (New York: Pegasus, 2011), Brian Landers contends that both Russia and the United States should be seen as imperialistic powers, which each use their power to extend hegemony in an attempt to control global resources. Landers's work, however, is a polemic and not a scholarly treatment of the subject. See also the recent article on the subject by Steven Sabol, "Comparing American and Russian Internal Colonization: The 'Touch of Civilisation' on the Sioux and the Kazakhs," *Western Historical Quarterly* 43:1 (Spring 2012): 29–51.

29. Quoted in G. J. Thurston, "Alexis De Tocqueville in Russia," *Journal of the History of Ideas* 37:2 (April–June 1976): 289–306.

30. David R. Jones, "Muscovite-Nomad Relations on the Steppe Frontier Before 1800 and the Development of Russia's 'Inclusive' Imperialism," in Wayne E. Lee, ed., *Empires and Indigenes: Intercultural Alliance, Imperial Expansion, and Warfare in the Early Modern World* (New York: New York University Press, 2011), 109–40.

31. Jones, "Muscovite-Nomad Relations"; C. M. Foust, "Russian Expansion to the East Through the Eighteenth Century," *Journal of Economic History* 21:4 (December 1961): 469–82.

32. Jones, "Muscovite-Nomad Relations"; Foust, "Russian Expansion to the East."

33. Kolchin, *Unfree Labor*; Jones, "Muscovite-Nomad Relations."

34. Mark Bassin, "Russia Between Europe and Asia: The Ideological Construction of Geographical Space," *Slavic Review* 50:1 (Spring 1991): 1–17; Robert I. Frost, *The Northern Wars: War, State, and Society in Northeastern Europe, 1558–1721* (London: Longman, 2000), chapters 9 and 10; Frost, *After the Deluge: Poland-Lithuania and the Second Northern War, 1655–1660* (New York: Cambridge University Press, 2004).

35. Foust, "Russian Expansion to the East," 471.

36. Foust, "Russian Expansion to the East"; Treadgold, "Russian Expansion"; Treadgold, *The Great Siberian Migration: Government and Peasant in Resettlement from Emancipation to the First World War* (Princeton, NJ: Princeton University Press, 1957).

37. Bergmann, *The American National State and the Early West*, 254–55; Francis Paul Prucha, *Broadax and Bayonet: The Role of the United States Army in the Development of the Northwest, 1815–1860* (Lincoln: University of Nebraska Press, 1973 [1953]), 11–13; Stephen J. Rockwell, *Indian Affairs and the Administrative State in the Nineteenth Century* (New York: Cambridge University Press, 2013), 57–126.

38. Mark Bassin, "Inventing Siberia: Visions of the Russian East in the Early Nineteenth Century," *American Historical Review* 96:3 (June 1991): 763–94; Bassin, *Imperial Visions: Nationalist Imagination and Geographical Expansion in the Russian Far East, 1840–1865* (New York: Cambridge University Press, 1999).

39. Henry Nash Smith, *Virgin Land: The American West as Symbol and Myth* (New York: Vintage Books, 1962); Peter Onuf, *Jefferson's Empire: The Language of American Nationhood* (Charlottesville: University of Virginia Press, 2000); Richard Slotkin, *Regeneration Through Violence: The Mythology of the American Frontier, 1600–1860* (Hanover, NH: Wesleyan University Press, 1973); Slotkin, *The Fatal Environment: The Myth of the Frontier in the Age of Industrialization, 1800–1890* (New York: Macmillan, 1985); Slotkin, *Gunfighter Nation: The Myth of the Frontier in Twentieth-Century America* (New York: Atheneum, 1992).

40. Theodore J. Karamanski, *Fur Trade and Exploration: Opening the Far Northwest, 1821–1852* (Norman: University of Oklahoma Press, 1983), 23–26; Foust, "Russian Expansion to the East."

41. Karamanski, *Fur Trade and Exploration*, 26–29; Howard I. Kushner, *Conflict on the Northwest Coast: American-Russian Rivalry in the Pacific Northwest, 1790–1867* (Westport, CT: Greenwood Press, 1975), 6–19.

42. Karamanski, *Fur Trade and Exploration*, 29–34; Kushner, *Conflict on the Northwest Coast*, 25–62.

43. Kushner, *Conflict on the Northwest Coast*, 81–105.

44. Howard I. Kushner, "Visions of the Northwest: Gwin and Seward in the 1850's," *Western Historical Quarterly* 4:3 (July 1973): 295–306, quote at 296.

45. Speech of William H. Seward, at the dedication of Capital University, Columbus, Ohio, September 14, 1853, "The Destiny of America" (Albany: Weed, Parsons, 1853), accessed at http://frontiers.loc.gov/cgi-bin/ampage?collId=mtfgc&fileName=1002/mtfgc1002.db&recNum=0&itemLink=r?intldl/mtftext:@field%28DOCID+@lit%28mtfgc1002_1%29%29%2310021&linkText=1.

46. Allan B. Cole, "The Ringgold-Rodgers-Brooke Expedition to Japan and the North Pacific, 1853–1859," *Pacific Historical Review* 16:2 (May 1947): 152–62; Kushner, "Visions of the Northwest"; Geoffrey Sutton Smith, "The Navy Before Darwinism: Science, Exploration, and Diplomacy in Antebellum America," *American Quarterly* 28:1 (Spring 1976): 41–55.

47. For more on the central role of the Navy to the expanding American empire, see Max Boot, *The Savage Wars of Peace: Small Wars and the Rise of American Power* (New York: Basic Books, 2003); William P. Leeman, *The Long Road to Annapolis: The Founding of the Naval Academy and the Emerging American Republic* (Chapel Hill: University of North Carolina Press, 2010); Michael B. Oren, *Power, Faith, and Fantasy: America in the Middle East, 1776 to Present* (New York: W. W. Norton, 2007).

48. Kushner, *Conflict on the Northwest Coast*, 117–55; N. N. Bolkhovitinov, "The Sale of Alaska in the Context of Russo-American Relations in the Nineteenth Century," in Hugh Ragsdale, ed. and trans., *Imperial Russian Foreign Policy* (New York: Cambridge University Press, 1993), 193–215.

49. Speech of William H. Seward, Sitka, Alaska, August 12, 1869 (Washington, DC: James J. Chapman, 1879), accessed at http://frontiers.loc.gov/cgi-bin/ampage?collId=mtfgc&fileName=1003/mtfgc1003.db&recNum=0&itemLink=r?intldl/mtftext:@field%28DOCI+@lit%28mtfgc1003_2%29%29%2310032&linkText=1.

50. Bassin, "Inventing Siberia," 784–91.

51. Federalist #14, in James Madison, Alexander Hamilton, and John Jay, *The Federalist Papers*, ed. Clinton Rossiter (New York: Signet Classic, 2003), 98

52. Federalist #14, in Madison, Hamilton, and Jay, *The Federalist Papers*, 99.

53. Federalist #14, in Madison, Hamilton, and Jay, *The Federalist Papers*, 99.

54. Quoted in Gordon S. Wood, *Empire of Liberty: A History of the Early Republic, 1789–1815* (New York: Oxford University Press, 2009), 484.

55. Quoted in Wood, *Empire of Liberty*, 699.

56. Bensel, *Yankee Leviathan*.

BIBLIOGRAPHY

Primary Sources

American State Papers.
Annals of Congress.
Carter, Susan B., Scott Sigmund Gartner, Michael R. Haines, Alan L. Olmstead, Richard Sutch, and Gavin Wright, eds. *Historical Statistics of the United States: Earliest Times to the Present* (Millennial Edition), volume 5. New York: Cambridge University Press, 2006.
Congressional Globe.
Gunnison, John Williams. *The Mormons or Latter Day Saints in the Valley of the Great Salt Lake, a History of Their Rise and Progress, Peculiar Doctrines, Present Conditions and Projects.* Philadelphia: Lippincott, Grambo, 1852.
Journal of the House of Representatives.
Journal of the Senate.
National Archives, Records of the Office of the Secretary of War.
Register of Debates.
Sollenberger, Mitchel A. "Presidential Vetoes 1789–Present: A Summary Overview." Congressional Research Service, Report 98-148, April 2004.
Stansbury, Howard. *An Expedition to the Valley of the Great Salt Lake of Utah.* Philadelphia: Lippincott, Grambo, 1855.
U.S. Serial Set.

Secondary Sources

Ablavsky, Gregory. "The Savage Constitution." *Duke Law Journal* 63:5 (February 2014): 999–1089.
Acemoglu, Daron, Francisco A. Gallego, and James A. Robinson. "Institutions, Human Capital, and Development." *Annual Review of Economics* 6 (2014): 875–912.
Acemoglu, Daron, Jacob Moscona, and James A. Robinson. "State Capacity and American Technology: Evidence from the Nineteenth Century." *American Economic Review* 106:5 (May 2016): 61–67.
Acemoglu, Daron, and James A. Robinson. *Why Nations Fail: The Origins of Power, Prosperity, and Poverty.* New York: Crown, 2012.
Adler, William D., and Andrew J. Polsky. "Building the New American Nation: Economic Development, Public Goods, and the Early U.S. Army." *Political Science Quarterly* 125:1 (Spring 2010): 87–110.
Ahrens, Joachim. *Governance and Economic Development: A Comparative Institutional Approach.* Northampton, MA: Edward Elgar, 2002.

Aldrich, John H. *Why Parties? The Origin and Transformation of Political Parties in America.* Chicago: University of Chicago Press, 1995.

Anderson, Fred. *A People's Army: Massachusetts Soldiers and Society in the Seven Years' War.* Chapel Hill: University of North Carolina Press, 1996.

Anderson, Fred, and Andrew Cayton. *The Dominion of War: Empire and Liberty in North America, 1500–2000.* New York: Penguin, 2005.

Angevine, Robert G. *The Railroad and the State: War, Politics, and Technology in Nineteenth-Century America.* Stanford, CA: Stanford University Press, 2004.

Atack, Jeremy. "The Impact of Access to Rail Transportation on Agricultural Improvement: The American Midwest as a Test Case, 1850–1860." *Journal of Transport and Land Use* 4:2 (Summer 2011): 5–18.

Atack, Jeremy, Fred Bateman, and William N. Parker. "Northern Agriculture and the Westward Movement," in Stanley L. Engerman and Robert E. Gallman, eds., *The Cambridge Economic History of the United States* (volume 2: *The Long Nineteenth Century*). New York: Cambridge University Press, 2000: 285–328.

Atack, Jeremy, and Peter Passell. *A New Economic View of American History.* 2nd ed. New York: W. W. Norton, 1994.

Baker, Pamela L. "The Washington National Road Bill and the Struggle to Adopt a Federal System of Internal Improvement." *Journal of the Early Republic* 22:3 (Autumn 2000): 437–64.

Ball, Durwood. *Army Regulars on the Western Frontier, 1848–1861.* Norman: University of Oklahoma Press, 2001.

Balogh, Brian. "Reorganizing the Organizational Synthesis: Federal-Professional Relations in Modern America." *Studies in American Political Development* 5:2 (Summer 1991): 119–72.

———. *A Government Out of Sight: The Mystery of National Authority in Nineteenth-Century America.* New York: Cambridge University Press, 2009.

Bassin, Mark. "Russia Between Europe and Asia: The Ideological Construction of Geographical Space." *Slavic Review* 50:1 (Spring 1991): 1–17.

———. "Inventing Siberia: Visions of the Russian East in the Early Nineteenth Century." *American Historical Review* 96:3 (June 1991): 763–94.

———. *Imperial Visions: Nationalist Imagination and Geographical Expansion in the Russian Far East, 1840–1865.* New York: Cambridge University Press, 1999.

Bates, Robert H. *Prosperity and Violence: The Political Economy of Development.* New York: W. W. Norton, 2009.

Bean, Richard. "War and the Birth of the Nation State." *Journal of Economic History* 33:1 (March 1973): 203–21.

Becker, Lawrence A. *Doing the Right Thing: Collective Action and Procedural Choice in the New Legislative Process.* Columbus: Ohio State University Press, 2005.

Bell, William Gardner. *Secretaries of War and Secretaries of the Army: Portraits and Biographical Sketches.* Washington, DC: Center of Military History, 1992.

Bensel, Richard Franklin. *Sectionalism and American Political Development: 1880–1980.* Madison: University of Wisconsin Press, 1984.

———. *Yankee Leviathan: The Origins of Central State Authority in America, 1859–1877.* New York: Cambridge University Press, 1990.

Bergmann, William H. *The American National State and the Early West.* New York: Cambridge University Press, 2012.

Bogue, Allan G., and Mark Paul Marlaire. "Of Mess and Men: The Boardinghouse and Congressional Voting, 1821–1842." *American Journal of Political Science* 19:2 (May 1975): 207–30.

Bolkhovitinov, N. N. "The Sale of Alaska in the Context of Russo-American Relations in the Nineteenth Century," in Hugh Ragsdale, ed. and trans., *Imperial Russian Foreign Policy*. New York: Cambridge University Press, 1993: 193–215.

Bonthius, Andrew. "The Patriot War of 1837–1838: Locofocoism with a Gun?" *Labour/Le Travail* 52 (Fall 2003): 9–43.

Boot, Max. *The Savage Wars of Peace: Small Wars and the Rise of American Power*. New York: Basic Books, 2003.

Brown, Alan S. "The Role of the Army in Western Settlement: Josiah Harmar's Command, 1785–1790." *Pennsylvania Magazine of History and Biography* 93 (April 1969): 161–78.

Browne, Susan M. "War-Making and U.S. State Formation: Mobilization, Demobilization, and the Inherent Ambiguities of Federalism," in Diane E. Davis and Anthony W. Pereira, eds., *Irregular Armed Forces and Their Role in Politics and State Formation*. New York: Cambridge University Press, 2003: 232–52.

Buchanan, James. *The Demand and Supply of Public Goods*. New York: McNally, 1968.

Burke, John G. "Bursting Boilers and the Federal Power." *Technology and Culture* 7:1 (Winter 1966): 1–23.

Burke, John P. "The Institutional Presidency," in Michael Nelson, ed., *The Presidency and the Political System*. 8th ed. Washington, DC: CQ Press, 2006: 383–409.

Callen, Zachary. *Railroads and American Political Development: Infrastructure, Federalism, and State Building*. Lawrence: University Press of Kansas, 2016.

Calloway, Colin G. *The Shawnees and the War for America*. New York: Viking, 2007.

Carpenter, Daniel P. *The Forging of Bureaucratic Autonomy: Reputations, Networks, and Policy Innovation in Executive Agencies, 1862–1928*. Princeton, NJ: Princeton University Press, 2001.

———. *Reputation and Power: Organizational Image and Pharmaceutical Regulation at the FDA*. Princeton, NJ: Princeton University Press, 2010.

Carpenter, Daniel P., and Colin D. Moore. "Robust Action and the Strategic Use of Ambiguity in a Bureaucratic Cohort: FDA Officers and the Evolution of New Drug Regulations, 1950–70," in Stephen Skowronek and Matthew Glassman, eds., *Formative Acts: American Politics in the Making*. Philadelphia: University of Pennsylvania Press, 2007: 340–62.

Carpenter, Daniel, and Gisela Sin. "Policy Tragedy and the Emergence of Regulation: The Food, Drug, and Cosmetic Act of 1938." *Studies in American Political Development* 21:2 (Fall 2007): 149–80.

Carter, John J. *Covert Operations as a Tool of Presidential Foreign Policy in American History from 1800 to 1920: Foreign Policy in the Shadows*. Lewiston, NY: Edwin Mellen Press, 2000.

Cayton, Andrew R. L. "'Separate Interests' and the Nation-State: The Washington Administration and the Origins of Regionalism in the Trans-Appalachian West." *Journal of American History* 79:1 (June 1992): 39–67.

Chaffin, Tom. *Pathfinder: John Charles Frémont and the Course of American Empire*. New York: Hill and Wang, 2002.

Chandler, Alfred D., Jr. *The Visible Hand: The Managerial Revolution in American Business*. Cambridge, MA: Belknap Press of Harvard University Press, 1977.

Chang, Ha-Joon. *Kicking Away the Ladder: Policies and Institutions for Economic Development in Historical Perspective*. London: Anthem Press, 2002.

Chervinsky, Lindsay M. "George Washington and the First Presidential Cabinet." *Presidential Studies Quarterly* 48:1 (March 2018): 139–52.

Cingolani, Luciana, Kaj Thomsson, and Denis de Crombrugghe. "Minding Weber More Than Ever? The Impacts of State Capacity and Bureaucratic Autonomy on Development Goals." *World Development* 72 (August 2015): 191–207.

Clark, Gregory. *A Farewell to Alms: A Brief Economic History of the World*. Princeton, NJ: Princeton University Press, 2008.

Coakley, Robert W. *The Role of Federal Military Forces in Domestic Disorders, 1789–1878*. Washington, DC: Center of Military History, 1988.

Cochran, Thomas C. *Frontiers of Change: Early Industrialism in America*. New York: Oxford University Press, 1981.

Cohen, Eliot A. *Supreme Command: Soldiers, Statesmen, and Leadership in Wartime*. New York: Anchor, 2003.

———. "The Unequal Dialogue: The Theory and Reality of Civil-Military Relations and the Use of Force," in Peter D. Feaver and Richard H. Kohn, eds., *Soldiers and Civilians: The Civil-Military Gap and American National Security*. Cambridge, MA: MIT Press, 2001.

Cole, Allan B. "The Ringgold-Rodgers-Brooke Expedition to Japan and the North Pacific, 1853–1859." *Pacific Historical Review* 16:2 (May 1947): 152–62.

Conron, Michael A. "Law, Politics, and Chief Justice Taney: A Reconsideration of the *Luther v. Borden* Decision." *American Journal of Legal History* 11:4 (October 1967): 377–88.

Cornell, Saul. *The Other Founders: Anti-Federalism and the Dissenting Tradition in America, 1788–1828*. Chapel Hill: University of North Carolina Press, 1999.

Costa, Dora L., and Naomi R. Lamoreaux, eds. *Understanding Long-Run Economic Growth: Geography, Institutions, and the Knowledge Economy*. Chicago: University of Chicago Press, 2011.

Crackel, Theodore J. *Mr. Jefferson's Army: Political and Social Reform of the Military Establishment, 1801–1809*. New York: New York University Press, 1987.

———. "The Military Academy in the Context of Jeffersonian Reform," in Robert M. S. McDonald, ed., *Thomas Jefferson's Military Academy: Founding West Point*. Charlottesville: University of Virginia Press, 2004: 99–117.

Cramer, Clayton E. *Armed America*. New York: Nelson Current, 2006.

Cress, Lawrence Delbert. "Radical Whiggery on the Role of the Military: Ideological Roots of the American Revolutionary Militia." *Journal of the History of Ideas* 40:1 (January–March 1979): 43–60.

———. *Citizens in Arms: The Army and Militia in American Society to the War of 1812*. Chapel Hill: University of North Carolina Press, 1982.

Cullum, George W. *Biographical Register of the Officers and Graduates of the U.S. Military Academy at West Point, N.Y., from its Establishment March 16, 1802 to the Army Reorganization of 1866–67*. Volume 1, 1802–1840. New York: D. Van Nostrand, 1868.

Cunliffe, Marcus. *Soldiers and Civilians: The Martial Spirit in America, 1775–1865*. New York: Little, Brown, 1968.

Dam, Kenneth W. *The Law-Growth Nexus: The Rule of Law and Economic Development*. Washington, DC: Brookings Institution Press, 2006.

Dauber, Michelle Landis. *The Sympathetic State: Disaster Relief and the Origins of the American Welfare State*. Chicago: University of Chicago Press, 2013.

de Tocqueville, Alexis. *Democracy in America: Historical-Critical Edition of De la démocratie en Amérique*, ed. Eduardo Nolla, trans. James T. Schleifer. Bilingual French-English ed. Indianapolis: Liberty Fund, 2010.

Dincecco, Mark. *State Capacity and Economic Development: Present and Past.* New York: Cambridge University Press, 2017.

Dincecco, Mark, and Gabriel Katz. "State Capacity and Long-Run Economic Performance." *The Economic Journal* 126:590 (February 2016): 189–218.

Donaldson, Dave, and Richard Hornbeck. "Railroads and American Economic Growth: A 'Market Access' Approach." *Quarterly Journal of Economics* 131:2 (May 2016): 799–858.

Dorsey, Leroy G., ed. *The Presidency and Rhetorical Leadership.* College Station: Texas A&M University Press, 2002.

Dougherty, Keith L. *Collective Action Under the Articles of Confederation.* New York: Cambridge University Press, 2001. Downing, Brian M. *The Military Revolution and Political Change: Origins of Democracy and Autocracy in Early Modern Europe.* Princeton, NJ: Princeton University Press, 1992.

Dunlavy, Colleen A. *Politics and Industrialization: Early Railroads in the United States and Prussia.* Princeton, NJ: Princeton University Press, 1994.

Edling, Max M. *A Revolution in Favor of Government: Origins of the U.S. Constitution and the Making of the American State.* New York: Oxford University Press, 2003.

———. *A Hercules in the Cradle: War, Money, and the American State, 1783–1867.* Chicago: University of Chicago Press, 2014.

Edling, Max M., and Mark D. Kaplanoff, "Alexander Hamilton's Fiscal Reform: Transforming the Structure of Taxation in the Early Republic." *William and Mary Quarterly* 61:4 (October 2004): 713–44.

Eisenhower, John S. D. *So Far from God: The U.S. War with Mexico, 1846–1848.* New York: Anchor Books, 1990.

Eisner, Marc Allen. *From Warfare State to Welfare State: World War I, Compensatory State Building, and the Limits of the Modern Order.* University Park: Pennsylvania State University Press, 2000.

Elkins, Stanley, and Eric McKitrick, *The Age of Federalism: The Early American Republic, 1788–1800.* New York: Oxford University Press, 1993.

Engerman, Stanley L., and Robert E. Gallman, eds. *The Cambridge Economic History of the United States* (volume 2: *The Long Nineteenth Century*). New York: Cambridge University Press, 2000.

Engerman, Stanley L., and Kenneth L. Sokoloff. "Debating the Role of Institutions in Political and Economic Development: Theory, History, and Findings." *Annual Review of Political Science* 11 (2008): 119–35.

———. "Once Upon a Time in the Americas: Land and Immigration Policies in the New World," in Dora L. Costa and Naomi R. Lamoreaux, eds., *Understanding Long-Run Economic Growth: Geography, Institutions, and the Knowledge Economy.* Chicago: University of Chicago Press, 2011: 13–48.

———. *Economic Development in the Americas Since 1500: Endowments and Institutions.* New York: Cambridge University Press, 2012.

Epstein, David, and Sharyn O'Halloran. "Asymmetric Information, Delegation, and the Structure of Policy-Making." *Journal of Theoretical Politics* 11:1 (1999): 37–56.

Ericson, David F. "The Nullification Crisis, American Republicanism, and the Force Bill Debate." *Journal of Southern History* 61:2 (May 1995): 249–70.

———. "The Federal Government and Slavery: Following the Money Trail." *Studies in American Political Development* 19:1 (Spring 2005): 105–16.

———. *Slavery in the American Republic: Developing the Federal Government, 1791–1861.* Lawrence: University Press of Kansas, 2011.

———. "The United States Military, State Development, and Slavery in the Early Republic." *Studies in American Political Development* 31:1 (April 2017): 130–48.

Ertman, Thomas. *Birth of the Leviathan: Building States and Regimes in Medieval and Early Modern Europe.* New York: Cambridge University Press, 1997.

Evans, Peter, and James E. Rauch, "Bureaucracy and Growth: A Cross-National Analysis of the Effects of 'Weberian' State Structures on Economic Growth." *American Sociological Review* 64:5 (October 1999): 748–65.

Farley, James J. *Making Arms in the Machine Age: Philadelphia's Frankford Arsenal, 1816–1870.* University Park: Pennsylvania State University Press, 1994.

Feaver, Peter D. *Armed Servants: Agency, Oversight, and Civil-Military Relations.* Cambridge, MA: Harvard University Press, 2005.

Fehrenbacher, Don. *The Slaveholding Republic: An Account of the United States Government's Relations to Slavery.* New York: Oxford University Press, 2001.

Ferejohn, John, and Charles Shipan. "Congressional Influence on Bureaucracy." *Journal of Law, Economics, and Organization* 6:1 (April 1990): 1–20.

Field, Ron. *Forts of the American Frontier, 1820–91: Central and Northern Plains.* Westminster, MD: Osprey, 2005.

———. *Forts of the American Frontier, 1820–91: The Southern Plains and Southwest.* Westminster, MD: Osprey, 2006.

Fishlow, Albert. *American Railroads and the Transformation of the Ante-bellum Economy.* Cambridge, MA: Harvard University Press, 1965.

———. "Internal Transportation in the Nineteenth and Early Twentieth Centuries," in Stanley L. Engerman and Robert E. Gallman, eds., *The Cambridge Economic History of the United States* (volume 2: *The Long Nineteenth Century*). New York: Cambridge University Press, 2000: 543–642.

Fogel, Robert William. *Railroads and American Economic Growth: Essays in Econometric History.* Baltimore: Johns Hopkins University Press, 1964.

Fortin-Rittberger, Jessica. "Exploring the Relationship Between Infrastructural and Coercive State Capacity." *Democratization* 21:7 (2014): 1244–64.

Foust, C. M. "Russian Expansion to the East Through the Eighteenth Century." *Journal of Economics History* 21:4 (December 1961): 469–82.

Frankel, Jeffrey A. "The 1807–1809 Embargo Against Great Britain." *Journal of Economic History* 42:2 (June 1982): 291–308.

Franklin, W. Neil. "Pennsylvania-Virginia Rivalry for the Indian Trade of the Ohio Valley." *Mississippi Valley Historical Review* 20:4 (March 1934): 463–80.

Frazer, Robert W. *Forts and Supplies: The Role of the Army in the Economy of the Southwest, 1846–1861.* Albuquerque: University of New Mexico Press, 1983.

Freehling, William W. *Prelude to Civil War: The Nullification Controversy in South Carolina, 1816–1836.* New York: Harper and Row, 1966.

French-Hodson, Ruth Anne. "New Economics of Organization and Nineteenth-Century Bureaucracies: A Study of the Bureau of Indian Affairs." M.Phil. thesis, Merton College, University of Oxford, 2007.

Friedberg, Aaron L. *In the Shadow of the Garrison State: America's Anti-statism and Its Cold War Grand Strategy*. Princeton, NJ: Princeton University Press, 2000.

Frost, Robert I. *The Northern Wars: War, State, and Society in Northeastern Europe, 1558–1721*. London: Longman, 2000.

———. *After the Deluge: Poland-Lithuania and the Second Northern War, 1655–1660*. New York: Cambridge University Press, 2004.

Frymer, Paul. "Building an American Empire: Territorial Expansion in the Antebellum Era." *UC Irvine Law Review* 1:3 (September 2011): 913–54.

———. "'A Rush and a Push and the Land Is Ours': Territorial Expansion, Land Policy, and U.S. State Formation." *Perspectives on Politics* 12:1 (March 2014): 119–44.

———. *Building an American Empire: The Era of Territorial and Political Expansion*. Princeton, NJ: Princeton University Press, 2017.

Fukuyama, Francis. "What Is Governance?" *Governance* 26:3 (July 2013): 347–68.

Furniss, Norman F. *The Mormon Conflict, 1850–1859*. New Haven, CT: Yale University Press, 1960.

Furstenberg, Francois. "The Significance of the Trans-Appalachian Frontier in Atlantic History." *American Historical Review* 113:3 (June 2008): 647–77.

Galambos, Louis. "The Emerging Organizational Synthesis in Modern American History." *Business History Review* 44:3 (Autumn 1970): 279–90.

———. "Technology, Political Economy, and Professionalism: Central Themes in the Organizational Synthesis." *Business History Review* 57:4 (Winter 1983): 471–93.

Gallman, Robert E. "Economic Growth and Structural Change in the Long Nineteenth Century," in Stanley L. Engerman and Gallman, eds., *The Cambridge Economic History of the United States* (volume 2: *The Long Nineteenth Century*). New York: Cambridge University Press, 2000: 1–55.

Gannon, Kevin M. "Escaping 'Mr. Jefferson's Plan of Destruction': New England Federalists and the Idea of a Northern Confederacy, 1803–1804." *Journal of the Early Republic* 21:3 (Autumn 2001): 413–43.

Gerhardt, Michael J. "Constitutional Construction and Departmentalism: A Case Study of the Demise of the Whig Presidency." *University of Pennsylvania Journal of Constitutional Law* 12:2 (January 2010): 425–59.

Goetzmann, William H. *Army Exploration in the American West, 1803–1863*. Lincoln: University of Nebraska Press, 1959.

———. *When the Eagle Screamed: The Romantic Horizon in American Diplomacy, 1800–1860*. New York: John Wiley and Sons, 1966.

———. *Exploration and Empire: The Explorer and Scientist in the Winning of the American West*. New York: Norton, 1978 [1966].

Golden, Miriam, and Brian Min. "Distributive Politics Around the World." *Annual Review of Political Science* 16 (2013): 73–99.

Goodrich, Carter. *Government Promotion of American Canals and Railroads, 1800–1890*. New York: Columbia University Press, 1960.

Gottschalk, Marie. "Hiding in Plain Sight: American Politics and the Carceral State." *Annual Review of Political Science* 11 (2008): 235–60.

Gourevitch, Peter. "The Role of Politics in Economic Development." *Annual Review of Political Science* 11 (2008): 137–59.

Greenberg, Amy S. "Pirates, Patriots, and Public Meetings: Antebellum Expansionism and Urban Culture." *Journal of Urban History* 31:5 (July 2005): 634–50.

Grenier, John. *The First Way of War: American War Making on the Frontier.* New York: Cambridge University Press, 2005.

Griffin, Patrick. *American Leviathan: Empire, Nation, and Revolutionary Frontier.* New York: Hill and Wang, 2008.

Haggard, Stephan, Andrew MacIntyre, and Lydia Tiede. "The Rule of Law and Economic Development." *Annual Review of Political Science* 11 (2008): 205–34.

Hall, Peter A., and David Soskice, eds. *Varieties of Capitalism: The Institutional Foundations of Comparative Advantage.* New York: Oxford University Press, 2001.

Hall, Peter A., and Kathleen Thelen, "Institutional Change in Varieties of Capitalism." *Socio-economic Review* 7:1 (January 2009): 7–34.

Hammond, Thomas H., and Jack H. Knott. "Who Controls the Bureaucracy? Presidential Power, Congressional Dominance, Legal Constraints, and Bureaucratic Autonomy in a Model of Multi-institutional Policy-Making." *Journal of Law, Economics, and Organization* 12:1 (March 1996): 119–66.

Handlin, Oscar, and Mary Flug Handlin. *Commonwealth: A Study of the Role of Government in the American Economy: Massachusetts, 1774–1861.* New York: New York University Press, 1947.

Hartz, Louis. *Economic Policy and Democratic Thought: Pennsylvania, 1776–1860.* Cambridge, MA: Harvard University Press, 1948.

———. *The Liberal Tradition in America.* New York: Harvest Books, 1955.

Heidler, David S., and Jeanne T. Heidler. *Old Hickory's War: Andrew Jackson and the Quest for Empire.* Baton Rouge: Louisiana State University Press, 2003.

Henderson, Dwight F. "Treason, Sedition, and Fries' Rebellion." *American Journal of Legal History* 14:4 (October 1970): 308–18.

Hendrickson, David C. *Peace Pact: The Lost World of the American Founding.* Lawrence: University Press of Kansas, 2003.

Herrendorf, Berthold, James A. Schmitz, Jr., and Arilton Teixera. "The Role of Transportation in U.S. Economic Development: 1840–1860." *International Economic Review* 53:3 (August 2012): 693–716

Heumann, Stefan, "The Tutelary Empire: State- and Nation-Building in the 19th Century United States." Ph.D. dissertation, University of Pennsylvania, 2009.

———. "State, Nation, and Empire: The Formation of the US." *Journal of Political Power* 4:3 (2011): 375–93.

Higginbotham, Don. "The Federalized Militia Debate: A Neglected Aspect of Second Amendment Scholarship." *William and Mary Quarterly*, 3rd ser., 55:1 (January 1998): 39–58.

Hill, Forest G. *Roads, Rails, and Waterways: The Army Engineers and Early Transportation.* Norman: University of Oklahoma Press, 1957.

———. "Formative Relations of American Enterprise, Government, and Science." *Political Science Quarterly* 75:3 (September 1960): 400–419.

Hilt, Eric. "Economic History, Historical Analysis, and the 'New History of Capitalism.'" *Journal of Economic History* 77:2 (June 2017): 511–36.

Hogan, Michael J. *A Cross of Iron: Harry S. Truman and the Origins of the National Security State, 1945–1954*. New York: Cambridge University Press, 2000.

Holt, Michael F. *The Rise and Fall of the American Whig Party: Jacksonian Politics and the Onset of the Civil War*. New York: Oxford University Press, 2003.

Hooker, Richard D., Jr. "Soldiers of the State: Reconsidering American Civil-Military Relations." *Parameters* 33:4 (Winter 2003–4): 4–18.

Horgan, Lucille E. *Forged in War: The Continental Congress and the Origins of Military Supply and Acquisition Policy*. Westport, CT: Greenwood Press, 2002.

Hounshell, David. *From the American System to Mass Production, 1800–1932: The Development of Manufacturing Technology in the United States*. Baltimore: Johns Hopkins University Press, 1985.

Howe, Daniel Walker. *What Hath God Wrought: The Transformation of America, 1815–1848*. New York: Oxford University Press, 2007.

Howe, John R., Jr. "Republican Thought and the Political Violence of the 1790s." *American Quarterly* 19:2 (Summer 1967), 147–65.

Howell, William G., and Jon Pevehouse. *While Dangers Gather: Congressional Checks on Presidential War Powers*. Princeton, NJ: Princeton University Press, 2007.

Hsieh, Wayne Wei-Siang. *West Pointers and the Civil War: The Old Army in War and Peace*. Chapel Hill: University of North Carolina Press, 2009.

Huntington, Samuel P. *The Soldier and the State: The Theory and Politics of Civil-Military Relations*. Cambridge, MA: Harvard University Press, 1957.

Hurt, R. Douglas. *The Indian Frontier, 1763–1846*. Albuquerque: University of New Mexico Press, 2002.

Irwin, Douglas A., and Richard Sylla, eds. *Founding Choices: American Economic Policy in the 1790s*. Chicago: University of Chicago Press, 2011.

Janowitz, Morris. *The Professional Soldier: A Social and Political Portrait*. Glencoe, IL: Free Press, 1960.

Jensen, Jeffrey L., and Adam J. Ramey. "Going Postal: State Capacity and Violent Dispute Resolution." *Journal of Comparative Economics* 48:4 (December 2020): 779–96.

Jensen, Laura. *Patriots, Settlers, and the Origins of American Social Policy*. New York: Cambridge University Press, 2003.

John, Richard R. *Spreading the News: The American Postal System from Franklin to Morse*. Cambridge, MA: Harvard University Press, 1995.

———. "Leonard D. White and the Invention of American Administrative History." *Reviews in American History* 24:2 (1996): 344–60.

———. "Governmental Institutions as Agents of Change: Rethinking American Political Development in the Early Republic, 1787–1835." *Studies in American Political Development* 11:2 (Fall 1997): 347–80.

———. "Affairs of Office: The Executive Departments, the Election of 1828, and the Making of the Democratic Party," in Meg Jacobs, William J. Novak, and Julian E. Zelizer, eds., *The Democratic Experiment: New Directions in American Political History*. Princeton, NJ: Princeton University Press, 2003: 50–84.

———. "Ruling Passions: Political Economy in Nineteenth-Century America." *Journal of Policy History* 18:1 (2006): 1–18.

Jones, David R. "Muscovite-Nomad Relations on the Steppe Frontier Before 1800 and the Development of Russia's 'Inclusive' Imperialism," in Wayne E. Lee, ed., *Empires and Indigenes:*

Intercultural Alliance, Imperial Expansion, and Warfare in the Early Modern World. New York: New York University Press, 2011: 109–40.

Kagan, Robert. *Dangerous Nation.* New York: Alfred A. Knopf, 2006.

Karamanski, Theodore J. *Fur Trade and Exploration: Opening the Far Northwest, 1821–1852.* Norman: University of Oklahoma Press, 1983.

Karp, Matthew. *This Vast Southern Empire: Slaveholders at the Helm of American Foreign Policy.* Cambridge, MA: Harvard University Press, 2016.

Katznelson, Ira. "Flexible Capacity: The Military and Early American Statebuilding," in Katznelson and Martin Shefter, eds., *Shaped by War and Trade: International Influences on American Political Development.* Princeton, NJ: Princeton University Press, 2002: 82–110.

Katznelson, Ira, and John S. Lapinski, "At the Crossroads: Congress and American Political Development." *Perspectives on Politics* 4:2 (June 2006): 243–60.

Katznelson, Ira, and Martin Shefter, eds. *Shaped by War and Trade: International Influences on American Political Development.* Princeton, NJ: Princeton University Press, 2002.

Kelly, Andrew S. "The Political Development of Scientific Capacity in the United States." *Studies in American Political Development* 28:1 (April 2014): 1–25.

Ketcham, Ralph. *Presidents Above Party: The First American Presidency, 1789–1829.* Chapel Hill: University of North Carolina Press, 1984.

King, Desmond, and Robert C. Lieberman. "Ironies of State Building: A Comparative Perspective on the American State." *World Politics* 61:3 (July 2009): 547–88.

Kingdon, John. *Agendas, Alternatives, and Public Policies.* New York: Harper Collins, 1995.

Klyza, Christopher McGrory. "The United States Army, Natural Resources, and Political Development in the Nineteenth Century." *Polity* 35:1 (Fall 2002): 1–28.

Kohn, Richard H. *Eagle and Sword: The Beginnings of the Military Establishment in America.* New York: Free Press, 1975.

Koistinen, Paul A. C. *Beating Plowshares into Swords: The Political Economy of American Warfare, 1606–1865.* Lawrence: University Press of Kansas, 1996.

Kolchin, Peter. *Unfree Labor: American Slavery and Russian Serfdom.* Cambridge, MA: Belknap Press of the Harvard University Press, 1987.

Korzi, Michael J. *A Seat of Popular Leadership: The Presidency, Political Parties, and Democratic Government.* Amherst: University of Massachusetts Press, 2004.

Kramon, Eric, and Daniel N. Posner, "Who Benefits from Distributive Politics? How the Outcome One Studies Affects the Answer One Gets." *Perspectives on Politics* 11:2 (June 2013): 461–74.

Kurland, Philip B., and Ralph Lerner, eds. *The Founders' Constitution.* Volume 1. Chicago: University of Chicago Press, 1987.

Kushner, Howard I. "Visions of the Northwest: Gwin and Seward in the 1850's." *Western Historical Quarterly* 4:3 (July 1973): 295–306.

———. *Conflict on the Northwest Coast: American-Russian Rivalry in the Pacific Northwest, 1790–1867.* Westport, CT: Greenwood Press, 1975.

Lamoreaux, Naomi R., and John Joseph Wallis. "Fixing the Machine That Would Not Go of Itself: State Constitutional Change and the Creation of an Open-Access Social Order in the Mid-Nineteenth Century United States." Available at https://economics.yale.edu/sites/default/files/files/Faculty/Lamoreaux/Lamoreaux%20Wallis%2C%20Fixing%20the%20Machine%2C%202018-09-16.pdf, 2018.

———, eds. *Organizations, Civil Society, and the Roots of Development*. Chicago: University of Chicago Press, 2017.

Landers, Brian. *Empires Apart: A History of American and Russian Imperialism*. New York: Pegasus, 2011.

Landes, David S. *The Wealth and Poverty of Nations: Why Some Are So Rich and Some Are So Poor*. New York: W. W. Norton, 1999.

Langguth, A. J. *Driven West: Andrew Jackson and the Trail of Tears to the Civil War*. New York: Simon & Schuster, 2010.

Langston, Thomas S. *Uneasy Balance: Civil-Military Relations in Peacetime Since 1783*. Baltimore: Johns Hopkins University Press, 2003.

LaPorta, Rafael, Florencio Lopez-de-Silanes, and Andrei Shleifer, "The Economic Consequences of Legal Origins." *Journal of Economic Literature* 46:2 (June 2008): 285–332.

Larson, John Lauritz. *Internal Improvement: National Public Works and the Promise of Popular Government in the Early United States*. Chapel Hill: University of North Carolina Press, 2001.

Lasswell, Harold D. *Who Gets What, When, How*. New York: Whittlesey House, 1936.

Latner, Richard B. "The Nullification Crisis and Republican Subversion." *Journal of Southern History* 43:1 (February 1977): 19–38.

Lee, Wayne E., ed. *Empires and Indigenes: Intercultural Alliance, Imperial Expansion, and Warfare in the Early Modern World*. New York: New York University Press, 2011.

Leeman, William P. *The Long Road to Annapolis: The Founding of the Naval Academy and the Emerging American Republic*. Chapel Hill: University of North Carolina Press, 2010.

Lepore, Jill. *The Name of War: King Philip's War and the Origins of American Identity*. New York: Vintage, 1999.

Levi, Margaret. "The State of the Study of the State," in Ira Katznelson and Helen V. Milner, eds., *Political Science: The State of the Discipline*. New York: W. W. Norton, 2002: 33–55.

Levine, Peter. "The Fries Rebellion: Social Violence and the Politics of the New Nation." *Pennsylvania History* 40:3 (July 1973): 241–58.

Lindberg, Timothy. "Legislating for American Empire: Territorial Policy and the House Committee on Territories." *Congress and the Presidency* 47:2 (2020): 153–74.

Lindert, Peter H., and Jeffrey G. Williamson. *Unequal Gains: American Growth and Inequality Since 1700*. Princeton, NJ: Princeton University Press, 2016.

Lipsky, Michael. *Street-Level Bureaucracy: Dilemmas of the Individual in Public Services*. New York: Russell Sage Foundation, 1983.

Lowi, Theodore J. "American Business, Public Policy, Case-Studies, and Political Theory." *World Politics* 16:4 (July 1964): 677–715.

Lowry, William R. "Can Bureaucracies Change Policy?" *Journal of Policy History* 20:2 (2008): 287–306.

Lucier, Paul. "Commercial Interests and Scientific Disinterestedness: Consulting Geologists in Antebellum America." *Isis* 86:2 (June 1995): 245–67.

Lustick, Ian. "History, Historiography, and Political Science: Multiple Historical Records and the Problem of Selection Bias." *American Political Science Review* 90:3 (September 1996): 605–18.

Macey, Jonathan R. "Organizational Design and Political Control of Administrative Agencies." *Journal of Law, Economics, and Organization* 8:1 (March 1992): 93–110.

Madison, James, Alexander Hamilton, and John Jay. *The Federalist Papers*, ed. Isaac Kramnick. New York: Penguin, 1987.

Madison, James, Alexander Hamilton, and John Jay. *The Federalist Papers*, ed. Clinton Rossiter. New York: Signet Classic, 2003.

Malone, Laurence J. *Opening the West: Federal Internal Improvements Before 1860*. Westport, CT: Greenwood Press, 1998.

Mann, Michael. "The Autonomous Power of the State: Its Origins, Mechanisms and Results." *European Journal of Sociology* 25:2 (1984): 185–213.

———. *The Sources of Social Power:* Volume 1: *A History of Power from the Beginning to A.D. 1760*. Cambridge: Cambridge University Press, 1986.

———. *The Sources of Social Power:* Volume 2: *The Rise of Classes and Nation-States, 1760–1914*. Cambridge: Cambridge University Press, 1993.

Mashaw, Jerry L. "Recovering American Administrative Law: Federalist Foundations, 1787–1801." *Yale Law Journal* 115:6 (April 2006): 1256–344.

———. "Reluctant Nationalists: Federal Administration and Administrative Law in the Republican Era, 1801–1829." *Yale Law Journal* 116:8 (June 2007): 1636–740.

———. "Administration and 'The Democracy'": Administrative Law from Jackson to Lincoln, 1829–1861." *Yale Law Journal* 117:8 (June 2008): 1568–693.

———. *Creating the Administrative Constitution: The Lost One Hundred Years of American Administrative Law*. New Haven, CT: Yale University Press, 2012.

Mason, Matthew. *Slavery and Politics in the Early American Republic*. Chapel Hill: University of North Carolina Press, 2006.

May, Robert E. "Young American Males and Filibustering in the Age of Manifest Destiny: The United States Army as a Cultural Mirror." *Journal of American History* 78:3 (December 1991): 857–86.

Mayer, David N. "'Necessary and Proper': West Point and Jefferson's Constitutionalism," in Robert M. S. McDonald, ed., *Thomas Jefferson's Military Academy: Founding West Point*. Charlottesville: University of Virginia Press, 2004: 54–76.

Mayhew, David R. "Wars and American Politics." *Perspectives on Politics* 3:3 (September 2005), 473–93.

McCarty, Nolan. "Presidential Vetoes in the Early Republic: Changing Constitutional Norms or Electoral Reform?" *Journal of Politics* 71:2 (April 2009): 369–84.

McCubbins, Matthew D., Roger G. Noll, and Barry R. Weingast, "Administrative Procedures as Instruments of Political Control." *Journal of Law, Economics, and Organization* 3:2 (Autumn 1987): 243–77.

McCubbins, Matthew D., Daniel B. Rodriguez, and Barry R. Weingast. "The Rule of Law Unplugged." University of Texas School of Law, Public Law and Legal Theory Research Paper Series Number 158, September 3, 2009.

Merry, Robert W. *A Country of Vast Designs: James K. Polk, the Mexican War, and the Conquest of the American Continent*. New York: Simon and Schuster, 2009.

Mettler, Suzanne. *The Submerged State: How Invisible Government Policies Undermine American Democracy*. Chicago: University of Chicago Press, 2011.

Minicucci, Stephen. "Internal Improvements and the Union, 1790–1860." *Studies in American Political Development* 18:2 (Fall 2004): 160–85.

Missall, John, and Mary Lou Missall. *The Seminole Wars: America's Longest Indian Conflict*. Gainesville: University Press of Florida, 2004.

Moe, Terry. "An Assessment of the Positive Theory of 'Congressional Dominance.'" *Legislative Studies Quarterly* 12:4 (November 1987): 475–520.

Mokyr, Joel. "Technological Inertia in Economic History." *Journal of Economic History* 52:2 (June 1992): 325–38.

Moore, Colin. "State Building Through Partnership: Delegation, Public-Private Partnerships, and the Political Development of American Imperialism, 1898–1916." *Studies in American Political Development* 25:1 (April 2011): 27–55.

———. *American Imperialism and the State, 1893–1921.* New York: Cambridge University Press, 2017.

Morris, Richard B. "Andrew Jackson, Strikebreaker." *American Historical Review* 55:1 (October 1949): 54–68.

Mulcare, Daniel M. "Restricted Authority: Slavery Politics, Internal Improvements, and the Limitation of National Administrative Capacity." *Political Research Quarterly* 61:4 (December 2008): 671–85.

Murrin, John M. "The Jeffersonian Triumph and American Exceptionalism." *Journal of the Early Republic* 20:1 (Spring 2000): 1–25.

Nackenoff, Carol. "The Private Roots of American Political Development: The Immigrants' Protective League's 'Friendly and Sympathetic Touch,' 1908–1924." *Studies in American Political Development* 28:2 (October 2014): 129–60.

Nichols, Roger L. "The Army and the Indians 1800–1830—A Reappraisal: The Missouri Valley Example." *Pacific Historical Review* 41 (1972): 151–68.

Niskanen, William A. "Bureaucrats and Politicians." *Journal of Law and Economics* 18:3 (December 1975): 617–43.

North, Douglass C. *Growth and Welfare in the American Past: A New Economic History.* Englewood Cliffs, NJ: Prentice-Hall, 1966.

———. *Structure and Change in Economic History.* New York: W. W. Norton, 1981.

———. *Institutions, Institutional Change, and Economic Performance.* New York: Cambridge University Press, 1990.

———. "Institutions and Credible Commitment." *Journal of Institutional and Theoretical Economics* 149:1 (March 1993): 11–23.

North, Douglass C., John Joseph Wallis, and Barry C. Weingast. *Violence and Social Orders: A Conceptual Framework for Interpreting Recorded Human History.* New York: Cambridge University Press, 2012.

North, Douglass C., and Barry R. Weingast. "Constitutions and Commitment: The Evolution of Institutional Governing Public Choice in Seventeenth-Century England." *Journal of Economic History* 49:4 (December 1989): 803–32.

Novak, William J. *The People's Welfare: Law and Regulation in Nineteenth-Century America.* Chapel Hill: University of North Carolina Press, 1996.

———. "The Myth of the 'Weak' American State." *American Historical Review* 113:3 (June 2008): 752–72.

Oakes, James. "The Political Significance of Slave Resistance." *History Workshop Journal* 22:1 (1986): 89–107.

O'Connell, Charles F., Jr. "The Corps of Engineers and the Rise of Modern Management, 1827–1856," in Merritt Roe Smith, ed., *Military Enterprise and Technological Change: Perspectives on the American Experience.* Cambridge, MA: MIT Press, 1985: 87–116.

Olmstead, Alan L., and Paul W. Rhode. "Cotton, Slavery, and the New History of Capitalism." *Explorations in Economic History* 67 (2018): 1–17.

Olson, Mancur. *The Logic of Collective Action: Public Goods and the Theory of Groups*. Cambridge, MA: Harvard University Press, 1965.

O'Neill, Karen M. *Rivers by Design: State Power and the Origin of U.S. Flood Control*. Durham, NC: Duke University Press, 2006.

Onuf, Peter. *Jefferson's Empire: The Language of American Nationhood*. Charlottesville: University of Virginia Press, 2000.

Oren, Michael B. *Power, Faith, and Fantasy: America in the Middle East, 1776 to Present*. New York: W. W. Norton, 2007. .

Orren, Karen, and Stephen Skowronek. *The Search for American Political Development*. New York: Cambridge University Press, 2004.

Paret, Peter. "The New Military History." *Parameters* 31 (Autumn 1991): 10–18.

Paskoff, Paul F. *Troubled Waters: Steamboat Disasters, River Improvements, and American Public Policy, 1821–1860*. Baton Rouge: Louisiana State University Press, 2007.

Peters, B. Guy, Jon Pierre, and Desmond S. King. "The Politics of Path Dependency: Political Conflict in Historical Institutionalism." *Journal of Politics* 67:4 (November 2005): 1275–300.

Peyton, Billy Joe. "'To Make the Crooked Ways Straight and the Rough Ways Smooth': The Federal Government's Role in Laying Out and Building the Cumberland Road." Ph.D. dissertation, West Virginia University, 1999.

Pierson, Paul. *Politics in Time: History, Institutions, and Social Analysis*. Princeton: Princeton University Press, 2004.

Pious, Richard. "The Presidency and the Nominating Process: Politics and Power," in Michael Nelson, ed., *The Presidency and the Political System*. 8th ed. Washington, DC: CQ Press, 2006: 195–218.

Pitcavage, Mark. "An Equitable Burden: The Decline of the State Militias, 1783–1858." Ph.D. dissertation, Ohio State University, 1995.

Polanyi, Karl. *The Great Transformation*. New York: Farrar and Rinehart, 1944.

Pollack, Sheldon D. *War, Revenue, and State Building: Financing the Development of the American State*. Ithaca, NY: Cornell University Press, 2009.

Polsby, Nelson W. "The Institutionalization of the U.S. House of Representatives." *American Political Science Review* 62:1 (March 1968):144–68.

Polsky, Andrew J. "'Mr. Lincoln's Army' Revisited: Partisanship, Institutional Position, and Union Army Command, 1861–1865." *Studies in American Political Development* 16:2 (Fall 2002): 176–207.

———. "The Presidency at War," in Michael Nelson, ed. *The Presidency and the Political System*. 8th ed. Washington, DC: CQ Press, 2006: 557–75.

Porter, Bruce D. *War and the Rise of the State: The Military Foundations of Modern Politics*. New York: Free Press, 1994.

Pressman, Jeffrey L., and Aaron B. Wildavsky. *Implementation: How Great Expectations in Washington Are Dashed in Oakland*. Berkeley: University of California Press, 1974.

Prucha, Francis Paul. *Broadax and Bayonet: The Role of the United States Army in the Development of the Northwest, 1815–1860*. Madison: State Historical Society of Wisconsin, 1953.

———. *The Sword of the Republic: The United States Army on the Frontier, 1783–1846*. Lincoln: University of Nebraska Press, 1969.

———. *The Great Father: The United States Government and the American Indians*. Lincoln: University of Nebraska Press, 1984.

Puls, Mark. *Henry Knox: Visionary General of the American Revolution*. New York: Palgrave Macmillan, 2008.
Rae, John B. "Democrats and the Dorr Rebellion." *New England Quarterly* 9:3 (September 1936): 476–83.
Rana, Aziz. *The Two Faces of American Freedom*. Cambridge, MA: Harvard University Press, 2014.
Rao, Gautham. "Administering Entitlement: Governance, Public Health Care, and the Early American State." *Law and Social Inquiry* 37:3 (Summer 2012): 627–56.
———. *National Duties: Custom Houses and the Making of the American State*. Chicago: University of Chicago Press, 2016.
———. "The New Historiography of the Early Federal Government: Institutions, Contexts, and the Imperial State. " *William and Mary Quarterly* 77:1 (January 2020): 97–128.
Rasler, Karen A., and William R. Thompson. "War Making and State Making: Government Expenditures, Tax Revenues, and Global Wars." *American Political Science Review* 79:2 (June 1985): 491–507.
Regele, Lindsay Schakenbach. *Manufacturing Advantage: War, the State, and the Origins of American Industry, 1776–1848*. Baltimore: Johns Hopkins University Press, 2019.
Riker, William H., and Steven J. Brams. "The Paradox of Vote Trading." *American Political Science Review* 67:4 (December 1973): 1235–47.
Risch, Erna. *Quartermaster Support of the Army, 1775–1939*. Washington, DC: Center of Military History, 1989.
Rockman, Seth. "The Unfree Origins of American Capitalism," in Cathy Matson, ed., *The Economy of Early America: Historical Perspectives and New Directions*. University Park: Pennsylvania State University Press, 2006: 335–61.
Rockwell, Stephen J. *Indian Affairs and the Administrative State in the Nineteenth Century*. New York: Cambridge University Press, 2013.
Rodenbough, Theophilus F., and William L. Haskin. *The Army of the United States: Historical Sketches of Staff and Line with Portraits of Generals-in-Chief*. New York: Maynard, Merrill, 1896.
Rodrik, Dani, Arvind Subramanian, and Francesco Trebbi. "Institutions Rule: The Primacy of Institutions over Geography and Integration in Economic Development." *Journal of Economic Growth* 9:2 (June 2004): 131–65.
Roland, Alex. "Science and War." *Osiris*, 2nd ser., 1 (1985): 247–72.
———. "Science, Technology, and War." *Technology and Culture* 36:2 (April 1995): S83–S100.
Ruttan, Vernon W. *Is War Necessary for Economic Growth? Military Procurement and Technology Development*. New York: Oxford University Press, 2006.
Ryan, Garry David. "War Department Topographical Bureau, 1831–1863: An Administrative History." Ph.D. dissertation, American University, 1968.
Sabol, Steven. "Comparing American and Russian Internal Colonization: The 'Touch of Civilisation' on the Sioux and the Kazakhs." *Western Historical Quarterly* 43:1 (Spring 2012): 29–51.
Saldin, Robert P. *War, the American State, and Politics since 1898*. New York: Cambridge University Press, 2011.
Samuels, Warren J. "The Political Economy of Adam Smith." *Ethics* 87:3 (April 1977): 189–207.
Samuelson, Paul. "The Pure Theory of Public Expenditure." *Review of Economics and Statistics* 36:4 (November 1954): 387–89.
Sanders, Elizabeth. "The Three American States." *Clio* 15:1 (Fall–Winter 2004–5): 1, 46–47.

Scheiber, Harry N. "Regulation, Property Rights, and Definition of 'The Market': Law and the American Economy." *Journal of Economic History* 41:1 (March 1981): 103–19.

Scherr, Arthur. "Thomas Jefferson's Nationalist Vision of New England and the War of 1812." *The Historian* 69:1 (Spring 2007): 1–35.

Schneider, Mark, and Paul Teske. "Toward a Theory of the Political Entrepreneur: Evidence from Local Government." *American Political Science Review* 86:3 (September 1992): 737–47.

Schnellenbach, Jan. "Public Entrepreneurship and the Economics of Reform." *Journal of Institutional Economics* 3:2 (2007): 183–202.

Schoen, Brian. "Calculating the Price of Union: Republican Economic Nationalism and the Origins of Southern Sectionalism, 1790–1828." *Journal of the Early Republic* 23:2 (Summer 2003): 173–206.

Schroeder, John H. *Mr. Polk's War: American Opposition and Dissent, 1846–1848.* Madison: University of Wisconsin Press, 1973.

Schubert, Frank N. *The Nation Builders: A Sesquicentennial History of the Corps of Topographical Engineers, 1838–1863.* Fort Belvoir, VA: Office of History, U.S. Army Corps of Engineers, 1988.

Schumpeter, Joseph A. *Capitalism, Socialism and Democracy.* New York: Harper and Brothers, 1942.

Shallat, Todd. "Engineering Policy: The U.S. Army Corps of Engineers and the Historical Foundation of Power." *The Public Historian* 11:3 (Summer 1989): 6–27.

———. "Building Waterways, 1802–1861: Science and the United States Army in Early Public Works." *Technology and Culture* 31:1 (January 1990): 18–50.

———. *Structures in the Stream: Water, Science, and the Rise of the U.S. Army Corps of Engineers.* Austin: University of Texas Press, 1994.

Sheingate, Adam D. "Political Entrepreneurship, Institutional Change, and American Political Development." *Studies in American Political Development* 17:2 (Fall 2003): 185–203.

———. "The Terrain of the Political Entrepreneur," in Stephen Skowronek and Matthew Glassman, eds., *Formative Acts: American Politics in the Making.* Philadelphia: University of Pennsylvania Press, 2007: 13–31.

———. "Why Can't Americans See the State?" *The Forum* 7:4 (2010).

Shipan, Charles R. "Congress and the Bureaucracy," in Paul J. Quirk and Sarah A. Binder, eds. *The Legislative Branch.* New York: Oxford University Press, 2005: 432–58.

Silverstone, Scott A. *Divided Union: The Politics of War in the Early American Republic.* Ithaca, NY: Cornell University Press, 2004.

Skelton, William B. "Professionalization in the U.S. Army Officer Corps During the Age of Jackson." *Armed Forces and Society* 1:4 (August 1975): 443–71.

———. *An American Profession of Arms: The Army Officer Corps, 1784–1861.* Lawrence: University Press of Kansas, 1992.

———. "High Army Leadership in the Era of the War of 1812: The Making and Remaking of the Officer Corps." *William and Mary Quarterly*, 3rd ser., 51:2 (April 1994): 253–74.

———. "The Commanding Generals and the Question of Civil Control in the Antebellum U.S. Army." *American Nineteenth Century History* 7:2 (June 2006): 153–72.

Skocpol, Theda. *Protecting Soldiers and Mothers: The Political Origins of Social Policy in the United States.* Cambridge, MA: Harvard University Press, 1992.

Skowronek, Stephen. *Building a New American State: The Expansion of National Administrative Capacities, 1877–1920.* New York: Cambridge University Press, 1982.

———. *The Politics Presidents Make.* Cambridge, MA: Harvard University Press, 1997.

Slotkin, Richard. *Regeneration Through Violence: The Mythology of the American Frontier, 1600–1860.* Hanover, NH: Wesleyan University Press, 1973.

———. *The Fatal Environment: The Myth of the Frontier in the Age of Industrialization 1800–1890.* New York: Macmillan, 1985.

———. *Gunfighter Nation: The Myth of the Frontier in Twentieth-Century America.* New York: Atheneum, 1992.

Smith, Adam. *An Inquiry into the Nature and Causes of the Wealth of Nations.* Chicago: University of Chicago Press, 1976 [1776].

Smith, Geoffrey Sutton. "The Navy Before Darwinism: Science, Exploration, and Diplomacy in Antebellum America." *American Quarterly* 28:1 (Spring 1976): 41–55.

Smith, Henry Nash. *Virgin Land: The American West as Symbol and Myth.* New York: Vintage Books, 1962.

Smith, Merritt Roe. *Harpers Ferry Armory and the New Technology: The Challenge of Change.* Ithaca, NY: Cornell University Press, 1977.

———. "Military Entrepreneurship," in Otto Mayr and Robert C. Post, eds., *Yankee Enterprise: The Rise of the American System of Manufactures.* Washington, DC: Smithsonian Institution Press, 1981: 63–102.

———. "Army Ordnance and the 'American System' of Manufacturing, 1815–1861," in Smith, ed., *Military Enterprise and Technological Change: Perspectives on the American Experience.* Cambridge, MA: MIT Press, 1985: 39–86.

Soifer, Hillel. "State Infrastructural Power: Approaches to Conceptualization and Measurement." *Studies in Comparative International Development* 43:3–4 (2008): 231–51.

Soifer, Hillel, and Matthias vom Hau. "Unpacking the *Strength* of the State: The Utility of State Infrastructural Power." *Studies in Comparative International Development* 43:3–4 (2008): 219–30.

Sosin, Jack M. "The British Indian Department and Dunmore's War." *Virginia Magazine of History and Biography* 74:1, part 1 (January 1966): 34–50.

Sparrow, Bartholomew. *From the Outside In: World War II and the American State.* Princeton, NJ: Princeton University Press, 1996.

Sparrow, James T. *Warfare State: World War II Americans and the Age of Big Government.* New York: Oxford University Press, 2011.

Spruyt. Hendrik. *The Sovereign State and Its Competitors: An Analysis of Systems Change.* Princeton, NJ: Princeton University Press, 1994.

Stagg, J. C. A. *Mr. Madison's War: Politics, Diplomacy, and Warfare in the Early American Republic, 1783–1830.* Princeton, NJ: Princeton University Press, 1983.

Stevenson, Charles A. *Warrior and Politicians: US Civil-Military Relations Under Stress.* New York: Routledge, 2006.

———. *Congress at War: The Politics of Conflict Since 1789.* Washington, DC: Potomac Books, 2007.

Stone, Geoffrey R. *Perilous Times: Free Speech in Wartime from the Sedition Act of 1798 to the War on Terrorism.* New York: W. W. Norton, 2004.

Storing, Herbert J., ed. *The Complete Anti-Federalist.* Volume 5. Chicago: University of Chicago Press, 1981.

Tarrow, Sidney. *War, States, and Contention: A Comparative Historical Study.* Ithaca, NY: Cornell University Press, 2015.

Tate, Michael L. *The Frontier Army in the Settlement of the West.* Norman: University of Oklahoma Press, 1999.

Taylor, Alan. "The Science of Distant Empire, 1768–1811," in Douglas Seefeldt, Jeffrey L. Hantman, and Peter S. Onuf, eds., *Across the Continent: Jefferson, Lewis and Clark, and the Making of America.* Charlottesville: University of Virginia Press, 2005: 16–44.

Taylor, George Rogers. *The Transportation Revolution, 1815–1860.* New York: Rinehart, 1951.

Teichova, Alice, and Herbert Matis, eds. *Nation, State, and the Economy in History.* New York: Cambridge University Press, 2003.

Teske, Paul, and Mark Schneider. "The Bureaucratic Entrepreneur: The Case of City Managers." *Public Administration Review* 54:4 (July–August 1994): 331–40.

Thelen, Kathleen. "Varieties of Capitalism: Trajectories of Liberalization and the New Politics of Social Solidarity." *Annual Review of Political Science* 15 (2012): 137–59.

Thompson, Paul M. "Is There Anything 'Legal' About Extralegal Action? The Debate Over Dorr's Rebellion." *New England Law Review* 36 (Winter 2002): 385–432.

Thonhoff, Robert H. "Taylor's Trail in Texas." *Southwestern Historical Quarterly* 70:1 (July 1966): 7–22.

Thurston, Chloe N. *At the Boundaries of Homeownership: Credit, Discrimination, and the American State.* New York: Cambridge University Press, 2018.

Thurston, G. J. "Alexis De Tocqueville in Russia." *Journal of the History of Ideas* 37:2 (April–June 1976): 289–306.

Tilly, Charles, ed. *The Formation of National States in Western Europe.* Princeton, NJ: Princeton University Press, 1975.

———. "War Making and State Making as Organized Crime," in Peter Evans, Dietrich Rueschemeyer, and Theda Skocpol, eds., *Bringing the State Back In.* New York: Cambridge University Press, 1985: 169–91.

———. *Coercion, Capital, and European States, A.D. 990–1992.* Malden, MA: Blackwell, 1990.

Ting, Michael M. "A Strategic Theory of Bureaucratic Redundancy." *American Journal of Political Science* 47:2 (April 2003): 274–92.

Treadgold, Donald. "Russian Expansion in the Light of Turner's Study of the American Frontier." *Agricultural History* 26:4 (October 1952): 147–52.

———. *The Great Siberian Migration: Government and Peasant in Resettlement from Emancipation to the First World War.* Princeton, NJ: Princeton University Press, 1957.

Turner, Frederick Jackson. "The Significance of the Frontier in American History." Presented at the July 12, 1893, meeting of the American Historical Association, Chicago.

Utley, Robert M. *Frontiersmen in Blue: The United States Army and the Indian, 1848–1865.* Lincoln: University of Nebraska Press, 1967.

———. *Fort Scott National Historic Site.* Western National Parks Association, 1991.

Vandenbroucke, Guillaume. "The American Frontier: Technology Versus Immigration." *Review of Economic Dynamics* 11:2 (April 2008): 283–301.

———. "The U.S. Westward Expansion." *International Economic Review* 49:1 (February 2008): 81–110.

Volpe, Vernon L. "The Origins of the Fremont Expeditions: John J. Abert and the Scientific Exploration of the Trans-Mississippi West." *The Historian* 62:2 (December 2000): 245–63.

Wallerstein, Immanuel. "The Rise and Future Demise of the World Capitalist System: Concepts for Comparative Analysis." *Comparative Studies in Society and History* 16:4 (September 1974): 387–415.

Wallis, John Joseph. "The Other Foundings: Federalism and the Constitutional Structure of American Government," in Douglas A. Irwin and Richard Sylla, eds., *Founding Choices: American Economic Policy in the 1790s*. Chicago: University of Chicago Press, 2011: 177–216.

Ward, Harry M. *The Department of War, 1781–1795*. Pittsburgh: University of Pittsburgh Press, 1962.

Warshaw, Shirley Anne. "The Formation and Use of the Cabinet," in Phillip G. Henderson, ed., *The Presidency Then and Now*. Lanham, MD: Rowman and Littlefield, 2000: 115–37.

Watson, Samuel J. "Professionalism, Social Attitudes, and Civil-Military Accountability in the United States Army Officer Corps, 1815–1846." Ph.D. dissertation, Rice University, 1996.

———. "United States Army Officers Fight the 'Patriot War': Responses to Filibustering on the Canadian Border, 1837–1839." *Journal of the Early Republic* 18:3 (Autumn 1998): 485–519.

———. "How the Army Became Accepted: West Point Socialization, Military Accountability, and the Nation-State During the Jacksonian Era." *American Nineteenth Century History* 7:2 (June 2006): 219–51.

Weber, Max. *The Theory of Social and Economic Organization*. New York: Free Press, 1997.

———. *The Protestant Ethic and the "Spirit" of Capitalism and Other Writings*. New York: Penguin Books, 2002.

Weigley, Russell. "The American Civil Military Cultural Gap: A Historical Perspective, Colonial Times to the Present," in Peter D. Feaver and Richard H. Kohn, eds., *Soldiers and Civilians: The Civil-Military Gap and American National Security*. Cambridge, MA: MIT Press, 2001.

Weingast, Barry R. "The Economic Role of Political Institutions: Market-Preserving Federalism and Economic Development." *Journal of Law, Economics, and Organization* 11:1 (April 1995): 1–31.

———. "The Political Foundations of Democracy and the Rule of the Law." *American Political Science Review* 91:2 (June 1997): 245–63.

———. "Caught in the Middle: The President, Congress, and the Political-Bureaucratic System," in Joel D. Aberbach and Mark A. Peterson, eds., *The Executive Branch*. New York: Oxford University Press, 2005: 312–43.

White, Leonard D. *The Jacksonians: A Study in Administrative History, 1829–1861*. New York: Macmillan, 1954.

———. *The Republican Era: A Study in Administrative History, 1869–1901*. New York: Macmillan, 1958.

———. *The Jeffersonians: A Study in Administrative History, 1801–1829*. New York: Macmillan, 1961.

———. *The Federalists: A Study in Administrative History*. New York: Collier-Macmillan, 1965.

White, Richard. *The Middle Ground: Indians, Empires, and Republics in the Great Lakes Region, 1650–1815*. New York: Cambridge University Press, 1991.

———. *"It's Your Misfortune and None of My Own": A History of the American West*. Norman: University of Oklahoma Press, 1991.

Whittington, Keith E. "The Political Constitution of Federalism in Antebellum America: The Nullification Debate as an Illustration of Informal Mechanisms of Constitutional Change." *Publius* 26:2 (Spring 1996): 1–24.

Whittington, Keith E., and Daniel P. Carpenter. "Executive Power in American Institutional Development." *Perspectives on Politics* 1:3 (September 2003): 495–513.

Wiecek, William W. "'A Peculiar Conservatism' and the Dorr Rebellion: Constitutional Clash in Jacksonian America." *American Journal of Legal History* 22:3 (July 1978): 237–53.

Williamson, Oliver E. *The Economic Institutions of Capitalism: Firms, Markets, Relational Contracting.* New York: Free Press, 1985.

Wilson, Mark R. *The Business of Civil War: Military Mobilization and the State, 1861–1865.* Baltimore: Johns Hopkins University Press, 2006.

———. "The Politics of Procurement: Military Origins of Bureaucratic Autonomy." *Journal of Policy History* 18:1 (2006): 44–73

Winders, Richard Bruce. *Mr. Polk's Army: The American Military Experience in the Mexican War.* College Station: Texas A&M University Press, 1997.

Wirls, Daniel, and Stephen Wirls. *The Invention of the United States Senate.* Baltimore: Johns Hopkins University Press, 2004.

Wolf, Charles. *Markets or Governments: Choosing Between Imperfect Alternatives.* Cambridge, MA: MIT Press, 1990.

Wood, Gordon S. *Empire of Liberty: A History of the Early Republic, 1789–1815.* New York: Oxford University Press, 2009.

Wright, Gavin. "The Role of Nationhood in the Economic Development of the USA," in Alice Teichova and Herbert Matis, eds., *Nation, State, and the Economy in History.* New York: Cambridge University Press, 2003: 387–403.

Young, James Sterling. *The Washington Community, 1800–1828.* New York: Columbia University Press, 1966.

Young, Tommy R., II. "The United States Army and the Institution of Slavery in Louisiana, 1803–1835." *Louisiana Studies* 13 (Fall 1974): 201–22.

Zegart, Amy B. *Flawed by Design: The Evolution of the CIA, JCS, and NSC.* Stanford, CA: Stanford University Press, 1999.

Zeisberg, Mariah. *War Powers: The Politics of Constitutional Authority.* Princeton, NJ: Princeton University Press, 2013.

Zolberg, Aristide R. "International Engagement and American Democracy: A Comparative Perspective," in Ira Katznelson and Martin Shefter, eds., *Shaped by War and Trade: International Influences on American Political Development.* Princeton, NJ: Princeton University Press, 2002: 24–54.

INDEX

ACKNOWLEDGMENTS

This book is the culmination of many years of work, but it could not possibly have been accomplished alone. Many friends and colleagues have provided excellent advice and suggestions along the way.

At the Graduate Center of the City University of New York I became friends with an incredible group of scholars: Jonathan Keller, Jennifer Hopper, Daniel Skinner, Patricia Stapleton, Shawna Brandle, Ben Epstein, and Jeffrey Broxmeyer. We have sustained each other and read each other's work and been conference buddies for years afterward. My professors at the Graduate Center provided me with the intellectual foundations for my own research and read innumerable drafts of this project as it progressed. In particular, I want to thank Thomas Halper for his always thoughtful suggestions; Susan Woodward for the best kind of critical advice that improved every aspect; and Andrew Polsky for his detailed readings and re-readings of every word across many years—his influence (if not a literal "AJP" comment) is on every page. I would also like to gratefully acknowledge the Graduate Center's support in the form of the Arthur Schlesinger Dissertation Proposal Award, the David Spitz Dissertation Fellowship in the Social Science, and a fellowship at the Center for Place, Culture, and Politics. During my two years at Johns Hopkins University as the Patrick Henry Postdoctoral Fellow (and ever since), Adam Sheingate has read my work, helped me improve it tremendously, and always given excellent professional counsel.

Others who read portions of this book as it was being written and provided constructive feedback include Rob Mickey, Julia Azari, Richard Bensel, Daniel Carpenter, Zachary Callen, Richard John, Ira Katznelson, Christopher Klyza, Rob Saldin, Peter Trubowitz, Sam Watson, Mark Wilson, Shamira Gelbman, and David Dagan. Rick Valelly and the editorial team at the University of Pennsylvania Press have been fantastic partners in helping make this book a reality. I would also like to thank the anonymous reviewers whose careful suggestions greatly enriched the final result.

At Northeastern Illinois University I have been blessed with a wonderful and supportive department, with the best colleagues any academic could ask for: Sangmin Bae, Russell Benjamin, Ellen Cannon, Martyn de Bruyn, Jeffrey Hill, Sophia Mihic, Gregory Neddenriep, Marshall Thompson, and our wonderful department secretary Uma Patel. I would also like to thank Northeastern Illinois University for awarding me a Committee on Organized Research grant that helped fund a research assistant, Jason LaBrosse, during the 2014–2015 academic year.

The staff and archivists at the National Archives in Washington, D.C., and at the New York Public Library did yeoman's work in helping me locate obscure material and in assisting me when I didn't even know what to ask for. Similarly, the librarians at the CUNY Graduate Center, Johns Hopkins University, and Northeastern Illinois University have been of tremendous help in tracking down every odd source I ever wanted to find.

Portions of the Introduction were previously published as "Building the New American Nation: Economic Development, Public Goods, and the Early U.S. Army," *Political Science Quarterly* 125:1 (Spring 2010): 87–110, reproduced here by permission of the Academy of Political Science; portions of Chapter 4 were previously published as "State Capacity and Bureaucratic Autonomy in the Early United States: The Case of the Army Corps of Topographical Engineers," *Studies in American Political Development* 26:2 (October 2012): 107–24, reproduced here by permission of Cambridge University Press.

And last but by no means least, to my family, each member of which has been supportive of this project in their own way. To my brother, Corey Adler, who could always be counted on to laugh every time I explained what incredibly abstruse thing I was writing about; to my mother, Ann Adler, whose love and support know no bounds; to my wife, Rachel Adler, for encouraging me and pushing me to keep going even when I felt stuck or lost; and to my children, Emily, Joey, and Nathan, for making it all worth it. Finally, to the memory of my father, James Adler, who taught me how to be the person I am.

CPSIA information can be obtained
at www.ICGtesting.com
Printed in the USA
JSHW021430090921
18555JS00002B/4

9 780812 253481